HOW TO START YOUR OWN SMALL BUSINESS
(Expanded Edition)

 Sterling Publishing Co., Inc.   New York

Library of Congress Cataloging in Publication Data

Main entry under title:

How to start your own small business.

    Includes index.
    1. Small business—Management. 2. New business
enterprises—Management.
HD62.7.H684 1982   658′.022   81-85067
ISBN 0-8069-7600-4 (pbk.)   AACR2

Copyright © 1982 by Sterling Publishing Co., Inc.
Two Park Avenue, New York, N.Y. 10016
Distributed in Australia by Oak Tree Press Co., Ltd.
P.O. Box K514 Haymarket, Sydney 2000, N.S.W.
Distributed in the United Kingdom by Blandford Press
Link House, West Street, Poole, Dorset BH15 1LL, England
Distributed in Canada by Oak Tree Press Ltd.
℅ Canadian Manda Group, 215 Lakeshore Boulevard East
Toronto, Ontario M5A 3W9
Manufactured in the United States of America

Contents

FINANCING YOUR VENTURE

If you have ever worked for someone else, you'll find that starting that job was a snap compared to starting your own business. You made a deal for wages and hours with your prospective employer, and you appeared for work on the appointed day, your skills in your head and a ballpoint pen in your pocket. Everything else was provided for you by the firm—the business with its fixtures and equipment; the merchandise or service you were to sell; the customers or clients; the recordkeeping; and, most important, an assured income.

Now you are thinking about opening your own business. The potential rewards are many, but so are the risks. And while the risks are certain, the rewards are not. If you make a mistake, there's no boss to give you a tongue-lashing, but you may find yourself in debt for life. You have to risk a considerable amount of money—either borrowed capital or your own slowly accumulated savings. The question at this point is, How much money, and where will you get it?

How Much Do You Need?

The problem of how much money to invest in your business is one of the toughest you'll have to face. It is closely tied in with the size of your business, its location, the amount of inventory you will have to carry or the scope of services you will provide, the number of people you will employ, and the income you expect to draw from the business.

The amount of capital you need compared to the amount you have available will probably determine whether you can go it alone or will need a partner to share the investment. Your success will depend on your having adequate capital for what you set out to do. It is important to be careful and thorough in figuring how much starting capital you need.

In general, your needs for capital can be classified under the following four heads:

1. *Fixed capital*

This is the money or credit you need for getting ready to open—preparing the premises and buying fixtures and equipment that can't be readily converted into cash.

2. *Working capital*

This is the money you need for running your business from day to day. It must cover such items as rent, light, salaries, insurance, telephone, installment payments, and so on. It must include enough funds to maintain daily business operations while you get your accounts receivable underway. Part of your working capital will be used for advertising and promotion. This continuing expense is most important when you are getting started, since you need to expand your business as quickly as possible. Many businesses spend from 5 to 10 percent of their gross income for promotions and advertising during the first few years they are in business. Later, as your gross sales increase, you may be able to reduce this percent—and even the actual dollar amount spent.

Working capital includes cash on hand and in the bank, accounts and notes receivable, and immediately marketable investments. How much you will need will depend on the volume of business you expect to do. It will also depend on whether you are buying an established business, including the accounts receivable. It should equal your expected expenses of doing business for at least 6 months—preferably a year. Neglecting to provide for enough working capital has brought failure or a poor credit rating to many new small businesses.

3. *Funds for living expenses*

Most new businesses don't show a profit for 2 or 3 years. Hold back enough funds to provide for your family during that time.

4. *A financial cushion*

Most prospective business owners underestimate the amount of money they need to get started. Don't overlook the need for cash to pay legal expenses, accounting expenses, fees for licenses and permits, utility deposits, interest and mortgage payments, installment payments on equipment, taxes, and so on. Allow some extra to take care of unexpected expenses— some of them are certain to come up.

Initial Cash Requirements

Make a worksheet to help you estimate how much capital you'll need for major items of furniture, fixtures, and equipment. Don't try to pull the figures out of a hat. Talk to suppliers of the various items. Listen to their advice, but don't accept it blindly. Study it in the light of the size and type of business you are planning and the money you have available. Here are some of the items you will have to provide for:

Salary of owner-manager—1 month or more.

All other salaries and wages—2 months or more.

Occupancy—2 months or more.

Advertising—one-fourth of your annual advertising budget.

Delivery expense—2 months or more.

Supplies—2 months or more.

Depreciation of fixtures and equipment—none, since no cash is involved when you start the business.

Telephone and telegraph—2 months or more.

Insurance (other than building)—you may have to pay premiums for 1 year or more.

Donations and dues—2 months or more.

Taxes, including F.I.C.A.—3 months or more.

Bad debts—no cash is involved here to start.

Interest (other than building)—2 months or more.

Maintenance (other than building)—2 months or more.

Travel and entertainment—2 months or more.

Legal and other professional fees—2 months or more.

Commissions to agents—2 months or more.

Miscellaneous—2 months or more.

You may also have to deal with the following nonrecurring initial capital requirements:

Purchase of real estate, if any—if you are buying real estate for the business and purchase it outright, the total price. If you are financing the purchase by a mortgage, the total cash payment. If you are going to build, the total cost of construction.

Decorating and remodeling—Total estimated cost.

Sources of Starting Capital

You've probably been saving your money for some time for the specific purpose of opening your own business. But suppose it isn't enough even after you've got your budget down to the lowest possible amount. Where can you look for the funds you still need?

Family and friends

Under some circumstances, it may be easier to get a loan from this source than from any other. But keep these two rules in mind:

1. Put the loan on a strictly business basis. Have properly drawn papers specifying the rate of interest and the terms of repayment.
2. Don't risk harming your business by listening to unsound advice from the person who makes the loan. You may not want to hurt his feelings, but you must be in control. He must be willing to rely on your training and experience.

Banks

If you apply for a bank loan, good banking practice demands that the banker protect himself, his depositors, and you. He'll want to know what sort of credit reputation you have, how much money of your own you are going to invest, what collateral you can offer. He'll want to see detailed plans for your business and a careful analysis of its prospects. He'll want to know what experience you've had to prepare you for running a business of your own.

Don't be discouraged if one banker turns you down. Shop around, and try to improve your application and approach each time.

Taking a partner

You may decide that taking in a partner is the solution to your problems of financing. But remember that you will be dividing the profits as well as the financing. Also, you should understand thoroughly the legal aspects of partnerships. Have a lawyer draw up the partnership agreement.

On the brighter side, a partnership may increase your skills as well as your financial resources if you can find a partner who is strong in areas in which you are weak.

Trade credit

If you have a topnotch credit reputation and can convince your suppliers of your ability and integrity, they may let you have your opening order on extended billing or promissory notes. You may even be able to get some merchandise on consignment, with the privilege of returning what you don't sell. In a new business, it may be hard to tell just what will sell in your area.

Another form of help that will ease the strain on your finances is the display material some manufacturers provide. Most suppliers offer seasonal units to dress windows and store interiors. Some have units of display cases that can be used as permanent show cases at no cost to you. This will reduce your fixture costs.

Small Business Administration

If you can't find a private lender, the Small Business Administration may be able to help you. An important feature of SBA assistance is that it includes counseling by management and financial specialists.

The counseling is available whether or not you are applying for a loan, and there is no charge for it.

The Small Business Administration is in existence to help the Nation's small firms. It performs this important function in a variety of ways. For instance, it participates with banks in financing small businesses; makes direct loans to small firms when private funds are not available; helps small businesses to get a fair share of Government contracts and sales; and licenses, regulates, and finances small business investment companies which in turn provide equity capital and long-term loans to small firms.

Additional information on SBA services is available by writing to the Superintendent of Documents, U.S. Government Printing Office, Washington 25, DC or the Small Business Administration, Washington, DC 20416.

BUYING A GOING BUSINESS

You may have a number of reasons for wanting to buy a going business rather than start a new one, but this is a step that should be taken only after the most careful investigation and thought. First, consider the pros and cons of this way of entering business.

Advantages

Here are some factors that tend to favor purchasing a going business over starting from scratch.

• The problem of finding a new location is avoided.

• Store layout has been completed. It may not be exactly what you'd like, but it is usable for the time being.

• Fixtures and equipment are purchased and in place.

• The store's name and location are known to the community.

• Some of the customers will probably continue to do business with the store when you take over. You have, to a degree, a ready-made clientele.

• A study of the records will tell you something about what you can expect in the way of sales and expenses. If you open a brand new store, you'll have no past to which you can refer.

• Suppliers are aware of the business. Salesmen will continue to call.

• You can start operating as soon as you wind up the purchase, with or without a "Grand Opening." The cost of calling people's attention to a new venture is avoided.

• If the store has employees, they will probably be willing to stay with you. This gives you a staff of persons who know the business.

• Office forms, letterheads, and machines are at hand. Records are set up. You may want to make changes later, but at the time you take over ownership, you'll be ready to go.

Disadvantages

You shouldn't necessarily be discouraged by the disadvantages of buying a going business, but keep them in mind while you are making the decision. Here are some of them.

• There will probably be a charge for "goodwill." This is the term used to describe the business potential that comes to the buyer of a going concern in the form of established customers and reputation. How much you will have to pay for it depends on many variables—sales volume, location, how long the business has been in operation, how the business's profits compare with those of similar establishments, and so on.

• You may inherit employees who will refuse to change their ways of doing business if you ask them to. You may have to dismiss them, and doing that can be "sticky"—depending on the employee's age and length of employment.

• You may have to settle for premises that aren't quite what you'd like in the way of location, size, or appearance—your choices are more limited than when you are starting up new.

• You run the risk, unless you check every aspect of the business carefully, of buying a lemon and having a hard struggle to save your investment or improve on it. Even with care, some risk remains.

• You have to expect a falloff of sales when you take over. Especially if the business you purchase is quite small, a large share of the sales may have come from the personal following of the present owner.

Questions to Ask

If you find a business for sale that seems to be just what you want—wait! You need the answers to a lot of questions before you commit yourself to anything. Here are a few of the questions you should consider.

• What is the real reason the owner wants to sell? If it is poor health or old age, that's one thing. But if the location is poor, with sales falling off and little prospect of improvement at the present location, or if poor management has given the store a bad reputation, look out!

• Do the city planners have urban renewal or a throughway in mind for the area? Is the neighborhood changing in such a way as to affect the store's prospects?

• What is the physical condition of the building? Will it need repair right away? Are the floors solid, the roof waterproof, the windows good?

• Is the heating system in good order? Is there air conditioning; will it keep the building at a comfortable temperature on a hot day?

• If the store is rented, what is the status of the lease? Does it have a renewal clause? Does it provide for a rate change at renewal time? Can it be transferred to you?

• Are the business records complete and accurate? Be sure to insist on a complete audit of the books before you make any commitment. Remember that many records, especially those required by governmental agencies, must be kept on file for specified lengths of time. If you buy the business, you may be answerable for faults that were not yours.

• How old are the lighting fixtures and exhibit cases? How old is the carpeting, if there is any? Will you have to replace these items in the very near future?

• How secure is the building? Is there an adequate safe? A burglar alarm?

• How much and what kind of merchandise is in the inventory? Will you be taking on a lot of slow-selling items?

• Is there enough insurance on the store, its contents, the employees? Public liability insurance? Can you assume the payments?

• How about the accounts receivable if they are included in your purchase of the business? Are customers prompt in making their payments? Is the ratio of accounts receivable to sales too high?

If You Buy Accounts Receivable

Suppose you are buying a business, including the accounts receivable. These accounts represent money that will come to you after ownership changes hands, so you owe the present owner something for them. How do you know how much they are really worth?

It is absolutely essential that all accounts receivable be carefully audited to establish their accuracy. Those that are being paid regularly are obviously worth the most, and you should be willing to pay almost total value for them. Delinquent accounts that will be paid only after further demands for payment aren't worth anywhere near their face value to the buyer.

The arrangement often made for handling accounts receivable in this situation is to establish a discount based on the age of the monies due. On, so-called "clean" accounts—those on which payments are met regularly—the buyer retains 10 percent of the amount collected. The rest is turned over to the seller. Older accounts receivable of more doubtful merit may be discounted at 20 percent, 50 percent, and so on.

Don't Try to Go It Alone!

Suppose you have decided to purchase a going business and have found an opportunity that looks good. Before you commit yourself in any way, get advice from the following experts:

• Someone who knows merchandise values well, so that you will have an accurate judgment as to whether the price asked for the inventory is fair.

• An accountant who will examine all books and records of the business to determine its financial condition.

• A real-estate expert who can tell you whether the rent you will be paying is proper and what the prospects for the area are.

• A construction expert to check the building and report on its condition.

• A lawyer to make certain that all legal papers are in order.

• An insurance representative to see that you have the coverage you need. Be sure he is thoroughly familiar with the insurance needs of your particular business.

LOCATION AND LAYOUT

No two factors will influence the success of your business, especially a retail store, more than its location and physical layout. True, some people will go out of their way to shop at a favorite store. Some, after they have learned that they can get fine merchandise at a fair price from pleasant salespersons, won't pay a great deal of attention to store layout.

But both these kinds of people are in the minority. As the owner of a new store, you must have one whose appearance says, "Come in, come in!" and it must be in a good traffic area.

Factors in Selecting a Location

Several questions have to be answered before you are ready to select a location. What type of store will you have? Be specific. Will sales be the main activity, or will you do mostly repair work? What quality of merchandise will you carry? Will you play up credit sales? Once you have made a firm decision about what type of store you want, you are ready to look for a location where such a store will have a good chance of success.

Your decision may be affected by the kind of community you prefer to live and do business in. It also may be influenced by time and by the wish to put your capital to work for you at once. Perhaps the purely personal considerations of past associations, friends, relatives, or family will guide your choice. These are certainly points to consider, but don't let them blind you to other factors. You must keep in mind and give careful study and thought to practical, bread-and-butter points.

Size of the community

The size of the market in which you open a store will affect the operation of your store and, to some extent, your profits. There are advantages and disadvantages in each market size.

Dun & Bradstreet, in studies conducted over the years, has found that small towns with a population of 50,000 or less offer the best chance of business survival. They also show a very satisfactory ratio of profit to sales. Large cities (populations of 200,000 or more) offer the highest percent of profit and the possibility of much greater sales volume. However, because of the greater competition from other businesses, the chance of failure is highest here. Costs of getting started and expenses of doing business are also higher.

Location within the community

Most small towns have only one business district, and that is where your store should be if it is in such a community. In a city, you can choose a downtown or a suburban location.

Downtown business areas have a heavy daytime traffic pattern. Business employees shop at noon and on the way home. Housewives go downtown during the day to shop. Though stores may be open one or more evenings a week, most sales are made during the day.

Suburban stores have a pattern of fair sales volume on weekdays, with heavy sales on weekends and during the evening hours. This means that a suburban store must have more open-for-business evenings.

For a downtown location

• Downtown is closest to the greatest number of people.

• Downtown stores have facilities that make it possible to provide more stock and better service.

• Downtown is the traditional center of business—the place of work—the changing scene. It is the place that draws the masses, the main tourist attraction, and still the largest shopping area.

For a suburban shopping center

• People are moving to the suburbs. More new homes are being built there.

• Downtown parking can be a problem—and expensive. Shopping centers provide ample and free parking.

• The downtown shopping area tends to be spread out. Shopping centers are complete and compact.

• Getting to a suburban shopping center is just a matter of minutes for the housewife.

Checklist for Selecting a Town

Here are some checklists to help you select a community and a site within the community. It is important to get as much solid information as you can about the area you are considering. Investigate carefully each point mentioned here.

Economic factors

Don't be misled by the outward appearance or climate of a city. Both should be considered, but much more important is a hard look at where the community is heading. If the main industry, for instance, is a buggy-whip factory, the outlook for prosperity for the residents is not favorable, to say the least. The best community for you is one that has a number of different industries, that is not dependent on seasonal peaks and valleys, and that shows growth both in industry and in population.

• Trend: Is the industry growing, stationary, or declining?
• Permanence: Is the industry old and well established, new and promising, or recent and uncertain?
• Diversification: Are the sources of income varied, or is the town dependent on one major industry?
• Stability: Is the industry very stable, average, or subject to wide fluctuations?
• Seasonality: Is there little or no seasonal change in industry, mild seasonal change, or extreme seasonal fluctuation?
• Outlook: Is the future of industry in the community promising, uncertain, or poor?

Population

• Trend: Is the population growing, stationary, or declining?
• Income: Is the community wealthy, well-to-do, moderately well off, or poor?
• Character: Is the population native born, mixed, or chiefly foreign born?

Competition

Competition can be a blessing or a curse. Lively stores selling up-to-date merchandise in an attractive setting give an overall tone to the business area that draws customers. On the other hand, your chances for success would be slim in a community that already has more than its share of your type of store or business.

 • Number of stores: Are there few, many, or too many?

 • Management: Is the management unprogressive, average, or alert and aggressive?

 • Chains: Are there any chain stores in your line of business in the community, a few chains, or many well-established chains?

 • Appearance: Are the stores attractive, average, unattractive?

 • Department stores: How many department stores have competing sections—none, a few, many?

Facilities of the town

You will want to be in a community that has good public transportation, ample parking space, good banks, active organizations, and other facilities for living as well as doing business. You should also be reasonably near your suppliers. Check these points:

 • Transportation facilities
 • Wholesale suppliers
 • Banking facilities
 • Civic associations
 • Schools
 • Churches
 • Medical and dental services
 • Amusements
 • Climate

The people

You wouldn't try to open a store in Zenobia unless you spoke and understood Zenobian. Be choosy about where you decide to go into business. Pick a community that is "you." You might succeed elsewhere, but why do things the hard way?

Checklist for Selecting a Site

Now that you have chosen a community, exactly where in the community will you open your store? Before you decide, take time to study the sites you find available and evaluate them carefully. When you find a store building that seems to have merit, check the surrounding area. Watch the street traffic. Ask yourself these questions.

The neighborhood

• How about the quality of the neighborhood? Does it appear to be changing? Many communities have areas that are either peaking or starting to run downhill. Other areas may be rising or at least retaining their vigor. Make sure, if you can, that no superhighways or throughways are planned for the area.

Traffic

• Is the street traffic fairly heavy at other than rush hours?
• Do the pedestrians impress you as being the kind of people who would be good prospects for your store?
• Is the foot traffic passing the store going to or between popular stores or office buildings?
• Are the people in a constant rush, or are they leisurely shoppers?

Customer access to the site

• How close is the store to transportation? Is there a bus or subway stop nearby?
• Are there adequate parking facilities in the area?
• Are the sidewalks wide and in good repair?
• Is the street lighting good?

Competition

• How many similar businesses are there in the vicinity?
• Do you honestly believe that you could do a better job in appearance, display, and salesmanship than the stores now doing business there? (Visit the stores. Get firsthand information. Leave nothing to guesswork if you can possibly get facts.)

Store Layout

When you have found the exact location for your store, the next problem is that of preparing the building—the interior layout and the exterior appearance. Whether you are starting from scratch or taking over a going business with the idea of renovating the building, you will be wise to get the help of a good architect. You'll have to pay him, but his services could save you much money later. An interior decorator can be helpful, but an experienced architect is the best bet.

Six keys

Remember these six keys to good layout as you plan your store:

- Attractive, eye-appealing design
- Good display of the merchandise
- Maximum use of space
- Customer convenience
- Free customer circulation
- Efficiency in handling the sale

Some Questions to Answer

As you study and plan the preparation of your building, consider the following points:

1. Is the store exterior pleasing? Does it have a modern, up-to-date look?

Weatherbeaten, unpainted sideboard may look good on a building in a Western movie, but it is not for you. A clean, bright exterior will give prospective customers a good impression.

2. Can you erect a good storefront sign?

Lettering on front windows is passé—and it blocks the view of merchandise.

3. Are the windows a good size?

Your window glass should be not less than 48 nor more than 54 inches high, depending on the type of storefront.

4. How deep is the display area inside your window?

It should be at least 30 inches deep. This gives plenty of space for display, yet places all merchandise within easy reach for trimming or removal upon customer request.

5. Is the floor in good condition? If it is carpeted, is the carpeting fairly new?

You may decide to start without carpeting and add it later. But nearly every store has it these days, and it is easier to install or replace before the display cases are in place.

A word of caution: Ordinary home carpeting will not bear up under store traffic. Be sure you buy commercial-grade material.

6. How good is the lighting?

The type of lighting you want will depend on the type of store you are trying to create, but be sure there is enough light.

Lighting can be used to set the tone of the store, to create atmosphere, to dramatize merchandise, and to arouse shopper interest. Your local electric power company can be helpful, and your architect will be a good source of advice. Detailed guides to store lighting can be obtained from the Illuminating Engineering Society, 345 East 47th Street, New York, N.Y. 10017.

7. Should you use an all-glass door?

Modern stores use them almost exclusively. Be sure the handle has an easily visible design to avoid the chance of people, especially children, accidentally walking into the closed door. Carry insurance on the door—repair can be costly.

8. Is there space for an office and storage?

9. How can you arrange your display cases so as to show your merchandise to the best advantage?

Counter-height cases are placed throughout the store for display and to make sales easier.

Be sure you have enough display area, but don't cramp the aisle space. If you do, customers will go elsewhere for service.

10. Can you provide ample space for wrapping merchandise?

Many items will be purchased as gifts. You'll need to gift wrap them and perhaps package them for mailing.

11. Are there any bottleneck areas where traffic tends to become tied up?

Free flow of customer and employee traffic is a must.

These points don't cover all the many aspects of store layout you'll have to consider. The shape and size of your store will play a big role. Remember, your wisest move will be to employ an architect.

Move slowly and surely. Be sure you have looked into and studied all the physical aspects of your store building. When you open for business, you should be able to rest assured that you have the best possible layout from the standpoint of security, customer comfort, color scheme, lighting, floor treatment, and employee movement.

And, finally, keep in touch with your lawyer. Don't commit yourself either to purchase or lease a site without consulting him.

Your Lease

One of the most important points in a lease is the length of time you are contracting for. You are starting with no business history behind you. You have lots of confidence in your ability to make a success of your store, but sometimes things do go wrong. For how long should you tie yourself up with a lease?

You will be making a considerable investment in fixtures, and you'll spend a good deal of money attracting customers to this specific location. A short-term lease, therefore, would be risky. If your business is successful, the landlord might demand much higher rent when your lease runs out. Or he may want you to vacate the premises if he gets a better offer—one you can't match. On the other hand, if you've made a mistake in selecting the location, you'll find yourself trapped if you've signed a long-term lease.

One method of hedging is to sign a lease for 2 or 3 years with an option to renew. In an arrangement of this type, you may have to offer an increase in rent for the second period.

Your lawyer may insist on a clause that protects you from competition within the building or shopping center for the life of the lease and its renewals.

TYPES OF BUSINESS OWNERSHIP

You may organize your business in any one of three basic legal forms: sole proprietorship, partnership, or corporation. There are also some variations of these three. Discuss the matter thoroughly with your lawyer and perhaps your accountant before you decide which form to use. Each one has advantages and disadvantages.

Sole Proprietorship

A sole proprietorship is the easiest form to get started. There are fewer legal problems, and you don't have to share control or profits with anyone else.

It does have some disadvantages, however. You are personally liable for the full amount of the debts of the business. You risk, not only the amount you invest in the business, but your personal assets as well. And, since you have only your own assets to offer as collateral, it's usually harder to borrow funds for the business than when there are two or more owners.

Partnership

A partner may be a source of needed capital, and a trustworthy and experienced partner can also be a great help to you in other ways. Work hours can be shared. You can feel confident that affairs are in good hands when you are away. Your partner may be able to teach you some things that would cost you time and money to find out for yourself.

On the other hand, personality problems can cause trouble. Are you sure that you can get along well with someone you are in constant business contact with day in and day out? How about your partner? Many a business has foundered because the partners couldn't get along.

Also, what would your partner bring to the business? Does he have ability and experience that would supplement yours? Would he bring solid knowledge, background, or money, or is he just a pal you think you'd like to have as an associate? Friendship tends to fray under the stress and strain of business problems, especially if one partner turns out to be weak—or, at the other end of the scale, stubborn or bossy. Does the size and potential volume you are planning justify a partner? Will the business be able to support the two partners adequately?

Do you have complete faith in the business judgment and honesty of the person you are considering as a partner? You will be personally liable for any debts or other contractual obligations he incurs in connection with the business.

If you are thinking seriously of a partnership, talk with your lawyer to make sure that you understand just what is involved. Have him draw up a detailed partnership agreement to be signed by both partners. This is important even though it isn't required by law. The agreement should cover not only how the partnership functions—what the duties and responsibilities of each partner are and so on—but also how the partnership is to be ended if one partner decides to quit.

Many highly successful retail businesses operate as partnerships, but they are stores whose owners checked all the pros and cons of the arrangement carefully *before* committing themselves. Clear thinking ahead of time may prevent heated arguments later.

Incorporation

Incorporating your business can be a way to raise additional capital. This form of organization gives you the safeguard of limited liability. Each stockholder or owner risks only the amount he invests in the business. (This is not too great an advantage when you are just getting started, since creditors will doubtless require that you sign obligations personally.) Also, an owner can sell or otherwise transfer his stock to another individual at will—provided he can find a buyer—without affecting the activities of the corporation.

There are other advantages and also some disadvantages. The principal disadvantages are the cost of setting up a corporation, additional taxes, and closer regulation by governmental agencies.

One of the first things your lawyer can do for you is to help you decide whether to incorporate your business. He'll explain the requirements, advantages, and disadvantages of each type of business organization. Your accountant may also enter into this discussion, since it involves taxes.

If you have a partner, your lawyer will draw up the partnership agreement. A legally executed partnership agreement isn't required by law, but it is an important safeguard for you, your business, and your heirs.

Where the Law Comes In

No business is so small that it doesn't come under some sort of government regulation—Federal, State, local—probably all three. Many of these regulations vary widely from one area to another.You'll have to find out just what regulations are in effect in your locality. You can, of course, check with the local authorities, but the safest way is to talk the matter over with your lawyer. He'll make certain that you comply with all regulations covering your type of business.

You'll be signing agreements with your fixture man, air-conditioning engineer, and others. Your lawyer will also see that you are protected in the performance and delivery of these jobs as ordered. Throughout your career as a business owner, matters will be coming up from time to time on which you must consult a lawyer. It will be to your advantage, if possible, to have one who is familiar with your business from the start.

YOUR BUSINESS RECORDS

Your record keeping system should be as complete as necessary and as simple as possible. It should also be well-organized and *kept up to date*. You'll have to keep some records in order to fulfill your legal obligations—payroll records, records of your income and expenditures, and so on. These required records, as well as others you should keep, are also an aid to good management. A good record keeping system will help you identify trouble spots and remedy them before they threaten the success of your business.

Getting Set

Get an accountant to set up your books for you. He can install a simple, easy-to-follow system that can be used as it is at first and expanded later as your business prospers. He can tell you about business procedures you must follow if your records are to be kept properly.

This is important, because records and systems are inseparable. The best record books in the world are of no use unless they are kept up to date. Have a system, and establish a pattern to make certain that all entries are made correctly, clearly, and without delay. If necessary, arrange to have an accountant keep the records and prepare the reports on a part-time basis.

The Basic Records

The financial records of your store will begin with bits and pieces of paper such as order forms, invoices, sales slips, credit memos, cash register tapes, written receipts, check stubs, petty-cash slips, bank statements, letters. These papers are important. They are the building blocks from which you put together your organized permanent records. Some sort of written record, however informal, should always be made *at the time a transaction takes place.*

The journal

The information from these various papers is first brought together in one or more journals; sometimes called "books of original entry." A journal is simply a record in chronological order of the daily transactions of your business. Each entry shows the date of the transaction; a brief description of it; the amount of money involved; and the assets, liabilities, capital, or type of income or expense affected by the transaction.

The ledger

To make the information record in the journal more usable, each entry is later transferred, or posted, to a ledger account. A ledger account is a record of the increases and decreases in *one type* of asset, liability, capital, income, or expense. A book in which several accounts are kept is called a ledger.

Financial Statements

At least once a year—every month would be better—your financial records should be summarized in the form of *financial statements.* The two most commonly used financial statements are the *balance sheet* and the *profit-and-loss statement.*

The balance sheet lists your assets, liabilities, and capital to show the condition of your business on a given date. It tells you how much of the assets you really own, which is simply the difference between the total assets and the liabilities, or debts of the business.

The profit-and-loss statement summarizes the activities of your business during the period covered. It shows the various types of income and expense for the business and the profit or loss that resulted.

If these financial statements are figured as percent of sales as well as in dollars and cents, you will be able to keep an eye on the trend of your business from one period to another and to compare your performance with the average performance of similar businesses. This can reveal areas that need special attention before they become real danger spots.

Your Bank Account

All receipts should be deposited daily in a bank account set up for your store. This account should be kept entirely separate from your personal bank account. When you draw funds for personal use, do so by writing a check on the store account made out to yourself.

Small purchases or other payments can be made from a petty-cash fund set up and replenished when necessary by cashing checks made out to "Petty Cash." (Be sure to keep a record of every payment from this fund.) *No* payments should be made from the cash drawer.

Keep an accurate record of each check on the stub provided in your checkbook, and reconcile your record with the bank statement you receive each month—regularly and promptly.

Inventory Records

If your stock is well organized, you can check fairly easily what you have on hand and what items must be reordered. A well stocked shop has hundreds of items for sale, and a complete perpetual-inventory system would be laborious to maintain. Therefore, many dealers keep detailed records only of their major items.

Get some 5″ × 7″ cards and a file box to fit. Use a separate card for each item for which you plan to keep an inventory record. Head the card with the name of the item. Then for each item purchased, list the name of the supplier, serial number of the item, date received, date sold, cost, and selling price. Also record to whom it was sold if you think you can use this information later in selling accessories.

With inventory cards like these, you can tell at a glance how many of a major item you have in stock, price changes, and rate of sale. Another benefit is that you will have an accurate record to prove a claim for loss in case of fire or burglary.

Many dealers also keep a "want book" and send written orders to their suppliers at the end of each day. If there is a rush request, the telephone is used to contact the vendor.

Advertisement file

Keep a file of copies of the ads you place in newspapers and the scripts for radio spot announcements if you use radio. Later, you can relate sales to ads and evaluate your advertising program.

Employment records

If you have any employees, you'll have to keep a careful record of hours worked, Social Security and income taxes withheld, and so on. Forms for this purpose can be purchased at an office-supply store, or your accountant can work out a system that fits your particular needs.

Records, Files, and Piles

Every business faces the continuing problem of accumulated records, overloaded files, and the piles of papers each year's business produces. What do you do with correspondence, canceled checks, paid bills, sales slips, charge records, repair-department slips, salary records, and the like?

First, find out how long the law requires that certain records be kept. However, although the law sets a retention period or a statute of limitations governing certain records (such as income tax returns and salary records), it is wise to hold some records longer than the required period. Your own experience will have to dictate how long you should keep other internal records, such as correspondence, before throwing them out.

Many stores list their record files on a "retention" card or a single sheet of paper. Opposite the title of each file there is a figure showing the number of years that records of that type are to be kept. On a specified date each year (it may be the calendar or fiscal year end, for example) the current file is closed and placed in dead storage. At the same time, the oldest file in dead storage is thrown out.

The retention card should be reviewed each year, and the number of years subject file is to be kept should be checked against experience. The retention time may need to be lengthened for some, shortened for others.

One of the big advantages of such a system is that you can tell quickly by referring to the retention card whether records of a certain past year are in the file. This can save much time that might otherwise be spent searching through dead files only to discover that the item you're looking for has been discarded.

Your lawyer and your accountant can be of great help in setting up your records-retention system. Once it is done, you'll have a valuable, orderly system for handling your records, files, and piles.

INSURANCE

Insurance is a complicated business. Most of us don't understand its details. You'll need an experienced and conscientious insurance broker to help you plan your insurance program.

Some kinds of insurance are required by law; others are optional but important for your own protection. Choose an insurance broker you can trust and then work out with him an overall program that will give you the protection you need without overlapping.

Building Insurance

You may decide to buy the building in which you open your business, or you may lease it. What you do will determine your insurance needs.

Insurance for your own building

If you own the building, check the following points:

• Do the policies cover fire, the extended-coverage perils including riot and civil commotion, and also vandalism and malicious mischief? A special extended-coverage endorsement that extends the policy to cover the building on an all-risk basis would be even better.

• Do you have a current and reliable record of both the replacement cost and the actual cash value of the building? If not, you should have a professional appraisal prepared for insurance purposes.

• Is the insurance written on a replacement-cost basis? A replacement-cost endorsement is necessary for this.

• Is the amount of insurance adequate? If you are in a riot-prone area, you may need to insure to 100 percent of replacement cost.

• Is breakage of window glass by riot and civil commotion covered? Breakage caused by vandalism that is not part of a riot? Should you consider plate glass breakage insurance?

Insurance for leased building

Suppose you lease your store space. You must then pay special attention to the provisions of your lease. You may have to cover your responsibility for damage both to the leased building or space and to your leasehold improvements. Take plenty of time to be *sure* that all questions are settled clearly *and in writing*. After a fire is no time to work out a mutually agreeable settlement on who is responsible for what. Among the points you should check are these:

• Does the lease clearly define the responsibility of the landlord or the tenant for repair or replacement of damage to the leased building and to tenant's leasehold improvements?

• Is there an agreement that the landlord will replace any glass broken by fire, riot, civil commotion, or other perils under the landlord's building insurance? If not, you should consider plate glass breakage insurance.

• Do you have an inventory of individual items of leasehold improvements and betterments with a current and reliable estimate of new replacement cost and actual cash value? If not, an appraisal is recommended.

• Does improvements and betterments insurance cover fire, the extended-coverage perils and vandalism?

• Does the improvements and betterments insurance insure on a replacement cost basis? A replacement cost endorsement is necessary for this. Is the amount of insurance enough to cover total destruction?

Business Interruption Insurance

Business interruption insurance covering riot and civil commotion as well as other perils is essential. It may mean the difference between life and death for your business. However, it has some limitations, and you must understand these clearly.

This insurance does not and cannot cover all loss of earnings resulting from a riot. More difficulty has arisen in connection with business interruption insurance than with any other form of insurance. There have been misunderstandings on the part of those insured as to the extent of coverage, disagreements as to the intent of the Civil Authority clause, and the problem of determining the loss of business actually covered by the policy.

Business interruption insurance insures only against loss of earnings resulting from damage to property on the premises of the insured person by an insured peril (except as extended by the Civil Authority clause). This difference is the key to understanding the limitations of business interruption insurance. In spite of the limitations, however, you must have this type of insurance.

Public Liability Insurance

Public liability insurance covers the owner of the store for any bodily injury sustained by a member of the public while on the store premises. Coverage can include medical payments for injuries to the public regardless of legal liability.

Bonding of Employees

Bonding employees protects the store owner against dishonesty on the part of the employees covered by the bond. For a small store, however, where the owner is working with a near relative or a close friend, this type of insurance may not be practical.

• Unless you are an insurance expert, get the services of a highly reputable broker and follow his advice. After you've been in business for several years, you may be able to make changes on your own; but at the start, with so much at stake, *don't underinsure!*

ADVERTISING

To make sure that the public knows your business exists, you'll have to advertise. Advertising costs money; and starting small, as you probably will, you're likely to have only limited advertising funds. Don't waste the little money you have. Use it effectively.

Where to Advertise

You should consider the following media, or methods of advertising.

• *Person-to-person advertising, or direct mail*

If your business is in a small town, you may find it best to use direct mail. Build a list of people you know or have reason to believe will be good prospects and those who have already purchased merchandise. Send them letters or cards promoting your store and its merchandise.

This is a rifle approach. It lacks the shotgun aspects of newspaper or radio advertising, but it may bring better results under some circumstances.

• *Newspapers*

Nearly every home receives a daily paper. It doesn't cost as much to advertise in newspapers as it does in some media, and you can use illustrations. If the paper covers too broad an area outside your immediate market, it may not bring the return you want; but if you are in a large market area, it may be your best kind of advertising.

• *Radio*

Spot radio announcements, if you can afford them, can be very effective. Your message must be unique, though, or it will be lost among all the others.

• *Television*

This is the most costly medium of all. It is used only by fairly large, well established businesses. For you, its use will come later. At the start, the cost will probably be too high.

• *Other forms of advertising*

Maintain a listing in the Yellow Pages of the telephone directory. Always have business cards on hand.

How Much to Advertise

Most stores use a combination of advertising media, starting with direct mail and newspapers and then branching out into radio and television as funds became available.

Keep this fact in mind: To be effective, advertising must be continuous. If you are just thinking of using newspaper advertisements or radio spot announcements once in a while, save your money. It's the regular, daily ad that produces impact and an identity and image for your store.

Window Displays

Your window displays can be a most effective form of advertising. The passerby who stops to look in your window becomes a potential customer *if* what he sees says, "Come in!"

The window area should be well lighted and the merchandise tastefully displayed. Be creative in your arrangement. Feature a few items rather than many—a cluttered window is just that and nothing more. Originality pays off, too. Use colored lights or spotlights to accent one item or an arrangement of items.

Many articles have been written about window displays. Pictures of stores in trade magazines will give you ideas, too.

Should you use the services of a professional window dresser? Many stores do, but with a limited budget you'd better have a go at it yourself until your business is producing a profit.

Interior Display

In arranging your store interior, keep in mind the idea of "suggestion selling." Suggestion selling is the art of persuading the customer, by spoken suggestion or by skillful display, to buy something he didn't intend to buy when he entered the store. This may be additional items or a higher priced article than he originally had in mind.

Display merchandise tastefully, and be sure it is well lighted. Logical tie-ins should be displayed close together.

Select a single item to feature on top of a counter or show-case. Watch to see if it catches customer interest and results in sales. If so, leave it there awhile. If not, try some other item.

BEAUTY SHOPS

I. RECOMMENDATION

The beauty care industry is among the fastest growing service industries in the United States but is also characterized by one of the highest industry failures. The reason for this is that beauty shops, or "salons," are usually very small in size and cater to a limited and demanding clientele. A few dissatisfied customers can have wide-ranging ill effects on the business.

Consequently, while beauty shops are good investments under the proper conditions, the entrepreneur must approach the venture with caution. Unless the manager can attract qualified and personable stylist employees, chances of success are limited. If a good staff is lined up and proper marketing analysis and planning precedes the venture, however, chances of success and a good return on investment are relatively high.

The shop should be planned and located only after the client population is defined and carefully analyzed with respect to current consumer patterns. While a successful existing firm has an initial competitive edge, there will always be women willing to try new establishments. If these trial customers are satisfied, the word will spread quickly, and a market of regular clients should soon develop.

Initial venture capital will run between $10,000 and $20,000 for medium-sized establishments (3 to 6 operators). Stylists can be found through industry sources, beauty schools, employment agencies, or classified advertisements.

The beauty care industry is one of the few in which a well-defined minority market segment can be identified. Minority-owned beauty salons tend to have an advantage in serving members of their own community, and the rapidly increasing beauty consciousness in the minority population provides a strong basis of support for the operations of a well-planned and operated salon catering to this group's needs.

II. DESCRIPTION OF THE BUSINESS

A. Identification

A beauty shop is any establishment primarily engaged in offering services to women involving hair, facial, hand, and nail treatment. While primarily providing services, some retail activities are included. In most shops wig sales, for example, are a new revenue generator.

Beauty shops are classified for statistical purposes as Standard Industrial Classification (SIC) 723 (and as SIC 7231 on the four-digit level). Included in SIC 723 are establishments that offer both beauty services for females and, secondarily, barber services for males. This profile, however, is restricted to the female-oriented services, which constitute the bulk of activities within this general classification.

B. Dimensions

There has been a steady growth in the beauty care industry in the United States during the past decade. The following statistics from the *Census of Manufactures* illustrate this growth:

Year	Number of establishments	Total receipts	Number of employees	Total payroll
1958	110,395	$1,028,077,000	140,336	$342,053,000
1963	151,720	$1,617,959,000	203,738	$572,910,000
1967	179,209	$2,354,398,000	255,037	$943,298,000

During this period, 1958–1967, growth was common to all parts of the United States. Only two States, Delaware and Montana, have experienced a decrease in the number of beauty establishments—and in both cases, total beauty shop revenues continued to rise despite the decrease in establishments.

More recent data suggest that the growth trend has continued beyond 1967. A Bank of America report on beauty salons indicated that in 1969 there was a 9.5 percent increase in sales over 1968 and an 8.2 percent increase in employees over this same year period as compared to annual rates of roughly 11 percent in sales and 6 percent in employment for both the 1958–1963 and 1963–1967 periods, as illustrated in the table above.

Using these rates as a basis, the beauty shop industry (as defined by SIC 723) in the United States was in 1971 a $3½ billion per year business, employing over 300,000 individuals in some 200,000 establishments. Over half of these establishments are small proprietorships with no paid employees. Of those with employees, the majority are single proprietorships with two or three employees on the payroll.

C. Characteristics

1. Nature of the Product

Women frequent beauty shops for the purpose of becoming better groomed and consequently more attractive. Also the beauty shop often serves as a social meeting place where weekly or monthly information is exchanged with other regular customers or with the staff.

The services offered include a wide spectrum of hair, facial, hand, and nail treatment. Among the more common services are hair and scalp conditioning, hair shampooing, dyeing or tinting, cutting, setting, and styling; facials and makeup, nail filing and polishing; and hairpiece sales and care. Hairdressing and manicures have typically accounted for the largest portion of receipts over the years.

For the most part, beauty shop services are required by their clients on a regular basis. There is in addition a sizeable number of clients who frequent beauty shops only on special occasions (before a wedding, dance, or similar event), choosing to use home care at other times. However, most customers are regular beauty shop users who visit the shop weekly or every 2 weeks.

Prices for beauty shop services vary widely from establishment to establishment, and sometimes even from stylist to stylist within the same establishment. For example, the price of a haircut—which takes relatively little time and minimal supplies and equipment—can range from $2 to $8 or more. Price ranges are determined primarily by the skill and/or reputation of the stylist; customer-type (income level primarily), time to complete service, cost of supplies and equipment, and market considerations (such as price lists of competitors).

The higher priced services, such as permanent waving or hair coloring (ranging from $15 to $25 and up), are required on a less frequent basis by regular customers than are the lower priced services (shampoo sets, for example, at $5 to $7 and up) which are required weekly or every 2 weeks.

Many salons complement their service sales by selling beauty products as well. Some offer more specialized services such as electrolysis for removal of unwanted facial and/or body hair and makeup treatments. Others compete with department stores and specialty shops by offering a full line of wigs and accessories (wig stands, cleaners, special combs and brushes). However, no more than 15 percent of all beauty shops offer this wide assortment of services—most focus almost wholly on hair treatment and styling.

2. Nature of the Customer

Virtually all women desire some continuous form of hair grooming and/or treatment. They have three alternatives: (1) do it themselves, (2) have relatives or friends do it, and/or (3) seek professional services. The decision to take the latter route—to seek professional services either by going to beauty shops or, in rarer cases, by having beauticians come to them—is based upon such considerations as availability of time, income, desire for expert services, lack of household alternative (e.g., no appropriate product on the market), and extent of interest, trust, or patience in home treatment.

Accordingly, the best source of customers for beauty shops are, first, middle-aged and elderly housewives who have time and money, and are extremely sensitive about their changing hair and facial features, and, second, working women who have their own incomes, a need to look well groomed at all times, and who don't want the burden of home grooming added to their already full week of activities. In an attempt to concentrate on younger clientele, some beauty shops have gone "mod," employing wild posters, rock music, and occasionally combining beauty services with retail sales of women's clothes and accessories (the so-called "boutique treatment").

One major determinant of each salon's customer mix is its established policy regarding appointments. There are recognized advantages and corresponding disadvantages to maintaining a standing list of appointments. On the plus side, a fully booked schedule of regular customers means a steady income from these regular patrons, fewer telephone calls and appointment changes, less style changes and learning problems, less idle time, and a more congenial atmosphere. On the other hand, the full book generally consists primarily of low-profit services (sets, manicures, etc.) and may result in a less challenging and more routine operation with little or no chance to increase profits by serving new patrons. Accordingly, a common strategy is for new shops and/or new stylists to begin by permitting customers to book time, but, upon establishing a reputation and a sound customer following, to reverse the booking policy and schedule customers according to the time and workload desired by the shop or stylist. This results in a more interesting schedule of services, combining profitable and less profitable items and permitting open time blocks for new patrons.

The location of the beauty shop will depend upon the target population being served and also upon the strategy adopted regarding customer scheduling. Women often combine the beauty shop trip with other shopping chores, and consequently the location of the shop in proximity to shopping areas is considered highly desirable.

Consequently, beauty shops are found in most shopping centers. In such cases, the shop may have an "exclusivity clause" within its lease, restricting the presence of competing businesses such as wig and cosmetic shops. Further, a beauty shop in a shopping center that does not accept appointments may be able to negotiate a higher favorable lease on the basis that customers may fill their waiting time frequenting the surrounding shops. Other common locations, in additon to shopping centers, are hotels, apartment house complexes, and downtown office districts.

3. Staffing Needs and Skills

The beauty operator must possess skills in shampooing, cutting, setting, styling, straightening, permanent waving, bleaching, and tinting, and in giving manicures, pedicures, scalp and facial treatments, makeup analysis, and in eyebrow shaping. A knowledge of the cleaning and styling of wigs and falls is becoming more necessary as well.

Operators in beauty salons must be licensed by the Board of Cosmetology in each State. To be eligible for licensing a prospective operator must possess a diploma from an accredited beauty school. Licensing is contingent upon passing the State board examination, meeting age requirements (usually 16 years of age), provision of certification of good health and having completed the minimum years of required formal schooling (ranging from grades 8 to 12, depending on the State). Cosmetology laws in most States require that an operator have at least 1 year of experience before opening or managing a beauty salon. Completion of a State-approved cosmetology course (6 months to a year) is recognized as adequate preparation for the examination in most States; sometimes this can be substituted for a period of apprenticeship.

The majority of beauty shops are proprietorships with no paid employees. The shops with employees generally have no more than three or four beauty operators, although much larger shops do exist. Operators may secure different types of arrangements with the shop owner. In most cases, their salaries will be based upon a percentage of their total service sales. A minimum guaranteed weekly income may also be set. The usual commission paid to an operator is 50 percent to 60 percent of sales. Inexperienced stylists will generally accept a lower rate at first. A few owners permit operators to act as independent agents who rent a station in the shop for a fee and/or a commission. In such cases, the operators generally furnish their own supplies. Weekly earnings for beauty operators range from $80 to $100 for beginning operators to $300 and up for top stylists.

In larger shops, auxiliary staff may also be required. Such staff might include a shampoo girl, manicurist, electrologist, receptionist (who may also handle retail sales), and maintenance help. Some salons keep a minimum full-time staff and increase personnel on the busiest days—Thursdays, Fridays, and Saturdays. Specialists such as a manicurist and electrologist are paid either on the same percentage basis as stylists or on the basis of concession arrangements. A shampoo girl must be a licensed cosmetologist in most States, but she is likely to be either a stylist just starting out or an older operator who is not skilled in recent styling techniques. Receptionists receive a flat salary (around $100 per week) or may work for commissions from retail sales. Maintenance staff are paid by the hour at a minimum wage level.

The major advantage of a full-service auxiliary staff is that stylists can be freed to engage in the more lucrative services while the more basic and smaller revenue producing services are performed by less expensive staff. In only relatively few shops, however, is there sufficient volume to permit such economies of scale.

4. Competition and Marketing

The success of a beauty shop rests squarely on satisfying the perceived needs of the client. If a customer is satisfied with the service she receives, she will continue to frequent the establishment on a regular basis. Moreover, she will serve as the single most effective form of advertisement for the shop ("Where did you get your hair done? It looks terrific!. . ."). On the other hand, if she is *not* satisfied with the services received, she will be certain to mention this to friends and associates. The negative consequences can be significant.

It has been found (by the National Hairdressers and Cosmetologists Association as a consequence of the collective experience of its members) that women will accept poor workmanship much quicker than bad treatment in the shop. Thus, customer relations is of even greater importance than quality of services in securing and maintaining a contented and growing clientele.

Beauty shops typically compete on the basis of service, quality, price, and image. The customers of a given beauty shop tend to be of a more homogeneous nature than in most other service establishments. The reason for this is that most stylists tend to favor certain hair styles and other beauty aids. Consequently their client groups quickly define themselves as those women who prefer this range of styles. More often than not, the style range will be more common among certain groups of women than others (the young, the middle class, housewives, office workers, the wealthy, the country club set, etc.). Shop decor and the price list also reflect customer range.

While customer recommendations are the best form of advertisement, it is usually recommended by industry experts that between 1½ percent and 3 percent of total sales be utilized for advertising, with perhaps 5 percent being spent in the initial year of operation. Direct neighborhood mailing has generally proven to be more effective than television or radio spots. Contributing free hairdos for school, church, and fashion shows and for local theatrical productions—with an accompanying credit line in the program—is also a typically effective method of advertising. Product distributors and manufacturers will sometimes contribute advertisement funds or materials to the shop in behalf of their product lines. Beauty shops in shopping centers may be required to contribute to a tenant association which, in turn, will handle all advertisements for the entire complex. Offering free introductory services (such as haircuts) or reduced introductory prices to newcomers to the area through organizations like "Welcome Wagon" will also help attract new customers.

Chains, especially those in department stores, and franchise operations are growing in numbers and in the volume of business they do. Even though at present they constitute less than 10 percent of the country's beauty shops, they present the independents with their major competitive threat. These big business salons achieve high sales either by using the "assembly-line" system of budget salons or charging high prices in luxury salons noted for their chic. Franchised operations are often given preferential consideration in shopping center developments.

The small salon also has competition from home beauty products —although national advertising can help increase salon sales by introducing women to new beauty aids and making them more beauty conscious. More than a few women have come to the beauty salon after damaging their hair by misusing home products.

5. Ease of New Firm Entry

All States require that a beauty salon manager be a licensed cosmetologist and hairdresser. However, the requirements for securing such a license vary from State to State and are obtainable from the bureau of licenses in each State and city. Locational requirements in relation to health and zoning regulations, as well as specifications of equipment conditions, may make difficult securing a specific site.

In addition to the initial capital investment of between $1,500 and $10,000 depending on size and decor, a cash reserve will be necessary to meet preoperating expenses, including advertising, legal services, and advance rent. The cash reserve must be large enough to cover both business and personal expenses until the business is on a paying basis. The minimum time for achieving profitable operations is estimated to be about 3 to 4 months. July and August are considered the slowest months in which to open a new salon, unless the location is a resort area.

Since there is a high turnover rate in beauty shops, the prospective owner might consider buying an existing salon rather than starting from scratch. An existing shop should have the proper electrical wiring and plumbing and the necessary equipment. However, the buyer should be careful to investigate why the shop is being sold. Was it so successful that the owner wanted to enlarge or was he discouraged by the lack of business? He should also find out whether any of the employees will stay on; if they leave, many of the present customers may go, too.

Minority-owned and operated beauty shops are quite common in minority neighborhoods. The ability to develop such an establishment in an all-white or racially mixed area will depend upon prevailing racial attitudes rather than on economic or other institutional factors.

6. Capital requirements and Financing

The amount of initial capital investment (or startup costs) required to begin a new beauty salon is dependent upon the target market, the types of services to be performed, and the number of operators to be employed. At a minimum, a shop selling to a lower income group will require from $1,600 to $1,800; one servicing a middle income group may need from $2,000 to $3,000; and a luxury type shop from $5,000 to $10,000 and up. The largest single cost factor in the beginning will be the equipment, including shampoo sinks, styling chairs, curler stands, dryers, and mirrors. This equipment usually costs $1,000 per station and may be purchased on installment.

In addition, inventories for the retail sales of beauty products and/or wigs and accessories as required must be added to the total cost. A typical wig room with display cases and counter can run an additional $500 to $1,000.

Typical operating costs include the following.

a. Rent, utilities, telephone, insurance (6 percent to 10 percent of sales).

b. Salaries (50 percent to 60 percent of sales).

c. Initial advertising (5 percent of sales).

d. Improvements in space, including plumbing, electricity, painting, and sign costs (5 percent to 10 percent of sales).

e. Supplies for shop use (7 percent to 10 percent of sales).

f. Reserve fund (5 percent of sales).

Financing may be accomplished through the use of equity, commercial bank loans under Small Business Administration guarantees, and occasional minority business financing. An excellent guide to local sources of financial and technical aid is the *Directory of Private Programs Assisting Minority Business,* Office of Minority Business Enterprise, U.S. Department of Commerce, 1970.

Franchise operations are growing in importance in the industry and now account for almost 10 percent of all establishments. The franchise fee entitles the entrepreneur to several advantages (such as use of company's name, preferential treatment in seeking locations, training programs, access to suppliers, etc.), which in turn should aid the entrepreneur in securing financial backing.

7. Profitability and Risk

Beauty shops have been able to raise their prices on a regular basis throughout the past decade to more than compensate for increasing costs of operation. The average gross margin for the industry is between 20 percent and 35 percent of total sales. Franchise operations are, on the average, even more profitable.

A high turnover rate of establishments during the 1960's, coupled with the rapid growth of the industry as a whole, suggest that while beauty shop operations can be highly profitable for successful entrepreneurs, the risks are great. Success is linked directly to satisfying the consumer through both quality of service and courteous delivery of these services. A few dissatisfied customers can literally destroy the market for the establishment. Consequently, the failure rate is high. The risk can be minimized substantially by selecting qualified and experienced beauty operators and by taking all measures possible to insure that every customer is well treated.

8. Dependence on Economic Conditions

Historically, the beauty shop business has been relatively resistant to general economic trends. Recepits have declined noticeably during periods of general economic slowdown only in those shops primarily serving the lowest income groups. Further, retail sales of cosmetic products do not decline significantly during periods of general economic recession. This would suggest that beauty services and products are considered by women to be relatively indispensable.

III. ANALYSIS OF BUSINESS FEASIBILITY

A. Review of Key Factors

The following factors are essential to successful development of a profitable beauty shop:

1. Market

As a general rule of thumb, a total population of roughly 1,000 persons is required to support a shop. The actual client group of a given beauty shop will tend to be relatively homogeneous. Clients will usually reside in the same general locale and belong to the same general socioeconomic group. They are also likely to be further defined by life-style.

2. Location

Proximity to the client group is the overriding locational determinant. Within this framework, a preferable location is one with good accessibility and visibility (such as a major shopping street or shopping center), preferably on the ground floor. Plenty of parking near the shop is considered a must. Locations near other shopping facilities are desirable.

3. Site Requirements

The space required for a beauty shop will average 100 to 150 square feet per operator. This space requirement will allow for reception areas and storage. Wig rooms, coloring rooms, and retail sales areas (including boutiques) will require additional space.

Beauty care equipment places heavy demands on plumbing and electricity, and the building chosen must be able to accommodate these utility needs.

4. Complementary Services

In addition to the required beauty services, additional items are recommended to enhance the shop: free coffee, food vending machines, outside telephone service, charge accounts, recorded or taped music, and retail sales of beauty accessories.

5. Equipment

The basic equipment required to operate the business will average around $1,000 per styling station and include vanity and shampoo bowl, mirror, styling chair, curler stand, and dryer. Expendable supplies will range between 7 percent and 10 percent of total sales.

6. Management

The manager must first and foremost be concerned about keeping the customers satisfied. This requires a sound working knowledge of the business, an ability to work well with employees, an ability to maintain good customer relations and to handle angry or dissatisfied customers, and good management sense (regarding inventory control, retail sales operations, hiring of additional employees, etc.). Both men and women are found as managers of successful beauty salons.

7. Work Force

Beauty shops are very labor intensive, with salaries generally accounting for between 50 percent to 60 percent of total revenues. It is the stylists and beauty operators who attract most customers and cause them to frequent the establishment on a regular basis. There are few economies of scale for smaller operations. However, the larger beauty shops can permit staff specialization and service differentiation in order to free the best stylists from routine functions to concentrate on the higher priced services. The number of operators will depend upon market demand—there is no optimum size.

In addition to beauty operators, larger shops will maintain a receptionist and possibly a maintenance worker. Part-time staff may be employed during the peak period (Thursdays through Saturdays).

B. Special Factors for New Minority Ventures

There are no known industrial barriers acting to prevent minority ownership of beauty shops. Beauty shops are highly market-oriented, and there are both a growing demand for beauty services among minority consumers and a general acceptance of minority-owned and managed beauty shops. Consequently, any beauty shop—white or non-white owned—that provides high quality service should be able to locate a favorable market area to serve.

Because of the high turnover of shops, a possibly attractive way to begin a new venture is to buy a shop about to close. The conditions leading to the closure should, of course, be investigated in detail before making such a move. Beauty salon failure due to poor service will usually not seriously hinder a totally new operation locating in the same facility with a new name and new operators.

C. Projections of Attainable Returns on Investment

Representative projections of revenues and profits attainable are furnished for three common sizes and types of beauty shops: a single proprietorship with no employees, a proprietorship with three beauty operators.

1. One-person Operation

Revenues
 Beauty services $15,000
 Retail sales   0
  Total revenues $15,000 100%

Operating expenses
 Rent .... $ 1,500
 Supplies 1,400
 Advertising   400
 Laundry rental service   200
 Utilities   500
 Maintenance and repairs   200
 Other (licenses and taxes,
  insurance, accounting fees, etc.).. 1,000
  Total operating expenses..... $ 5,200 35%

Gross operating profit .... $ 9,800 65%

Other expenses (equipment,
 depreciation, and interest) .... $ 750

Net profit before taxes .... $ 9,050 60%
 (before owner's compensation)

2. Proprietorship With Three Beauty Operations (including owner)

Revenues
 Beauty services $40,000
 Retail sales 2,000
  Total revenues $42,000 100%

Operating expenses
 Salaries and wages $21,000
 Rent 3,600
 Supplies 3,700
 Advertising 1,800
 Laundry rental service   700
 Utilities 1,500
 Maintenance and repairs   500
 Other   800
  Total operating expenses $33,600 80%

Gross operating profit .... $ 8,400 20%

Other expenses .... $ 2,400

Net profit before taxes .. .. $ 6,000 14.3%

IV. SUMMARY: ESTABLISHING THE BUSINESS

A. Approaching the Market

In determining where to set up a beauty shop, the overriding consideration is to be reasonably accessible to the target client group. In turn, the target group should be selected on the basis of perceived divergence between demand and available services. In this latter regard, a detailed analysis of (1) the services offered by competition and (2) the dominant client group of existing establishments in each alternative location should be undertaken.

Upon determining the target client group to be served and the general locale, a detailed analysis of alternative sites should be undertaken. Special consideration should be given to sites near shopping centers that offer adequate parking.

In the actual planning of the facility, the decor, complementary services, and the price list should be designed with the target client group specifically in mind. Stylists should be recruited on the basis of their interest in creating styles and providing beauty services for the target group. In the case of a franchised operation, the franchisee will help with both the shop layout and the hiring of personnel, as well as in setting up books and records.

There are several options open to a new firm wishing to introduce itself to the general public and particularly to its target population. Placing a large advertisement in a neighborhood shoppers' newspaper is generally a good investment. A mimeographed letter announcing the opening might also be sent profitably to selected addresses (neighborhood associations may exist and will have names and addresses for their areas). Radio and/or television spots are costly, but do reach sizeable numbers of persons. In the case of a shopping center location, the announcement of the opening probably will be handled through the center's tenant association. In the case of a franchised operation, the franchiser will arrange the grand opening and local advertising and may provide a guest star.

As a longer term marketing project, reduced rates may be offered to newcomers to the area through the local Welcome Wagon organization. Free styling for fashion shows and local theatrical productions may also be offered in return for a credit in the program. However, as stated several times already, the best form of advertising is through the satisfied customer.

B. Facility and Capital Requirements

As indicated above, roughly 100 to 150 square feet of floor space per operator is required for a typical beauty shop. This space requirement includes room for a reception area and for storage. Wig rooms, coloring rooms, and extensive retail sales areas will require additional space, depending on the scale of the operation. The building must be capable of accommodating the electricity and plumbing needs of the shop. The land must be appropriately zoned.

Equipment can be supplied by a single supplier. Installment terms are available. Usually a one-third downpayment (roughly $400 per operator) is required. Furniture, leasehold improvements, initial advertising, and supplies may run as high as $5,000 for a small four-operator venture. Larger operations (10 or more operators) will have proportionately higher startup costs.

A franchised operation will cost a little more to start than an independent operation. A franchise fee must be paid, plus future monthly payments of between 5 percent and 10 percent of monthly sales.

C. Financing

As indicated above, equipment can be purchased on installments, with a one-third downpayment typically required. Bank loans may be available to cover other capital requirements. A 90 percent loan guarantee from the Small Business Administration will be of assistance in obtaining a commercial loan.

A franchised operation should have an easier time securing a loan. The franchiser may be unwilling to offer a franchise to an entrepreneur lacking sound financial backing, however.

D. Labor Force

As indicated above, the beauty shop operation is highly labor intensive. At least half of the revenues are returned to the operators as salaries or owner's profit (in the case of an owner/operator). The labor force performance is also the single most important marketing vehicle. Accordingly, selection of a qualified and personable staff is a sine qua non for a successful venture.

The entrepreneur must be sure that each of his operators has met the requirements of the State's board of cosmetology or other regulatory agency responsible for setting standards and issuing licenses for hair stylists. In some States, other shop employees such as manicurists, electrologists, and those who service wigs need licenses.

CHILDREN'S AND INFANTS' WEAR

I. RECOMMENDATION

Entry into the dynamic industry of children's and infants' wear sales is recommended only for those who are experienced retailers, who have experience in following apparel fashion trends, and who have access to at least $80,000 of risk equity capital from personal savings or investors. The children's and infants' wear industry has become an increasingly important part of total apparel industry sales, with a dollar volume of approximately $500 million in 1969. Yet the children's and infants' wear retail trade had a failure rate of 49 firms out of every 10,000 in 1968, according to Dun and Bradstreet, making its industry failure rate higher than average for the retail field.

The dynamic changes that are continually taking place in the industry can, however, offer rewards to the retailer who knows both his local market and the trends in children's fashion to which the buyer is increasingly sensitive. The minority entrepreneur who meets the above qualifications and who is able to locate so as to take best advantage of his desired market segment will be in a position to capitalize on growth trends in the industry.

II. DESCRIPTION

A. Identification

Standard Industrial Classification (SIC) 5641 defines children's and infants' wear stores as those stores stocking and selling a variety of clothing sized and designed especially for children from infancy to the age of 12 years. An assortment of children's furniture, toys and accessories is also included.

B. Industry Dimensions

Trends within the industry indicate a movement toward fewer but larger stores. The number of specialty stores decreased from 4,879 establishments with payroll in 1963, to 3,556 in 1967, while the average annual sales per store went from $79,960 in 1963 to $92,700 in 1967. The typical selling space in a specialty store has increased from 1,800 to 2,500 square feet in the same time period. These trends have continued since that period.

Industry sources indicate that several other trends have become apparent. Departments devoted to infants' and children's wear have proliferated in department stores on an increasingly subdepartmentalized basis, breaking merchandise down into increasingly narrower age groupings, such as preteen or teen. This has also been the case in specialty stores where emphasis has been on merchandising to children by breaking them into age categories. There has also been growth in the selling of children's and infants' wear in men's and women's shops, supermarkets, drugstores, and variety chains, resulting in increased competition for those specialty and department stores that base their market appeal on greater convenience and lower price. Sales of suburban retailers are also increasing at a faster rate than downtown, reflecting, in part, demographic patterns and the convenience and increased appeal of shopping centers.

C. Industry Characteristics

1. Nature of the Product

The infants' and children's wear industry is designed to satisfy clothing needs of children to the age of 12, including diapers, underwear, nightwear, day wear, coats, shoes, and accessory needs. The apparel is increasingly styled for adaptability to children's activities, ease of care, and durability. These items may thus be considered both staple and impulse and are for the most part repeat sale items.

Infants' and children's clothing and accessories are available in a wide range of prices. Price range bears a functional relationship to quality and, therefore, to the nature of the particular merchant's target market. "Big ticket" products may include those items which are specially designed or novelty creations or which are sold as accessories to children's wear such as jewelry and toilet items.

The marketing or sales approach is very much dependent upon the type of store and the target market. It may reflect a higher price, high quality, and service orientation, as does the department or specialty store, or a lower price, less quality conscious, self-service approach characteristic of the discount or drugstore. Higher price department stores and discount stores currently lead the children's wear industry in terms of growth in sales volumes.

2. Nature of the Customer

Despite the fact that children are the ultimate wearers of the merchandise sold by children's and infants' wear stores, adults are usually the purchasers. Adults develop preferences toward a particular seller on the basis of price, quality of merchandise, service, selection, style, and goodwill.

Children's wear retailers have found the most profitable locations for business to be those areas with a heavy concentration of families, with adequate housing facilities for future growth, and with business and commercial activity capable of sustaining local population growth. Locational determinants to be considered in the selection of a particular site include the extent of customer traffic (including pedestrian) and the nature of the existing stores in both the immediate vicinity and in the community.

3. Competition

Infants' and children's wear stores may take any of several organizational forms—proprietorships, corporations, franchises. No single form predominates, though the growth in the number of department stores that include infants' and children's wear departments and the trend in the industry toward larger size and multiple stores suggest increasing use of the corporate form. One of the most significant features of the industry from the competitive aspect is the large variety in the types of business operations which stock and sell infants' and children's wear; outlets include everything from department stores and specialty stores to discount operations, supermarkets, and mail order houses.

Fashion consciousness has become more and more significant in the industry, particularly at the higher quality outlets. Department stores and specialty shops in particular have based their approach on quality and fashion, competing with each other largely on the basis of price and service. The low-end price lines tend to be "fashion followers" and are handled primarily by stores such as discounts, chains, mail order firms, supermarkets, and varieties which depend on high turnover for success. Use of a merchandise buying service may offer the smaller retailer a source of information about price changes, new merchandise, best sellers, and other trade features on which success in his chosen market is based.

There are three major types of buying services which an infants' and children's wear retailer may use. All fulfill the same function, market representation for the stores served, but differ from one another in the matter of ownership. Wholly owned services include Allied Purchasing Corp. and the May Company; association buying offices (owned and operated by members and stockholders) include Associated Merchandising Corp. and the Specialty Stores Association; and privately owned independent buying offices include Kirby Block & Co. and Youth Fashion Guild. Unless the prospective entrepreneur is very experienced in the trade, he should investigate affiliation with an established buying service.

4. Promotional Techniques

Every infants' and children's operation needs sales promotion to attract customers. But too often, store owners equate merchandise promotion with reduced prices alone. This is usually a mistake. Unless the store is purely a bargain operation, it has other things to offer—values, assortment, service, and fashion. Some of its promotional efforts should, therefore, be keyed to these themes.

The major methods for promotion used in the industry are newspaper advertising, direct mail, and store window displays. While newspaper advertising gets its major share of the large store's promotional dollar, smaller stores with smaller budgets have tended to avoid the newspaper because they cannot afford professional advertising staffs. However, some smaller stores have found that running small ads regularly keeps the store's name before the public, and that the extra cost of professional advertising help is often offset by the extra sales for which the ads are responsible.

With respect to direct mail, this technique has the virtue of being available to any store, no matter how small the amount it can invest. A mailing list should be developed from customer records, supplemented by birth lists and school rosters.

Perhaps the most economical form of promotion is the store window display, and specialty stores have found this to be the best way of attracting customers. Effective windows tell a story, and each item displayed should be an integral part of that story, with no extraneous merchandise present.

5. Ease of Entry

The industry is characterized by relatively easy entry, the one restrictive factor perhaps being the trend toward bigness and the consequent financing problems. Licensing is usually required at the local level, but this, as a rule, does not pose a serious or costly problems.

In a major city, a specialty store with an $80,000 or more annual sales volume and with a selling area of 20 by 100 square feet requires a minimum capital investment of about $45,000. This figure by 1970 standards represents a rather small initial investment. Once a general area has been selected in which to locate, feasibility planning should be done on the basis of available store space, sources of supply, and licensing and capital requirements. One means by which a businessman new to infants' and children's wear may become better acquainted is by joining an infants' wear and children's wear merchandising group, such as Youth Fashion Guild and the National Retail Merchants Association.

6. Capital Requirements

Financing in the infants' and children's wear business today must be thought of only in "big" terms. Insufficient financing at the outset is extremely dangerous. In 1967 an estimated capital investment of $35,000 was required to finance a 20 by 100 foot shop capable of generating a sales volume of $80,000 in the first year, with $15,000 to $18,000 going for fixturing, $17,000 for inventory, and $3,000 for other expenses. Capital needs for almost all types of shops have since climbed. In 1970, a recommended minimum capital investment for an infants' and children's wear store was about $45,000. However, this figure will vary considerably with the particular store's situation—rents, anticipated price and quality level of the merchandise, and amount of service offered.

Determination of the initial capital needs may be accomplished through a valuation of opening merchandise inventory, a summation of projected fixture and equipment costs, and an estimate of such operating expenses as credit costs, payroll size, and startup expenses such as licensing and advertising.

Other important factors to be considered in determining the capital investment required in infants' and children's wear retailing include the intended markup on the merchandise to be carried and the expected annual turnover of inventory. The children's and infants' wear trade average of three stock turnovers per year (calculated by dividing annual net sales by average monthly inventory) is lower than is usually found in men's and women's wear sales and is the main reason for a relatively high initial capital requirement in children's and infants' wear stores. This turnover rate will often vary by specific items within the store's stock, and successful stores are adept at stocking these high turnover items.

7. Profitability

Trade data on infants' and children's wear stores throughout the U.S. indicate the following operating ratios for the "average" children's and infants' wear store:

1969

Item	Percentage
Net sales	100.0
Cost of goods sold	61.0
Gross margin	39.0
Total operating expenses	36.8
Owner's compensation	10.4
Employee wages and benefits	8.2
Occupancy	8.4
Advertising	1.8
Depreciation, fixtures	1.5
Buying expenses	1.0
All other expenses	5.5
Net profit before taxes	2.2
Inventory turnover (annual)	2.9

Gross margins in the industry have improved from 32.5 in 1957 to 39.0 in 1969, and the annual turnover rate has risen slightly from 2.6 in 1957 to 2.9 in 1969. These figures should not be taken to indicate an industrywide strengthening of margins, as they are suggestive primarily of the growing market strength of the department store outlets at the upper end of the market.

8. Outside Factors Affecting Business Success

The seasonal cycles exert a strong influence on the apparel business in general, and children's and infants' wear stores are no exception. There is generally slower activity in the winter months, a gradual upswing into the spring, a leveling off during the summer months, and an upswing in the fall lasting through Christmas. A notable feature in this industry is a general insensitivity to economic downturns, particularly in the discount lines and their outlets. This is an important factor in the projection of sales and turnover rates and offers a favorable margin of stability to this industry.

III. BUSINESS OPPORTUNITIES IN THE INDUSTRY

A. Success Determinants

There are several features of the industry which affect the probabilities for business success.

• The requirement for substantial display and selling square footage is high, due to the necessity for a large stock assortment both in depth and breadth of styles, sizes, and colors.

• There is a relatively large amount of "detail" work in the business due to the breadth and depth of the stock assortment which must be carried. This also requires greater buying and inventory control skills.

• An average annual turnover which is slower than men's and women's wear entails a relatively large initial capital investment.

• During economic and business downturns this industry is less affected than many retail industries since customers seem to continue spending on their children.

• Considerable departmentalization now characterizes the businesses in the industry since fashion considerations have become more essential to selling and since both children and parents are increasingly interested in and aware of clothing. Children prefer to find their clothing broken down by age groups, and their growing interest and awareness has tended to increase their influence on parents' buying habits.

B. Examples of Returns Attainable in the Industry

1. Small Suburban Shopping Center Partnership

Two partners open an infants' and children's wear store in a shopping center centrally located with respect to several middle income housing developments consisting primarily of young families. This location affords 8,000 square feet of selling space, good pedestrian traffic, and convenient parking facilities. The merchandise to be carried is in the medium price range. There is a weekly regional advertiser available. The initial capital investment is $80,000, $70,000 of which is financed by a long term bank loan with a 90 percent Small Business Administration guarantee, with the remaining $10,000 provided by the owners. The business is established as a proprietorship by obtaining a license from the county at a nominal cost. The two proprietors expect to hire additional sales clerks necessary to provide a high level of customer service. First-year sales are good, with operating results as follows:

Sales		$300,000	100%
Cost of goods sold		183,000	
Gross margin		$117,000	39%
Operating expenses		$ 94,600	
Fixtures	$15,000		
Wages and benefits	36,000		
Rent	3,600		
Interest	5,000		
Advertising	5,000		
Buying expense	3,000		
Owner's compensation	26,000		
Depreciation	1,000		
Net profit before taxes		$ 22,400	7.4%

2. Downtown Specialty Shop

A proprietor opens a small downtown children's wear shop featuring relatively low prices and self-service. High volume is expected to provide enough revenue to cover relatively high operating costs. It is expected that advertising will be important to the operation, and advertising space is bought in the local newspaper. Only 4,500 square feet of selling space is available; display area fixtures are crowded but arranged for maximum traffic. The assortment in terms of style, color, and size is somewhat limited. The strategy is to achieve a faster turnover than is generally found in the industry through lower pricing catering to the lower income level of the majority of the pedestrian traffic. Sixty thousand dollars of financing is needed to open the store; capital sources include:

$20,000	Bank loan (5-year, 10%)
10,000	Owner's equity
10,000	Grant, local urban development foundation
20,000	Loan, MESBIC (10-year, 8%)
$60,000	

First-year operating results for the store:

Sales	$161,000	100%
Cost of goods sold	112,700	
Gross margin	$ 48,300	30%
Operating expenses	$ 46,280	
Fixtures and equipment $18,000		
Wages and owner's compensation 12,880		
Rent 4,800		
Advertising 3,220		
Buying expense 1,980		
Depreciation 1,800		
Interest costs 3,600		
Net profit before taxes	$ 2,020	1.3%

In the first example, the market was segmented predominantly on the basis of price, quality, and service. A middle-income area offers good consumer spending potential at the level associated with a higher price range, since this income level is in a position to demand and to pay for a certain quality and to expect service when a purchase is being considered. The second example portrays a store oriented more toward a market based on daily commercial center traffic. Pricing policy is aimed at capturing impulse sales from passers-by and from respondents to the media advertising which emphasize price specials. Depth of selection and service are sacrificed for the lower-priced levels.

IV. ESTABLISHING THE NEW BUSINESS

A. Establishing the Market

The first step in starting a new children's and infants' wear store is to determine the market which the store is intended to serve. The prospective entrepreneur must identify the general type of consumer he wishes to cater to. He may wish to locate downtown, for example, and make his appeal to inner-city residents; or he may take a location in a suburban shopping center and cater to the suburban population.

Whatever the decision, it will affect where the new store is to be located, what it's total market is, and what kind of merchandise it should carry. If the market is an upper income one, willing to pay higher prices, it will require higher quality merchandise, dressing room space, merchandise displays, and gift boutiques. The entrepreneur who wishes to cater to this market will have to invest considerably more in a wide range of merchandise, store fixtures, and in trained sales staff than the discount operator.

The general procedure to be followed in selecting a store location begins with the identification of several potential locations where space is known to be available, the computation of the number of potential customers within the shopping area of each location (statistics from the local school system may be of value), and determination of the amount of annual expenditures on children's wear. An analysis of competition from department stores, discount operations, and other children's wear stores will suggest where underserved markets exist.

B. Securing Capital

A number of cities have organizations which specialize in assisting minority entrepreneurs to secure capital. A prospective entrepreneur should seek out these sources and go over his plans with them.

The local Small Business Administration office or OMBE affiliate may help to put the prospective entrepreneur in touch with sources of capital and to provide the names of banks which have made minority loans. Minority-owned banks may also provide capital.

MACHINE SHOP JOB WORK

I. Recommendation

Successful operation of a machine shop which specializes in job work requires technical experience and strong managerial talents. Individuals wishing to enter the industry as shopowners should have considerable experience and very high motivation.

If a new machine shop is located in a metropolitan area where manufacturing activities are growing, it should have good prospects for success—if management is technically competent, resourceful, willing to work long hours, and dedicated to controlling costs. Risk can be minimized if the market for the proposed new job shop is clearly defined and substantiated by information received from prospective customers.

Investment requirements are minimal provided that the owner shows ingenuity in finding inexpensive space, securing second-hand machinery, and/or arranging for leasing more expensive equipment. Careful attention should be paid to the availability of a technically competent work force, particularly when there is a high demand for machine shop services. At such times, it is often difficult to secure the skilled labor which is required.

II. Description of the Machine Shop Industry

A. Identification

A machine job shop, Standard Industrial Classification (SIC) 35993, is a service-oriented activity providing custom service to repair, make, or otherwise improve an existing manufactured product or a new product of the same kind. All items are custom made. There is some overlapping between the operation of a machine job shop and a tool-and-die shop, since many machine job shops manufacture tools and dies, and some tool-and-die shops machine parts to order, as well as design and build special machinery. Many machine job shops specialize in the repair and reconditioning of machinery, and a typical aspect of their work is the availability of repair service on a 24-hour basis.

Many of the technical, financial, and operational aspects of machine job shops and tool-and-die makers are similar. However, tool-and-die makers tend to have more complicated and expensive machinery, often using numerical controls, and they are somewhat larger. The average tool and die shop employs about twice as many persons as the average job shop.

The essential operation of a machine job shop is to take a piece of metal and alter it to the customer's specifications. This may include plating, assembly welding, fabricating, diecasting, stamping, or grinding, or any combination of these operations. In most cases the metal is supplied by the customer. Various types of metal forming machinery, such as lathes, presses, planers, millers, and drills are used for this purpose. The most important shop costs are labor and investments in machines. An operation which can be accomplished quickly on a small and inexpensive machine will be less costly than a complicated and time-consuming operation on an elaborate machine. However, labor is more costly than machinery, and it is usually more profitable to use a more expensive faster machine than one which is slow but inexpensive.

B. Dimensions

There were some 3,000 machine shops employing 66,500 workers doing jobwork, according to the 1967 Census of Business. Their total sales were reported to be above $1.2 billion. The National Tool, Die, and Precision Machining Association, which includes tool-and-die manufacturers as well as job machine shops in its definition of the industry, reports that there are about 7,000 firms in the industry doing $3 billion of business annually. There are many other operations which are captive operations of other firms, and these latter do machine work only for the company by which they are owned.

Growth in the industry is directly related to growth in manufacturing and particularly the growth in the use of machinery. Thus, it can be expected that, with the continuing increase in population and standard of living, there will be corresponding increases in the value of manufactured output and the need for contract machining. Continuing introduction of laborsaving devices and other machinery are also bound to increase the output of machine shops.

There are significant factors affecting the independent contract firm. These include:
Cyclical factors,
Single-industry ties,
Captive operations.

Cyclical factors. Machine job shops generally tend to be hurt by the ups and downs of business. When industrial output is not expanding, machines are used less intensively, and there is less need for repairs and special machine work. The machine shop industry generally has considerable excess capacity when industrial production is lagging and has insufficient capacity when production is booming.

Single-Industry Ties. Unless a machine job shop is large and located in an area where industry is diversified, its output tends to be specialized to serve one or two customers or a single industry. This leaves the machine shop operation overly dependent on customers over whom it has no control. This can result in seasonality of work, abrupt loss of work when a customer closes his plant or moves, loss of work if a particular industry is declining, and so on.

Captive Operations. Captive operations, which are shops owned by the companies which purchase their output, are always a threat to the independent. In recessions, captive operations get the work before a company provides any orders to outside suppliers.

Machine job shops tend to be located in the industrial concentrations of the Nation. They are particularly concentrated in and around the automotive industry and in places like Chicago. However, agriculture centers have machine shops serving agricultural machinery, and there are other concentrations serving the mining industry, the petroleum industry, and the logging industry. While urban centers are good locations because of their proximity to diversified manufacturing operations and the availability of used machinery and skilled labor, there are often opportunities to be found in other areas near industries which are expanding or which are introducing new machinery into their operations. For example, the rapid mechanization of coal mining and the surge in the demand for coal has resulted in a very rapid upsurge in machine shops in West Virginia and Kentucky.

There has been very little penetration into the machine shop industry by black or Spanish-speaking entrepreneurs. Ownership in the industry is concentrated among a group of persons, many of European extraction, who have established close working relationships with each other over a period of years. The National Tool, Die and Precision Machining Association does, however, report that at least one of its members is a black owner of a machine shop.

C. Characteristics

1. Nature of the Product

The contract machine shop serves other industries. It provides machine time, technical skills, and know-how. It uses its customers' materials and works them to repair or produce new parts for existing machines, and turns out relatively small quantities of parts and other metal items needed in the manufacturing process.

2. Nature of the Customer

The customer of a machine shop is anyone who uses machinery, whether he be manufacturer, farmer, miner, logger, transporter, etc. The basis for choosing a particular machine shop can be any one or combination of the following:

a. *Convenience.* The machine shop is handy and can quickly provide and deliver the required service.

b. *Quality.* The machine shop can be relied upon to provide accurate machining to very close tolerances, or to repair machines.

c. *Price.* The machine shop can perform work at an economical cost. (Much business is secured through competitive bidding.)

d. *Ingenuity.* The machine shop can figure out a way of doing something more quickly or more economically, or can modify a machine to make it work more effectively.

A machine shop may have a number of different types of customers. If the shop makes tools, dies, molds, and other forms, its customers will be the manufacturers who produce other products (such as automobiles, appliances, aerospace products, etc.).

Other types of machine shops specialize in one-of-a-kind jobs, machining or welding a particular part needed for the operation of another machine. Many shops also specialize in repairing and maintaining machinery particular to a specific industry such as textile manufacturing, mining, agriculture, and the like.

In most cases, the machine shop must be located close to its customers. There are some exceptions, particularly in imports from Canada and Europe in tool-and-die production, but the imports have a cost advantage in labor rates which would not be applicable to operations in the United States located at a distance from customers.

3. Technology

The machine job shop is an outgrowth of the Industrial Revolution. It had its first development in the early 19th century when Eli Whitney invented interchangeable parts for guns. Most of the early equipment was used on wood, and much of the basic machinery performs the same operations today which were performed by the early wood-working machinery of the 19th century. Technological changes have come from size of machines, speed of operation, ability to work with more complicated metals, closeness of tolerances, and capability of using more highly automated controlling devices.

The technology involved in operating a modern machine shop is quite complex. The manager must know mathematics, mechanics, metal engineering, the theory of metal cutting, the properties of various metals and alloys, and the workings of machines.

In addition, a manager must know cost estimating, plant layout, and wage and salary administration. Quality control is an essential ingredient of successful machine shop management, as are careful estimating and rigid control of costs.

Machine shops may be classified by the size of job orders and the degree of precision to which they work. For example, a shop may specialize in light jobs weighing less than 10 pounds when completed, medium work, weighing between 10 and 50 pounds, and heavy work, which may weigh up to several tons when completed.

Rough work is that in which finishes are seldom smoother than 125 micro-inches and tolerances seldom better than 0.007 inches. Medium work finishes are seldom smoother than 63 micro-inches and tolerances down to 0.002. In fine work, finishes may be as smooth as 8 micro-inches and tolerances as close as 0.0002.

Machine shops may specialize in different types of metal, such as steel, aluminum, or bronze, or in the case of the aerospace industry such exotic alloys as titanium, beryllium, and the like.

The machines to be purchased for a machine shop will depend upon the nature of the market the owner wishes to serve and the technical requirements for machinery to produce for that market. The prospective owner must have a clear idea of how large his work will be, what precision will be expected, the type of metals with which he will be working, whether numerical tapes will be available for automatic operation, and so on.

There are some one-machine shops where the total output is performed on one machine having unique properties such as the ability to perform very heavy work, or the ability to work at very high speeds with consequent savings in costs. Such machines are usually automatically controlled and expensive.

A machine shop is generally labor-intensive with a moderate investment of $7,000 to $10,000 per worker required. Total wages for the industry as a whole represent about 44½ percent of the total value of the work performed in the industry.

The basic skill utilized in the labor force is that of the skilled machining worker. The various occupational titles for this skill are listed in D.O.T. 600 through 607.886, 609.280 through .782 and 609.885, in the *Dictionary of Occupational Titles,* U.S. Department of Labor, third edition (1966).

Most training authorities believe that apprenticeship is the preferred way to learn the machinist trade. While a typical apprentice program lasts 4 years, many companies have training programs that qualify their employees as machinists in less time. Training includes the operation of various types of machine tools and such skills as chipping, filing, handtapping, dowel fitting, riveting, and other hand operations. A machinist must also know blueprint reading, mechanical drawing, shop mathematics, and shop practices. The National Tool, Die and Precision Machining Association conducts an apprenticeship program in cooperation with those of its members who wish to participate.

Depending on the type of work done, the average machine shop might have about half the work force skilled, a third semiskilled, and the balance in unskilled or learner category. About 75 percent of the workers in the industry are nonunion, although in some areas union membership is the practice. Wages are generally high, ranging in 1970 from about $3.50 an hour in low-wage areas to about $6 an hour in the areas where higher wages are more common.

4. Competition

As in most industries where there are generally a large number of small suppliers and it is relatively easy to enter, competition can be intensive. When work is scarce, competitors tend to shave prices and forget about overhead. However, during rush seasons, work can be found very easily, particularly if delivery schedules can be maintained.

The machine shop also faces competition from the captive operation that is owned by a manufacturer or by the in-plant toolroom. Many manufacturing operations which reach a certain size will install a toolroom of their own to do many machining operations and to maintain and repair machinery. This can often result in the machine shop's losing an important customer. However, a job shop offers a manufacturer many advantages over an in-house operation, including lower cost in some instances, greater flexibility, and higher skills. These can be marketed aggressively.

The introduction of new machinery can often make business difficult for a machine shop that is attempting to compete on a relatively large scale for the production of tools and dies or molds. Financing must often be found for new machinery or else the business must be given up.

As noted above, there is a certain amount of clannishness within the industry, and competitors may help each other by making machine time available on certain types of machines. While this has advantages for those who are already in business, it may pose problems for a newcomer not known by or friendly with existing shopowners.

5. Ease of Entry

Machine job shops still offer opportunities for small entrepreneurs because customers are always looking for reliable suppliers who can be depended upon to deliver orders quickly and according to exact specifications. This places a premium on geographical proximity to customers, flexibility of operations, and careful craftsmanship, all of which become more difficult characteristics to maintain as the size of operation increases. Given the qualifications for operation of a machine shop and a market for his services, an individual can become a machine shop operator with relative ease. There are no special licensing requirements or unusual capital needs.

Many owners of job shops got their start by picking up one second-hand machine for less than $1,000, reconditioning it themselves, and operating it at nights and weekends in their basements or garages. As business increased, they secured more machines, hired some friends or relatives, and eventually moved into a small garage-type building.

On the other hand, the industry would be impossible to enter successfully if one did not have solid experience in the field and a broad range of acquaintanceship with potential customers. Moreover, the industry would be particularly difficult to enter during one of its many periods of excess capacity. Entry is most easily accomplished when work is easy to find and customers are desperately searching for places to get their contract machining accomplished.

6. Financing

An experienced operator with some connections with potential customers and a good personal credit record should experience relatively little difficulty securing the necessary financing. Little or no investment is required for materials. Used machines can be purchased relatively cheaply or new machinery can be leased. Firm orders can usually be used as collateral to obtain bank loans for wages and supplies; the loans are expected to be retired by order payments.

The actual amount of money needed for investment will vary greatly. An individual wanting to purchase all new machinery for cash in a building all his own would need perhaps $125,000 in capital for a relatively small operation with sales of about $250,000 annually. However, as noted above, it is possible to use someone else's machine and start with nothing. Somewhere in between, an experienced individual who has enough work for two or three others, in addition to himself, and who can secure some leased space without putting up a lot of money for a lease, ought to be able to get started with about $2,500 of his own capital and about $7,500 of borrowed funds.

7. Profitability

Although the potential for profitability in a job shop operating at 100 percent of capacity over a long period of time is high, the actual profitmaking potential for the average shop is relative low and is often achieved only at the expense of long hours of work and overtime by the owner-manager. Profit-reducing factors include:

a. Keeping workers on the payroll when there is no work. Many owners will keep workers on the payroll when there is no work out of consideration for the worker's welfare or because work is expected and the owner does not want a valuable employee to go elsewhere. If the expected work is delayed or does not materialize, the drain on profits can be significant.

b. Investment in new machinery and equipment. While an individual starting on a small scale may be content with secondhand machinery, there is always a temptation, once a business is established, to invest in more elaborate machinery on the assumption that the addition will make it possible to bid on a greater variety of potential contracts. If the assumption proves overoptimistic, the payments on the idle machine can drain away profits. However, it is better to have idle machines than idle men.

c. Seasonal and cyclical factors. Shops generally tend to have too much work or not enough. During rush seasons or a booming economy, extra help must be found, productivity goes down, overtime goes up, and profits are not as great as might be expected. During slack time, machines and men are idle, and profits are affected correspondingly.

d. Quality control. As business grows, it becomes more and more difficult to control quality. This means that material is sometimes wasted and must be replaced at a cost. It may also mean taking longer to perform an operation than estimated, a factor which would reduce profits on individual contracts and may even result in losses.

e. Competition. Competition is often intense, not only from captive shops and in-house toolrooms, but from new entrants into the business whenever times are good and work is plentiful.

There are no specific figures on actual profitability, but the range of profits for firms in the miscellaneous machinery field (SIC 3599) and metalworking machinery and equipment, which includes tool-and-die, suggests an average rate of net profit somewhat under 4 percent of sales. Thus, a firm employing about 15 persons and doing an annual business of approximately $250,000 might generate annual profits of somewhat less than $10,000, not including the owner's direct labor.

8. *Dependence on Outside Factors*

As pointed out above, there are many factors outside the control of the owner of a machine job shop which would affect his profitability. These would include the following:

a. Decision by major customers to install or expand their in-house machining capabilities.

b. National business cycle. Machine shops would be affected more than most businesses by the ups and downs of the national economy.

c. Long-range or short-range trends in the industries served. The prosperity of machine job shops is affected by what happens in the major industries they serve. Those catering to the automotive industry tend to do well or poorly on the basis of how well the auto industry is doing. Others are affected by mining, aerospace industry, etc.

III. Feasibility Analysis

A. Review of Key Factors

These factors are essential to feasibility of a machine job shop:

1. *Management*

The proposed management must be technically competent, experienced, and highly motivated toward making profits. In the absence of other factors suggesting unusual competence, at least 10 years of experience in the industry, 3 of which have been spent in supervisory capacities, are the very minimum which should be required of the management. In addition, there must be something in the proposed management's background which indicates a profit orientation, such as skill in handling his personal finances, or previous successful experience. The extent to which a prospective manager knows his precise market, where he is going to get his machinery, and has shown cost consciousness in his initial projections would also be indicative of the likelihood of success.

2. *Market*

A very specific market should be identified to assure feasibility. Such a market may be identified by the following:

a. A nearby booming industry which is unable to get all the contract machining it needs. Interviews with purchasing agents can establish the existence and size of such a market. Some judgment should be made as to the prospects for continuation of the boom.

b. Acquaintanceship by the proposed management with sources of business and reasonable assurances by such sources of an adequate volume. There may be special factors here, such as a willingness to help minority entrepreneurs, but reliance on such a special factor should be approached cautiously.

c. Knowledge of a need for a new technical procedure or introduction of a new machine which can be offered by the proposed new shop at a competitive advantage. This, too, can be documented by interviews.

d. A special factor such as location or technique that offers an opportunity to prospective customers to get work more conveniently or more inexpensively. The requirement for such convenience or economy should also be documented by interviews.

3. Location
The proposed location should be such that the proposed market can be served inexpensively and conveniently and rental is minimal.

4. Machinery
The machinery required must be available at a cost commensurate with the sales and cost projections for the proposed shop.

5. Work Force
Depending upon the size needed, there should be assurance that the required work force is available. It is often true that the available work force, more than any other factor, limits capacity. Thus, if there is an unfilled demand for contract machining in a particular area or region, the problem is more apt to be related to the inability to secure a work force than to any other. If there were existing manpower competent to perform the required work, the existing shops could put them to work by putting on second and third shifts or adding machines. Thus, a newcomer to the business within a specific area cannot expect to succeed because there is an unfilled demand for contract machining unless he has a solution to the manpower shortage.

B. Special Factors for New Minority Ventures

A minority entrepreneur seeking to establish a new machine shop would have one potential advantage and one potential disadvantage with regard to existing shops. All other factors would be potentially neutral.

1. Advantage
As indicated above, many large manufacturing and other concerns are under somewhat extensive pressures to exhibit concern for minority economic development. Thus, a minority-owned machine job shop might receive special considerations from purchasing agents.

It should be stressed, however, that such special considerations would not extend to paying a premium for the work or accepting work that is not up to standard. Thus, a minority business would be expected to produce quality work at competitive cost.

There would be limitations on the amount of preference which might be exhibited toward minority machine job shops. With many small existing jobs already in the business, a small shift in work might well have a disastrous effect on one or two existing shops, and such an eventuality would have to be taken into account by all concerned.

2. Disadvantage

As also indicated above, existing owners of machine job shops tend to have ethnic and family relationships and might tend to view entrance of a minority entrepreneur with more hostility than that normally felt with the advent of a business competitor: This might lead to excessively competitive practices, such as heavy price-cutting, to the detriment of the new business. At the very least, it would make it difficult to secure the cooperation that now exists among many firms in the industry.

C. Projections of Attainable Returns in Industry

Projections are furnished below for two different types of operations. The first is for a small three-man operation on two or three basic machines. The second is for a larger operation employing about 15 persons.

1. Small, three-man operation

a. Revenues (includes small amount of income from sale of waste materials such as metal cuttings)	$40,000	
b. Operating expenses (all materials supplied by customers)		
1) Direct labor (including proprietor's direct labor)	25,000	
2) Other (includes power, selling expense, cost of transportation, consumable supplies, rent, etc.)	8,000	
Total operating expenses	33,000	
Percent of sales		82.6%
c. Gross operating profit	7,000	
Margin		17.4%
d. Other expenses (interest, depreciation, taxes)	4,000	
e. Net profit	3,000	
Percent of sales		7.6%
f. Investment	5,000	
g. Return on investment		60.0%

A high return on investment is shown for an operation of this type, because it is assumed that relatively little investment is required and that the entrepreneur has been able to find a facility (such as his garage or comparable) which does not require heavy preparation for machines. It is also assumed that the machines can be secured on lease or secondhand with relatively small downpayment. Very little depreciation is assumed. It is also assumed that there is relatively steady work for the three persons and that they are able to work on billable contracts for about 80 percent of the time. This may require some unpaid overtime on the part of the owner.

There are three major risks involved in setting up an operation of this type: (1) the work may not come in; (2) the machinery will break down; (3) the workers will not be available. However, an experienced man who knows the machinery and who has lined up reliable workmen and sufficient contracts may reasonably expect profitable operations from the very beginning. Due to the cyclical nature of this business, however, the prospects of maintaining profitability at this level will probably diminish as the volume of available work fluctuates over time. It is unlikely that an operation of this size can last long since it will either go out of business as soon as there is no work, unless the new firm is unusually well capitalized, or else it will attract enough business to grow and expand, secure more machinery, and hire a larger work force.

2. Medium-sized 15-man operation

a. Annual revenues $250,000
b. Operating expenses
    1) Direct labor (includes overtime and owner's direct labor) ... 112,500
        Percent of Revenue 45.0%
    2) Manufacturing expense (incudes indirect labor, fringe benefits,
        depreciation, tools and supplies, power, light, heat, etc.) ... 61,875
        Percent of direct labor 55.0%
    3) Selling expense (includes delivery) 39,375
        Percent of direct labor 35.0%
    4) Administrative expense 16,875
        Percent of direct labor 15.0%
        Total operating expenses 230,625
        Percent of sales 92.2%
c. Gross operating profit 19,375
    Gross margin 7.8%
d. Other expenses (interest on capital of about $100,000) 10,000
e. Net profit 9,375
    Percent of sales 3.7%
f. Investment 25,000
g. Return on investment 37.5%
    NOTE: The above figures exclude materials. These are most often supplied by the customer, but even when they are supplied by the vendor, they are generally furnished at cost.

Given good management and a carefully chosen location with respect to markets, the chances are better than even that the above profit can be earned on the average over a number of years. However, the risk would be slightly higher in any given year depending on the business cycle and the current conditions in the principal industry being served.

IV. Establishing the Business

A. Approaching the Market

Whether he is contemplating a small operation or a medium sized operation, the prospective entrepreneur for a machine job shop should have a very clear idea of his market, backed up by interviews with prospective customers, and commitments, if possible.

This should be the first step in establishing a machine job shop, and if it has not been accomplished, there is no point in going any further in planning to establish a business.

The approaches to the prospective market may be based upon convenience, technical competence, price, friendship, or good will, or any combination of these. The prospective entrepreneur should establish the basis on which he expects to solicit the business and then visit potential customers to determine whether such a basis is valid.

The new entrepreneur should be careful not to depend upon promised opportunities to bid on contracts in formulating his own business plans, unless the potential customer's assurance appears based on a realization of cost advantages (by virtue of location, skill, machines used) in the proposed business relationship.

B. Plant Requirements

The small operation should seek minimum space, either in a garage or some similar structure. An existing business (not a competitor) may be willing to rent out a small amount of space. Room will be needed for a workbench and for whatever machines are considered essential to the type of work which is available and which the operator plans to get.

For the medium-sized operation, the operator should seek ground level space of about 1,200 to 1,500 square feet in a cement floor building, with enough room for a small office, a storeroom, a tool-crib, a space for finished parts, three workbenches, milling machine, two turret lathes, engine lathe, hacksaw, three drills, and three grinding machines. A furnace may also be required for heat treating tools, and electric welding equipment may also be desirable.

Most metropolitan areas have a number of suppliers of machine tools and a prospective job shop operator should make the rounds of these suppliers to ascertain the availability of secondhand machinery. Assuming the purchase of good secondhand machinery, and the acquisition of one or two real "bargains" at an auction, it is estimated that the necessary equipment can be secured for about $100,000. This would include special costs of installation.

C. Financing

The basic investment involved in machine job shops is the purchase of machinery. Since machinery has considerable value in secondhand condition, most machines can be financed with relatively little difficulty. Often, the seller will arrange for financing, or arrangements can be made for leasing machines from the seller or from an equipment leasing firm with an option to buy. Some cash outlay would be required for installation of machines and for expendable supplies such as office supplies, transportation equipment, cutting bits, hand tools, and the like. About 1 month's working capital would be required to cover rent, operating expenses, and wages.

Some typical financial arrangements might include the following:

Small Operation

Capital required:
Machinery installed	$ 5,000
Working capital	3,000
Supplies, etc.	2,000
	$10,000

Source:
Own funds	$ 2,500
Bank loan	7,500
	$10,000

Given the requisites for successful operation, it should be relatively easy for a bank officer to approve a small loan for such an operation. If the requisite conditions are not present, the business is not viable and should not qualify for a loan.

In most cases, the bank loan could be secured through a guarantee by the Small Business Administration, which has a special program to promote minority enterprises, and which might be expected to cooperate.

Medium-Sized Operation

Capital required:
Machinery installed	$ 90,000
Working capital	25,000
Supplies, etc.	10,000
	$125,000

Source:
Equipment loan	$ 75,000
Own funds	25,000
Bank loan	25,000
	$125,000

It is likely that most of the machinery can be financed and that the bank loan can be secured through a Small Business Administration guarantee. In the event the proposed operator does not have the required $25,000, it would be well to consider a small operation, per-haps employing one to three men. However, in exceptional circum-stances, where an unusual individual with the necessary experience and business management ability has an opportunity to enter a market and make a success of contract machining on a somewhat larger scale, and he cannot secure $25,000 from his own funds, he may be able to secure funds from a local source specializing in providing equity for minority businesses.

D. Labor Force

As indicated above, a skilled work force is essential to the successful operation of a machine job shop. For a small operation, the work force should be nearly all skilled. (For a three-man operation, two skilled machinists and an apprentice might be appropriate.)

A labor force breakdown for a 15-man operation might include:

Manager	1
Foreman	1
Skilled	6
Semiskilled	4
Unskilled	2
Office	1
	15

The foreman or shop supervisor is a key to successful operation. He can see to it that the work force is kept busy, that the machines are scheduled for maximum productivity, that work commitments are met, and that quality control standards are maintained.

It is often possible to start a shop of this size with two principals, one serving as the foreman-supervisor, and the other as the business manager-salesman.

Prospective operators of a new business should have a very clear idea of where they will get their key employees. In boom times, skilled machinists are exceptionally hard to recruit, and unless a new entrepreneur knows of some men who are capable and willing to come with him, it would be wise to give up the idea until such men are found.

Wage scales and union affiliation are influenced heavily by local conditions and cannot be generalized on a national basis. While most machine job shops are nonunion, it is important in certain areas that they be unionized. Wage scales can vary extensively from one section of the country to another. A prospective operator of a job shop should know the going level in the area in which he intends to locate and adjust his figures accordingly.

V. Summary

For an individual who knows the machine shop technique, who is experienced in the trade, and who is a good businessman, there are opportunities to establish and to make money in the ownership and operation of a machine job shop. Such an individual will know in advance what his market is and how he intends to capture it and keep it. He will know who his customers are going to be and why they will purchase from him rather than from others. He will know what machines he wants and how he can get them at a bargain and for relatively little investment. He will know where he will get a reliable labor force. If he does not know these things, then he is not ready to establish a machine job shop.

MOBILE CATERING

I. RECOMMENDATION

Success in the mobile catering industry requires both managerial ability and a technical knowledge of food service operation. While entry may be attempted on a very small scale with little prior experience, at least 1 year of experience is necessary for an operation of moderate to large scale, especially where food product purchasing and preparation is involved. The prospective entrepreneur must have a personality readily adaptable to selling and public relations activities, since he is meeting customers on a recurring basis. Establishing firm agreements with customers and following through with provision of good service is the best insurance for maintaining a route and against loss of sales to competitors.

An awareness of growth patterns in major market segments as well as of current developments in associated food manufacturing industries is an essential part of the mobile catering field. A metropolitan area with high concentrations of industrial locations and with a high construction rate should offer an excellent opportunity for a mobile catering operation. Since labor is significant to the mobile catering industry, careful attention should be paid to determining the availability and proximity of an adequate labor supply.

Investment requirements may be minimal if the operation is begun on a small scale and if a perceptive selection of routes, equipment, and supply location is made. Each year, however, the food service industry accounts for 20 percent of all retail failures, reflecting the necessity for careful planning and some understanding of the industry prior to committing capital and beginning operations.

II. INDUSTRY DESCRIPTION

A. Identification

Mobile catering is one type of fast food operation within the broad field of the food service industry. Food service applies to all types of facilities or operations serving food to people while they are away from home. The food service industry may be broken into three major categories. The largest of these provides meal service to the general public. The second category includes organizations in which meals are prepared and served by employees who are part of the organization, such as a day-care center. The third category covers employee, student, and hospital patient feeding, which has increasingly relied on outside contractors for food service.

Fast food services comprise the major part of the first category and make up the largest portion of the away-from-home food services. Included in fast food operations are coffee shops, cafeterias, snack bars, carryouts, drive-ins, and vending machines. Mobile catering has become an increasingly important form of this fast food service, fulfilling the needs of a particular segment of the food service market.

Mobile catering, Standard Industrial Classification (SIC) 5812, provides food service at locations where, because of the number of employees or the geographical location, vending machines or contract food services are either infeasible or uneconomical. Mobile catering operators today use specially built truck bodies, generally with swing-out doors that cover display trays for food products, urns for liquids, and soft drink storage dispensers.

Mobile catering trucks follow routes that consist of a series of sales stops during the business day. Routes are established for the most part through informal agreements with customers, usually construction companies, businesses, and industrial locations in a given area. The nature of these agreements is such that the particular mobile catering operator will have access to the premises at specified times during the day and on specified days of the week. The operator establishes these contracts by directly contacting the organization and, in effect, selling his services. Once agreements are made, the operator "owns" the route and may lease or sell it to other operators.

The mobile catering truck driver may operate under several conditions. He may be independent, owning his truck and developing his own route. Or he may be semi-independent, owning his truck and leasing a route from a commissary company. Also he may be a contractor, leasing both truck and route from a commissary company. Mobile catering companies are organized to operate a number of routes that they lease to independents, or for which they purchase their own trucks and hire drivers to utilize some combination of both leasing and working their routes.

Nearly all companies operate out of commissaries, whether trucks are owned by independent routemen or by the catering companies. Most established companies began operating their own commissaries at about the same time they began mobile catering. Those commissary facilities purchase, prepare, package, and dispense food products to route trucks. Commissaries may take one of several forms: (1) total food preparation facilities on the premises; (2) purchase of food from other suppliers and operation as a distributor or wholesaler; and (3) a combination of these two forms, both buying and preparing food for resale.

B. Industry Dimensions

The retail value of all food served through food service outlets— restaurants, snackbars, drive-ins, caterers—is currently greater than $27 billion annually, a 56 percent increase in total retail value of meals served away from home since 1960. American families spend an average of $400 to $500 per year on food-away-from-home, an amount equal to approximately 5 percent to 6 percent of the household budget.

Currently, fast food services account for approximately 80 percent of the total $27 billion food-away-from-home dollar value. These fast food operations, of which mobile catering is a part, concentrate on food products served quickly and conveniently, with a relatively low emphasis on such esthetic factors as decor, space, and personal service.

The mobile catering business is a fast-growing component of this fast food industry. Nearly 1,100 operators sold $1.1 billion worth of food products and merchandise in 1970, representing an $80-million increase over 1969 industry sales with a nearly equal number of operators and a $290 million increase over 1968 sales. The number of catering routes similarly expanded from 21,830 in 1969 to 23,271 in 1970 Route sales, however, averaged $171 per day in 1970, as compared with the $181 per day average of 1969. Industry size is growing in terms of employees as well; some 30,000 people were directly employed in the industry in 1970 as compared with 28,400 in 1969.

C. Industry Characteristics
1. Product

Fast food products are selected and prepared for the customer who is "necessity or convenience food" oriented. Mobile catering food products are primarily frozen and convenience foods, prewrapped and prepackaged prior to being served to the customer. The following is a breakdown of sales share by product in 1970:

Sandwiches	29.0%
Hot drinks	12.9
Dairy products	12.0
Cold drinks	11.5
Pastries	10.6
Canned entrees	6.4
Commissary prepared foods	5.3
Miscellaneous	12.3
	100.0%

Commissaries purchase the majority of food products sold on trucks directly from the manufacturer or processor; of secondary importance are local suppliers for fresh produce, meat, and similar items. Prepackaged items and convenience products are generally obtained from the manufacturer on a direct basis, and local distributors are of only minor importance.

Mobile caterers' menus are frequently cycled on a weekly, monthly, or quarterly basis. Cycling prevents the serving of identical foods on the same day of consecutive weeks or months or quarters, and cycle menus may be planned and scheduled by commissary managers in the larger operations and by the owner-manager in smaller companies. Several considerations with reference to customers are taken into account when making a selection of foods: (1) average customer age (younger customers tend to buy more dairy products); (2) sex of customers (men tend to prefer heavier foods in larger proportions than women); (3) ethnic composition of customers (menus tend to be reflective of neighborhoods); (4) income levels of customers (high-priced platters tend to sell well only in higher income areas).

Industry sources indicate that usually the only food prepared on the truck is coffee and, in a few cases, sandwiches. Time, health laws, and weather conditions are factors that greatly limit preparation of food on the trucks. The driver salesmen, however, in most cases select the food products they stock in their trucks, since they are in the best position to evaluate the varying tastes and requirements of the customers on each route.

2. Customer

Customers of mobile catering services may be considered captive markets in the sense that they require food service not immediately available at their particular locations. That is, they may not be able to leave the worksite and have no internal food service facility or access to eating places close by. Since there are limitations on the types of foods and the manner in which they may be prepared and served in this type of situation, interesting, varied menus and good service are essential to maintaining a route. It is for this reason that cycle menus have become a more important marketing approach in addition to the advantages of eliminating monotony, time and expense in planning, and buying and preparation of food.

Customers are found at the following types of locations:

	1969
Construction sites	15.20%
Industrial locations (less than 100 persons)	50.30
Industrial locations (more than 100 persons)	27.30
Office	6.40
Parks and recreational areas	0.43
Special events	0.37
	100.00%

As indicated by the chart, industrial locations employing fewer than 100 persons make 50 percent of total industry sales and have retained the lead in sales in the industry through the 1960's.

On the average, a good customer requires about four stops a day—before work, lunch meal, and two coffee breaks.

When determining the market size necessary for operating a route, three factors are usually taken into consideration: the mileage length of the route, the types of location stops available (i.e., construction sites), and the number of stops. These factors determine the sales revenues that may be expected of a potential route.

3. Technology

The entrepreneur who begins on a small scale with one truck and one route may require few specific skills to start. However, several abilities are immediately essential. The most important function fulfilled by the independent truckdriver is the selling function, which involves making a selection of food products that have the highest salability value, handling routine cash transactions, and performing public relations type activities on a regular basis. The operator with more than one route and at least one commissary must employ labor and must manage truckdrivers in the performance of all the functions indicated for an independent; he must supervise commissary operations (involving food purchasing, cooking and preparation, packaging, and dispensing to trucks), menu planning, fleet traffic management, and general management functions. The management of a company with fewer than 20 routes will generally find it necessary to perform sales duties as well, including locating, establishing, and maintaining routes. Companies with more than 20 routes employ on the average:

1 management or supervisory employee for every 3 routes;
1 salesman for every 30 routes;
1 maintenance employee for every 5 routes;
1 commissary employee for every 2 routes.

There is a high degree of labor required in nearly all the activities of the mobile catering industry. This feature reflects the importance of labor to the industry and the additional personnel problems and costs that may result. Food preparation facilities may be made more capital intensive as new equipment and methods become available, reducing the need for labor intensity in the commissary operation.

The mobile catering industry, and the fast food industry in general, are relying more and more heavily on prepared foods. Prepared foods are processed products that have undergone all preparation except heating or cooking. Frozen prepared meals is one of the fastest growing categories of prepared foods. This trend is particularly noted in the case of mobile catering, where almost all food products are selected for ease and speed of preparation.

There has been a recent industry trend toward leasing operations. This leads to greater diversity in wage rates within the industry, since commissions on sales constitute a major form of income, and commission rates vary as do the revenues yielded by routes. However, according to U. S. Department of Labor statistics, the 1968 average hourly earnings for employees in eating and drinking places was $1.57. Federal minimum wage laws require operators grossing $500,000 annually to pay $1.60 per hour. This affected fewer than 2 percent of all public eating places in 1968 and, when in 1969 the gross ceiling was lowered to $250,000, still only about 5 percent of eating places were affected. Some States do have their own minimum wage laws, however, that might also affect the entrepreneur's labor costs.

4. Competition

The mobile catering industry has a real competitive advantage over other forms of fast food facilities, since by definition it fulfills a food service need, the response to which has already proven uneconomical for other types of food services. To this extent other types of food service do not pose a competitive threat since they may not be easily substituted for the mobile catering service. Mobile caterers are competing in a market that again is relatively captive and where the demand is for low-priced, fast foods, or where the slant is toward necessity and convenience in away-from-home food service. However, competition within the industry is often quite severe, especially for establishing ownership and control of new routes. Getting control of a route as an independent may be quite difficult, since existing operators are constantly on the lookout for new market areas and may be well informed far enough in advance to lock out prospective newcomers.

Good service and quality and variety of prepared food products remain the most essential competitive factors within the industry. The most essential and recent form of change or development in the industry is menu cycling and innovative, prepared food products. The operator of either an independent or multiroute company with its own commissary operation, who is perceptive enough to successfully introduce new products marketed by prepared food manufacturers and the frozen-food industry, will be ahead in providing better quality and variety to customers. An awareness of developments in associated industries is a basic facet of competition.

However, other fast food businesses are increasingly interested in diversifying into the mobile catering service. Industry sources indicate that vending companies may be the most immediate competitive threat; many have already expanded to include mobile catering in their total operations. The vending companies apparently recognize advantages in having both internal and external sales locations, for when a potential market need cannot be satisfied by installing vending machines, it can be served by mobile catering, which offers both mobility and low capital investment. On the other hand, mobile catering companies have shown distinct disinterest in diversifying into vending operations. In fact, in 1969 several mobile caterers with vending machine operations completely divested themselves of their vending operations. Most mobile caterers involved in other food service activities are in party and special function catering.

Almost all of the medium and large companies are corporations. Small independents are for the most part proprietorships (and to a lesser extent corporations). Franchising plays a continually more important role in the fast foods field, but it has not lent itself to mobile catering as well. This may be attributed to the fact that the increasingly important leasing arrangements prevailing in the industry reduce the appeal of the franchise form of business organization somewhat.

5. Ease of Entry

Entry into the mobile catering industry depends on several factors:

1. Licensing requirements: As a rule, each State has its own set of minimum health and sanitation laws and the associated licenses and permits required to begin and maintain operations. Permit fees in the food industry generally range from $1 to $60 per unit.

2. Capital requirements: Initial capital requirements may be quite low if a prospective entrepreneur is willing to begin at a very modest scale. The cost of catering truck, route, and beginning inventory are the major expense factors.

3. Locational requirements: The mobile catering industry's greatest advantage is the mobility factor. Easy access to a commissary location is extremely important both in the case of the operator with one or more commissaries and in the case of the one-truck independent. Usually a commissary should be located in as central a position as possible relative to the total number of routes.

The development of a route is an essential prerequisite to the establishment of a mobile catering business. The new entrepreneur in many cases does not even purchase capital equipment until he has had the opportunity to cover a route for several days, assuring himself of expected revenues. Existing operators are sure to have a strong market position in established market areas. While established routes are available for lease or purchase in most cases, the best, least-cost opportunity for newcomers may be in the development of new routes as new construction sites and industrial complex locations spring up. However, intense competition may be expected when new markets of this nature become available.

6. Capital Requirements

The four major items included in the initial capital investment for a mobile catering operation include:

1. Cost of route(s) (buy lease. etc.),
2. Cost of truck(s)
3. Cost of commissary facilities,
4. Warehousing and office space.

In addition, whether independent or franchised, the operator's cash investment will typically require:

- Lease deposit (usually 2 to 4 months' rent);
- Operating capital sufficient to cover operating expenses for 3 to 6 months;
- Initial food inventory;
- Equipment financing for the commissary—a minimum down-payment of 25 percent and 3 to 5 years to pay off.

Route values are assessed on the basis of daily sales. Currently, for every $1 of daily sales revenue a route draws a market value of from $40 to $50. A good route area ideally should be 20 to 30 miles one way from point of supply pickup. A good 8-hour working route will require a 10- to 12-hour day and have 40 to 50 stops along a 15- to 20-mile run.

The complete unit for a mobile catering truck costs between $6,000 and $8,000. These trucks are generally financed over a 3-year period, but some security is often required by financiers due to the single purpose nature of the vehicle. On the average, truck chassis are retired after 4 years, the bodies every 6 years; tire replacement varies from 20,000 to 25,000 miles.

In addition to trucks, warehousing, and office space, companies intending to own and operate one or more commissaries to supply their routes will require a minimum of 1,000 square feet for kitchen, preparation, and packaging. Costs approximate those of a regular food service kitchen facility, which runs between $15 and $25 per square foot. Kitchen equipment costs average $25 per square foot of kitchen area. The following types of equipment were most frequently included in equipment buying plans for 1969:

Slicers
Mixers
Ovens
Grills
Coolers
Compressors
Sandwich wrapping units
Walk-in boxes
Filling machines
Coffee makers
Walk-in freezers

This equipment is considered basic to the operation of a commissary. Analysis of the failure of food service ventures indicates that one of the major factors is undercapitalization. In many cases lenders require that the prospective businessman have 35 percent to 50 percent of the total cost of the initial investment in cash before the balance of the capital requirement is made available. This is often the minimum extent of participation—equity or risk capital—expected for the operator to obtain financing.

7 Profitability

The mobile catering company has three main sources of revenue:

1. Commissary sales of drivers (food and supplies) — 60% to 70%
2. Truck lease to drivers (typically $12 to $30 per day including gas, insurance, and maintenance) — 20% to 25%
3. Route lease to drivers (route rental frequently based on 5 percent to 10 percent of truck's daily gross, or on percentage of food purchased from commissary) — 15% to 20%

Industry sources determine that a fairly typical annual return on investment figure is 10 percent. The following industry operating ratios are based on a survey made by Vend magazine and reflect the experience of many mobile catering companies:

	Average for Responding Companies	Range for Responding Companies
Gross sales	100.0%	
Operating expenses		
Cost of goods sold (including commissary overhead)	52.7	23% to 77%
Gross profit	47.3%	
Other expenses		
Driver salaries and commissions (2)	17.3%	5% to 24%
Office and general overhead (including salaries)	10.2	2% to 31%
Truck depreciation	3.6	1.8% to 4.0%
Truck maintenance (including downtime)	3.9	0.1% to 5.0%
License fees	1.0	0.01% to 2.1%
Other depreciation (equipment and buildings)	2.9	1% to 10.4%
Building rental	2.9	1% to 10%
Sales taxes	2.8	0.2% to 4.75%
Total	44.6%	
Projected net profit (before State and local income taxes)	2.7%	

Operators leasing all routes to independent contractors are primarily involved in the preparation and sale of merchandise to truck drivers. This type of operator shows considerably higher product costs than a company that employs its own drivers and sells its own products at retail. Generally, the larger the company the higher the product cost among those companies that do employ their own drivers. Companies with less than 10 routes tend to have lower product costs of from 24 percent to 48 percent, while companies with more than 10 routes tend to experience product cost from 52 percent to 54 percent. The median for salaries and commissions is 18 percent; this cost figure shows rather wide variations within the industry.

Average industry gross profit per year is $42,500, with an average net profit of from $7,000 to $9,000 including owner's compensation. For the independently owned, one-truck, one-route operation, the following are ranges for average operating ratios:

Gross sales	100%
Food and supplies	55% to 60%
Maintenance (including downtime), repairs, and insurance	10% to 15%
Depreciation, interest, taxes and licenses	1% to 3%
Net profit, including owner's compensation	27% to 32%

Trucks are usually depreciated over 5 years.

8. *Effects of Outside Factors*

There are several factors external to the industry which greatly affect sales revenue. The mobile catering industry is greatly influenced by weather hazards, which can limit and even prevent sales. Also since construction sites account for over 15 percent of the market, construction slow-downs in the shortrun can have a serious effect on the fortunes of a company. From a long-range point of view, economic and industrial slow-downs may directly affect the mobile catering industry, in that new industrial locations and complexes potentially yielding new routes and greater sales are to some extent diminished.

Another factor greatly influencing mobile catering is the product research and development in the food manufacturing industry, particularly in frozen and instant foods, which have contributed toward improved quality foods with lower preparation times.

III. FEASIBILITY ANALYSIS

A. Key Factors

The factors of major importance in terms of contribution to successful performance in the mobile catering industry are the following:

1. *Management*

An independent one-truck type operation in which food products are purchased from an existing commissary requires less knowledge and experience than would be necessary in a company with one or more commissaries, multiroutes and a truck fleet to operate. The one-truck independent with sufficient risk capital to invest in a route and truck, however, should at least be informed as to what constitutes a good route, what the relative operating costs are likely to be, and what types of food products are most likely to be successfully sold. In addition, basic salesmanship and public relations abilities are equally important when this type of direct sales contact is made repeatedly each day. While these same requirements apply to larger operations, a much higher technical competence is needed for commissary operations and fleet management. Knowledge of commercial kitchen equipment and layout, menu planning, food product purchasing and processing, as well as the managerial functions, including traffic management, is needed. In all scales of operation a willingness and ability to cope with the intense competition frequently characteristic of the industry is also a basic ingredient of success. A prospective newcomer to the industry should be certain of a high degree of motivation well in advance of actual investment.

2. Service

Once routes have been established through promotion efforts, a high level of quality food products and service is absolutely essential to the maintenance of customers. This, of course, is due to the fact that most agreements with customers are merely verbal. This has the effect of making ownership of routes vulnerable to "pirating" by other operators, especially when service begins to drop off. For the most part, foods served by mobile caterers are convenience items, and, if the operator does not make his products available at the times customers want them, another operator will. Another aspect of service is menu variety. The operator who relies on cycling is capable of marketing much more interesting food products to his customers.

3. Location

Location is important especially where growth patterns for construction and industrial sites are concerned. The operator interested in expansion must be well informed about such development if he expects to arrive there first and secure new markets.

B. Minority Ventures

Mobile catering can be a particularly suitable business opportunity for a minority entrepreneur. It lends itself well to low capital investment and requires little experience. An associated advantage in this instance may be the better market acceptance of a minority entrepreneur in a community area where the majority of residents are members of the minority group to which the entrepreneur belongs. The entrepreneur in this case would also have some awareness of the types of food products that would be likely to have the greatest market acceptance and highest demand.

The bulk of the markets, however, will be places of employment such as corporations and construction sites. The minority entrepreneur must usually sell to the general market, therefore, and he is likely to have little comparative advantage in lining up routes. The beginning entrepreneur may find it useful, then, to obtain an existing route (that may feature a fairly high portion of minority workers) and to obtain experience in serving this market before attempting to establish a new route. Service and food quality will in any case be the basis of competition.

C. Projection of Attainable Returns

A description of the business and projection of attainable returns are furnished for a one-man independent operation and a small company operation. These examples are meant to be representative of each of two common forms of businesses in the industry and may be particularly illustrative of returns attainable by minority ventures.

1. One-Man Independent Operation

This type of operation would generally involve a single truck purchased at a cost of about $6,000. The average route, which would itself have a marketable value of approximately $6,800, would be developed and owned by the operator. The workweek would generally entail 5¾ working days of 8 to 10 hours each day during which 43 stops are made. The route is expected to yield approximately $170 in sales revenue each day. Total initial capital requirement would be about $10,000. Startup capital is obtained from both equity and debt sources; the entrepreneur obtains a $5,000 bank loan on his personal guarantee and finances the purchase of his truck over 3 years. Capital requirements are broken into the following categories: Downpayment on truck, $1,800; food, supplies, equipment, $4,000; operating capital and licenses, $4,200. First year projections are as follows:

Gross sales	$44,200	100%
Food and supplies	25,600	58
Butane, oil, and gas	1,800	4
Repairs, maintenance, and insurance	3,500	8
Depreciation, interest, taxes, and licenses	1,300	3
Net profit before tax (including owner's compensation)	$12,000	27%

The profit earned in this operation is representative of only one hypothetical situation and may vary widely, depending on a variety of factors both internally and externally related. While prior experience in the field is not essential on this level, day-to-day observation of commissary operation will contribute toward accumulating technical knowledge if and when expansion should be considered. This does not, however, eliminate the need for careful planning and good management from the beginning. A high level of service will have to be maintained to assure sales and to retain the route.

2. Small Company Operation

This type of operation would own and operate six routes and a commissary. The company would have the option of either leasing its routes or hiring its own drivers, and in this case the company hires its own drivers. The total labor requirement would generally be at least two managerial level employees (presumably at least one would be an owner), one maintenance employee, and three commissary employees. The use of one commissary for six routes requires a fairly central location, which means being situated in an area highly competitive with other mobile catering companies. An emphasis on service and menu cycling becomes increasingly important in this type of situation. Leasing of a building with sufficient parking area for the six trucks and at least 1,000 square feet of food preparation area, plus an additional 400 square feet for warehousing and a small office area, would be required.

Capital requirements for this operation would be approximately the following:

Downpayment on 6 trucks	$ 18,000
Initial food inventory	10,000
Lease deposit	1,800
Licenses, etc.	2,000
Building preparation and adaptation, office equipment	20,000
Operating capital	30,000
Food preparation equipment financed over 5 years	25,000
	$106,800

The capital structure of such a business might be as follows:

Owner's equity	$ 43,000
Bank loan with 90 percent SBA guarantee	63,800
	$106,800

Trucks would generally be in use 6 days a week, 8 to 10 hours per day, with 45 stops per day per truck. Estimated daily sales revenue per truck ranges from $170 to $175.

Projected sales revenues and operating costs for the 1st year are as follows:

Gross sales	$324,500	100%
Cost of goods sold (including commissary overhead)	172,000	53
Gross margin	$152,500	47%
Operating expenses	$139,500	
Driver salaries and commissions		18%
Office and general overhead (including salaries)		10
Truck depreciation		3
Truck maintenance		4
License fees		1
Depreciation—equipment and building		3
Building rental		2
Interest—trucks		2
Net profit, before taxes (including owner's compensation)	$ 13,000	4%

This net profit is only a single, though representative, example of what might be earned in the 1st year for an operation of this nature and size.

INDUSTRIAL LAUNDERERS
AND LINEN SUPPLY

I. RECOMMENDATION

The industrial launderers and linen supply industries are both growing sectors of the U.S. service industry. Since the technology and markets are basically similar, these industries are often combined in one business. A new business can be started at any level of capitalization between about $20,000 and $200,000. The technology is simple, and the skills needed are primarily related to managerial capacity.

The ability to "sell" is an important one. The industries are highly competitive, and selling is vital. The enterpreneur must have the confidence to respond to closed bid competition, the main method by which clients select a laundry or linen supply firm. This confidence will come from experience, good management, and cost control. The industries have had a fairly high failure rate, due largely to poor cost accounting which results in the submission of bids on which the firm can only make a loss (for a contract period as long as 2 to 3 years).

Since the labor productivity has traditionally been low in the industries, and labor costs often represent 50 to 75 percent of total costs, the ability to manage labor is also important. Indeed, every effort must be made to accumulate capital quickly so that the expensive labor saving machinery available can be used.

There is a critical size in the growth of firms in these industries of about $500,000 to $1 million annual revenue, at which labor productivity is often too low to compete with larger firms, while overheads are so much higher than those of small firms that underbidding is frequent. The small entrepreneur should be able to outbid all but the cheapest of the larger companies—but only if he is capable of controlling his overhead costs carefully, while being constantly aware of the need to increase labor productivity at a rate faster than the growth of his total revenues.

This is a critical management problem, and it requires considerable managerial aptitude. With this aptitude the entrepreneur can succeed; without it he will probably fail very quickly as his firm begins to grow beyond a small-size operation.

II. DESCRIPTION OF THE INDUSTRIES

A. Definition

This report treats two industries in parallel. They are:

SIC 7218 Industrial launderers providing cleaning and reconditioning service for uniforms, towels, safety equipment, work clothes, dust control items. Items are owned either by company or customer, and establishments may or may not operate their own laundries.

SIC 7213 Linen supply (or services) supplying uniforms, gowns, bed and table linens (on a rental basis) to commercial and service establishments may or may not operate their own laundry.

B. Dimensions of the Industries

1. General

Both of these industries are part of the Nation's $600 billion "services" sector, and because of this orientation, are growing fast. There are, of course, many features contributing to the growth and to the differences in the growth rates of the two industries.

TABLE 1

Growth of Output and Establishments

	Linen supply			Industrial launderers		
	Number of establishments	$ Mil-lions	Output Percent of growth	Number of establishments	$ Mil-lions	Output Percent of growth
1958		433				
1959		463	6.9			
1960		491	6.0			
1961		498	1.4			
1962		540	8.4			
1963	1,469	571	5.9	768	272	
1964		611	7.0			10% average
1965		664	8.6			annual
1966		734	10.6			growth
1967	1,435	804	9.5	918	408	
1968		885	10.1			

The Standard Industrial Classification (SIC) definitions suggest more of a distinction between the two industries than actually exists; the industries are in most respects very similar. Almost all industrial laundries (IL) do some "flat work" (sheets, tablecloths) and many linen supply establishments (LS) supply industrial-type goods such as mats and dust mops. Both industries devote much of their output to garment supply, but it is within this latter activity that they are somewhat distinct.

Both industries are fairly small. Linen supply has an output now of about $970 million per year, and industrial laundries about $700 million, while in terms of numbers of establishments, 1,435 were classified as linen supply and 918 as industrial launderers in 1967.

2. Size Distribution

Size distribution is important since it indicates the degree to which small businesses share in the market. Both industries have many small companies with low revenues and few employees serving a small segment of the market. At the other extreme there are a few large companies with fairly large revenues occupying an increasingly large part of the market as they grow by amalgamation and through the purchase of smaller companies. Data presented in Table 2 reveal the preponderance of small reporting units in the industries in both 1965 and 1970, with possible indication of increasing size in the latter year. Nevertheless, the heavy concentration of facilities in the lower employment group categories (46 percent of total employment in 1970 was in reporting units employing less than 20 employees) indicates continuing opportunities for small businessmen.

TABLE 2

Distribution of Reporting Units With Employees, by Employment Size (1965, 1970)

Employment size	Number [1] 1965	Number [1] 1970	Linen supply [2]	Industrial launderers [3]
1–7	693	530	374	156
8–19	371	445	322	123
20–49	442	475	324	151
50–99	339	348	213	135
100–249	220	262	188	74
250–499	36	44	31	13
500 and more	3	4	4	—
Total	2,104	2,108	1,456	652

[1] Reporting units—linen supply and industrial launderers combined
[2] Reporting units—linen supply, 1970
[3] Reporting units—industrial launderers, 1970

Bureau of the Census, County Business Patterns, 1965 and 1970.

3. Location

Firm location is a function of population and population density, and all major metropolitan areas have industrial launderers and linen service representatives. National chains try to place at least one establishment in each metropolitan area. Exceptions to this occur where there is a component of demand greater than the population would seem to indicate. Hospital centers, State capitals, university towns, and cities near large military establishments are particularly attractive locations to the industry.

C. The Market

1. General

An idea of the general orientation of the market is available in Table 3, estimated from the 1963 market structure. In an industrial laundry, over 60 percent of the business comes from renting garments owned by the industrial laundry itself. Only 5 percent of business is done with articles owned by the client. Other categories of the market are wiping cloth rental (12 percent) and dust control rentals (8 percent). In the linen supply industry 80 percent of total revenues are derived from renting to businesses, but most of this is in "flatwork" (sheets, towels, tablecloths) rental which is the linen service's main business. However, 28 percent is now garment rental to businesses—a growing proportion, up from perhaps 20 percent in 1963, and bringing the two industries closer in the types of business they do and the markets they serve. This major distinction (in degree to which the two industries are specializing in garment rental) is perhaps the single most important factor in their growth differences. Garment rental is not only the fastest growing market sector, but also the most profitable. Originating in a "uniform" rental business, garment rental has now expanded to "career apparel" including clothes for all types of service workers—in hospitals, banks, restaurants, retail shops, garages, academic institutions, car rental agencies, transportation companies, public utilities, and so on.

TABLE 3

Market Structure

A. Industrial launderers

	Percent
Garment rental	63.2
Wiping cloth rental	11.6
Dust control	7.6
Garments and wiping cloths owned by customer	5.3
Linen supply rental	4.1
Other sources	8.2
Total	100.0

B. Linen supply

	Percent
To homes (linen supply)	1.0
Garment rental (to business)	28.0
Flatwork (to business)	52.0
Drycleaning work	1.3
Family work	1.7
Commercial work	3.5
Industrial laundry work	11.8
Other	0.7
Total	100.0

Details of the linen service market are available in Table 4, showing that restuarants, motels, and hotels are the major customers. Receipts from these customers are growing primarily as a function of the garment rental rather than "flatwork" rental; the latter is also less profitable except in very large quantities for major clients.

TABLE 4

Sales, linen supply, industry — 1968

Customer category	Percent of annual volume *
1. Restaurants (includes country clubs)	25.9
2. Food stores (grocery stores, supermarkets)	8.0
3. Industrial (other than food processors: includes gasoline service stations and new/used car dealers)	7.6
4. Hotels and motels	11.6
5. Medical (doctors, dentists, clinics, nursing homes, hospitals)	10.9
6. Other	36.0

* Results of a 1968 membership study conducted by the Linen Supply Association of America.

In both industries, growth is taking place by:

a. Expansion of rental service into homes—particularly for towels, and

b. Expansion of services to existing clients by introducing the idea of prestige, image-producing "career apparel," mainly in the customer contact industries.

2. The Supply Chain

The service provided by industrial laundries/linen service companies varies in at least two ways. First, the articles can be owned by the client, or the industrial laundries/linen service, or (increasingly) by the manufacturer of the articles in a licensing or franchising agreement with the industrial laundries/linen service. Second, the service can be initiated by the client, as a request; from the industrial laundries/linen service, in a sales bid; or from the clothing manufacturers, some of whom are realizing that the rental clothing market is a very fast growing one indeed.

3. Economic Threshold for Entry into Market

Several factors have a bearing on the scale of operations which must be obtained before market entry is feasible.

Both industries are highly labor intensive. This characteristic is changing due to more activity by unions and expanded research into more capital intensive methods designed to cut labor costs and increase labor productivity. The large firms (with access to capital) are in the forefront in this trend, and are able to hold down prices as a result, while smaller operations are being forced to close if lack of capital prevents them from investing in the "new" machinery. "Minimum threshold size" is, therefore, growing.

Another major component of cost (over 25 percent in most cases) is attributable to the distribution of clean articles and collection of soiled items. These costs are increasing due to road taxes, trucking industry wages, fuel bills, and the costs of vehicle servicing. This means that there is an advantage in securing large clients who have large orders, and a disadvantage (even a loss) in serving a small client. Interviews in the industries suggest that the current cost of making one service call may be about $5 to $7. The advantage of a large client is obvious:

100 customers, 10 pieces each = 100 calls per week = $500-$700

10 customers, 100 pieces each = 10 calls per week = $50-$70

4. Ease of Entry

The "minimum threshold," therefore, tends to be a function of both contract size and total business, and this makes it difficult for the small firm, since entry with small capacity prevents access to the most profitable large order market.

Initially, at the "mom and pop" size, the firm might be quite competitive in bidding for contracts as labor and overhead costs would be low. Despite low labor productivity due to low capitalization, survival would be feasible even serving small clients with small orders where distribution costs are high per item. Capital investment totaling $10,000 would be sufficient for this type of operation, with the following items of equipment probably required:

1 100 lb. washer	$2,000	Employment: 4-5 persons
1 press	2,000	
1 tumble dryer	2,000	Plant size: 2-4,000 sq. ft.
2 delivery vehicles	3,000	
stock (setup costs)	1,000	
	$10,000	

However, expansion beyond this stage is difficult. As soon as the firm is able to secure larger contracts (inherently more profitable), then a change of scale is needed, entailing new machinery, a larger, and possibly unionized, work force, a sales effort to keep the new machines fully occupied, and administration costs, all of which tend to raise the operating costs despite higher labor productivity. Prices in bidding will then be higher than both "mom and pop" size stores with low overhead and large companies with high productivity.

In effect, the cost per item processed is higher in the size range $50,000 to $100,000 than it is for companies of smaller and larger size.

5. Market Potential

Future growth of linen supply and industrial launderers will no doubt be considerable, but there are many complicated factors to be taken into account.

The two industries have grown because of the great convenience which their services offers—it relieves the client of an unpleasant, costly, time-consuming, job, and the market for rental garments and other items will grow because of this. An even more convenient method, however, is now available to solve this problem and is on the market—the use of disposable items in flatwork (wiping cloth, sheets, towels, napkins, tablecloths) and in the garment areas (coveralls, surgical aprons, patient coveralls, and so on). The economics of disposables are making them more attractive as the price of labor (and therefore of linen supply and industrial launderers services) grows.

The Linen Supply Association of America (LSAA) is aware of this trend and is encouraging its members to expand into the disposable market by adding disposables to their services to be used where most economical. Given this possibility, the industrial laundries/linen service might grow even faster. The linen supply industry expects the market for career apparel to grow to $70 billion by 1980.

This optimistic LSAA estimate of the market for "career apparel" based on the penetration of the "career clothing" idea to some very large markets, such as banks, utilities, and university communities, where uniforms are not as yet fully accepted. Recently, for example, Minnegasco (Minneapolis Gas Co.) outfitted all its employees from president to janitor with several alternate types of clothing, including various lines of dresses (evening wear included) and pant suits for women employees, all imaginatively styled and updated on a fashion conscious basis. This "image" building activity may well provide a very important market for linen supply/industrial launderers.

D. Competition

1. General

Competition within the industries is severe in most metropolitan areas, and survival depends largely on two factors:

a. The success of the firm's marketing effort.
b. The degree to which the firm can reduce labor costs.

Most large companies, institutions, hospitals, restaurant chains, and the like take care of their laundry needs by asking for bids from the industry. The ability to assess one's own costs in relation to the types of items needed, the frequency of service, and the quality required is a critical feature. Bidding tends to be highly competitive, and in some areas a price-cutting "war" develops in which firms "steal" contracts from each other by bidding below cost.

Great variation in local labor rates, due to the differing bargaining power of local unions, causes significant differences in the competitive stance of firms. Currently, wage rates in Oakland, California, are 60 cents per hour higher than those in Los Angeles, allowing Los Angeles companies to compete successfully for Bay Area business despite the 400-mile distance. As a result, all but two of the existing Oakland firms are now for sale.

Recent expansions by the national chains have also increased competition, since the large companies have greater resources in marketing and bidding. By mid-1970, 50 percent of the industrial laundries market was controlled by the top eight companies and 60 percent of the linen service market by only five companies. The swing toward higher capitalization in response to rising labor costs favors the large companies.

2. Form of Organization of Competition

Tables 5a and 5b feature the industry structures from the point of view of organizational form. It is clear that the dominant organizations are corporations (70 percent of all ownership), which control 90 percent of the market. Small businesses, individually owned and in partnerships, represent over 20 percent of the firms, sharing 3 to 5 percent of the market. Despite this, however, in 1963 the industries were still composed primarily of single establishment firms, with only 20 percent of industrial laundries having more than 11 branches (21 percent of market). Today the leading chains control perhaps 50 percent of the market. This growth in chains has steadily lessened the available opportunities for small businessmen during the last decade, particularly in the linen supply industry.

TABLE 5a

Legal Form of Organization — 1963

	Industrial launderers				Linen supply			
	Establishments		Receipts		Establishments		Receipts	
	Number	Percent	$ Millions	Percent	Number	Percent	$ Millions	Percent
Individual owner	201	23.2	$ 12.4	3.8	366	22.5	$ 25.8	4.7
Partnership	76	8.9	31.0	8.3	143	9.0	33.1	7.0
Corporation	587	67.9	326.9	87.9	1,079	67.5	505.4	88.3
Other legal forms	4	—	2.1	—	3	—	2.3	—
Total	868	100.0	$372.4	100.0	1,591	100.0	$571.6	100.0

Source: 1963 Census of Business

TABLE 5b

Single and Multibranch Firms

	Industrial launderers					Linen supply				
	Firms	Establishments		Receipts		Firms	Establishments		Receipts	
	Number	Number	Percent	$ Millions	Percent	Number	Number	Percent	$ Millions	Percent
Single	567	567	65.3	$182.2	49.8	1,010	1,010	63.5	$257.6	45.2
2-10	74	163	18.8	113.0	29.5	96	194	12.7	106.9	18.7
11+	11	138	15.9	77.2	20.7	17	387	23.8	207.1	36.1
Total	652	868	100.0	$372.4	100.0	1,123	1,591	100.0	$571.6	100.0

E. Technology

Recent attempts to increase productivity in response to rising labor costs have resulted in many new processes and machines being introduced. Yet the technology used by both industries remains basically simple.

Standard equipment includes the following *:

Washers 25-400 lb. capacity	$20,000
Washer/extractors	17,000
Tumble dryer, up to 400 lbs.	3,000
Flatwork ironers	55,000
Steam presses (hand)	5,000
Steam presses (machine operated)	10,000
Tunnel steamer	10,000
Solvent drycleaning, up to 400 lbs.	30,000

* Prices are averages for one item of the largest capacity.

Additional necessary equipment includes conveyor (overhead and ground), loading and unloading equipment, parcelling machines, a hot water system of large capacity, and perhaps dye vats. Trucks for delivery are also needed. All of this equipment is simple and can be maintained "in-house"; it is also fairly reliable and downtime is normally not excessive.

Major technological changes include the recent introduction of the "hot box" by LSAA—a heating and steaming box operating at high temperatures (300° to 400° F) for cleaning garments. This major innovation performs some of the functions of washers, driers and presses, and labor saving possibilities are large. Some hot boxes are now in use, permitting increases in productivity of 80 to 200 percent and cutting down on the labor force proportionately.

Another major technological change without which the hot box cannot be used is the development of increasingly long-lasting, manmade fiber mixes and manmade/natural fiber mixes. In uniforms the 65-percent dacron 35-percent cotton garments can last up to 2 years (four times their cotton equivalents) at an extra initial cost of only 30 to 80 percent. They are essential if a firm is to take advantage of such methods as the hot box. Item replacement is an important component of cost in the industry.

Finally, new continuous process machinery developed in Europe is now being brought into the U. S. market, permitting even lower labor handling costs. The LSAA is increasing productivity at the distributor end of the business by providing advice to the salesmen's problem of least-cost delivery with optimum service to customers.

All of these improvements require high volumes to justify them-selves economically. Capitalization in the industry is growing rapidly, raising the economic threshold for entry into the market.

F. Cost Structure

The extent of labor productivity has been the major factor in the structuring of costs in the industry. During the past decade there has been a gradual substitution of capital for labor as labor costs have risen. Nevertheless, the recent technological breakthroughs have been associated with increasing union pressure for better wages and work-ing conditions.

Annual replacement ratios for items in the linen supply industry vary considerably. Industry statistics show the ratio for continuous towels to be 1.623 per 100 whereas that for pants is 5.316 per 100. The use of "new" fiber in garments is expected to close this gap, and ratios may change considerably as the need for hot processing methods (to raise labor productivity) forces companies to use the long-lasting product mixes.

G. Productivity

Productivity is a different concept to deal with in a service industry. Clearly it is important to raise output per man-hour but such efforts could conceivably lower the quality of service to the customer, which is ultimately the only measure of success that is relevant. The very low labor productivity figures which have until recently been common in the industry (Table 6) are more an indicator of the degree to which the industry has been dependent on labor (instead of capital) than in indicator of "inefficiency" per se.

During the period 1963 to 1967, output per man-hour grew at a rate of 4½ percent per year in industrial launderers and 6 percent per year in linen supply. However, in both cases, output per dollar of labor cost declined.

TABLE 6

Productivity of Labor
(Estimates only)

	Industrial launderers		Linen supply	
	1963	1967	1963	1967
Output per $1 of labor cost	$2.65	$2.63	$2.68	$2.60
Total receipts per man-hour	$5.55	$5.95	$4.01	$4.90

This low productivity feature is related to low capital investment figures, which even after the relatively heavy investment of the 1965-1970 period range only between $1,500 and $6,000 per employee, with an average of about $3,000, depending on the size of the company.

Data on productivity in relation to revenue and to weight of goods processed are in Table 7, which distinguishes between firm sizes. The table shows that productivity per pound increases as firms increase annual volume to $1 million of revenue while revenue per employee increases up to companies doing $2 million worth of business. Beyond these points average productivity begins to decline.

TABLE 7

Productivity Measures
Linen Supply Industry — 1968

| | Productivity | |
Company size	Revenue per lb. (cents)	Revenue per employee
Under $200,000	—	—
$200,000 to $500,000	20.1	$ 8,178
$500,001 to $1,000,000	21.5	$10,934
$1,000,001 to $2,000,000	20.0	$12,017
Over $2,000,000	18.8	$11,426

Source: LSAA survey 1968

These data indicate that the smaller firms with low productivity of labor receive a fair revenue per pound of work processed. Above $1 million in sales, revenues per pound start to fall due to increasing overheads (such as sales, administration, and equipment amortization costs) despite increasing labor productivity.

Economies of scale do not emerge in these figures, but they certainly are available in many forms. The advantages of having large clients and large volume in lowering distribution costs have already been discussed. Almost all capital expenditures in these industries cut down labor costs and produce economies since the larger and faster machines use so much less labor per pound of output. One problem associated with capital intensity, however, is the need to generate quantum increases in business in order to run new machinery at full capacity, involving much greater expenditures on sales and the marketing function. Lowering production-labor costs, therefore, involves an increase in administration and sales-labor costs. There is no evidence that these types of overhead eventually make further expansion less profitable. The available economies of scale do not seem to have a cutoff point as long as advances in technology take place.

H. Pricing Policy

Pricing is one of the critical skills affecting success in industrial launderers, linen supply industries. Most sales made to large- and medium-sized organizations take place by the bid method in which 20 or more firms are requested to submit bids from which the client makes his selection. Bid prices are based on the cost of processing individual types of items and vary considerably from such simple items as towels to the complex "career apparel" items. Competition is severe, and accurate knowledge of costs is, therefore, a requisite for survival in the industries.

TABLE 8

Average Price Received for Selected Clean Items Delivered

	Percent of total sales	Price per item	Price per lb.
Office towels	5.4	9¢	55¢
Pants	5.8	45	34
Shirts	4.7	39	20
Wiping cloths	1.2	3	15
Sheets	9.1	13	17
Tablecloths	3.7	13	18
Dresses	5.4	35	33

Source: LSAA Handbook 1970

These data show great variation in the price per pound received. These prices must cover labor costs, the machine-hour rate (MHR) and replacement costs for the items due to wear and tear and loss. Obviously, bidding on a contract which might include many different items is a difficult process and requires great skill and good cost accounting. It is common for many firms to bid at "below-cost" prices, not only because of their desire to get the contract, but because of ignorance over certain aspects of the costs of one or two items in the total contract. The price per pound to process shirts and pants (which need to be pressed) is obviously greater than that of towels. Sheets and tablecloths require a special item of equipment—a flatwork ironer—which represents a $50,000 investment, and large volumes of business are needed to fill the capacity of even the smallest flatwork ironer. Margins are slim and small slips cost money.

I. Profitability

Profitability per item is difficult to generalize about because of all the variables involved, but industry sources stress the profit potential of garment rental (given adequate new machinery) and the difficulty of making money in flatwork. Indeed, firms will often offer flatwork as a "loss-leader" in order to gain associated garment contracts.

The LSAA Survey of 1968 (44 firms) indicated the following average operating ratios:

Gross profit (margin) 42.2%
Operating expenses 34.4
Operating profit 7.8
Income taxes 2.8

Net profit 5.0%

The average after-tax return on investment was about 19.5 percent. These margins are fairly wide by service industry standards, exceeding much of the retailing industry in operating and net profit. Return on investment is handsome.

Variation in profitability varies considerably by size of company.

TABLE 9

Linen Supply Industry — 1968
Operating Ratio Percentages by Annual Receipts Categories

	Under $500,000	$500,000 to $1 million	$1 million to $2 million	$2 million +	$30 million +
Gross margin	42.9%	39.1%	41.8%	40.5%	31.7%
Expenses	35.2	34.2	32.3	30.7	21.1
Operating profit	7.7	4.9	9.5	9.8	10.6
Taxes	2.2	1.1	3.7	4.4	5.2
Net profit	5.5%	3.8%	5.8%	5.4%	5.4%

Expenses decline systematically with size—a function of the economies of scale discussed earlier. This means that operating profit tends to increase with size, apart from the "dip" in the medium-size company which experiences low-profit levels.

III. ANALYSIS OF BUSINESS FEASIBILITY

A. Major Factors Determining Industry Success

1. Marketing and Sales

The industry is selling a service, and growth takes place by extending the range of those services. This takes a great deal of skill and persuasiveness by the firm. Bidding is at the heart of the company-client relationship and competition is severe. A good sales staff, adequately paid, is an essential. Subscription to lists of "contacts" is invaluable.

2. Cost Control

The pressure placed on margins by the increasing cost of labor in this industry means that efficiency in all other areas is essential. This applies particularly in distribution where good management can reduce costs effectively.

3. *The Critical Growth Gap*

Entry can be achieved with a very small amount of capital, but growth beyond the $500,000 per annum level is difficult as overhead becomes larger. At this point, access to larger amounts of capital is essential in order to reduce labor requirements and raise productivity. Failure to do this reduces net profit to critically small margins, and it becomes difficult to win any contract at "above cost" prices.

4. *Size of Client*

Of all the critical features this is the most difficult to deal with. It is clear that very small clients cannot be served profitably once the firm grows beyond the "mom and pop" stage, and many firms have a minimum contract value ($5 to $10 per week) below which they will not service a client. This feature is a difficult one from the point of view of a new small business.

5. *Product Mix*

Garments are the most profitable end of the business but require larger sums of investment both on behalf of the firm (in processing machinery) and the client (in his stock of garments). Unless entry is made at a fairly large size, this valuable market may not be open to the new firm with little experience.

B. **Problems of Minority Enterprise**

A new minority enterprise in these industries must face all of the problems discussed above and probably several others. But, there may be opportunities not open to nonminority competitors.

In Detroit, Cleveland, and Oakland, California, and some other large cities, the minority community clientele may be sufficient to support a fair-sized industrial laundry, given guarantees of support from minority company trade associations. Most of these companies are relatively new, however, and are unlikely to be very receptive to attempts at selling "career clothing" or other industrial launderers/linen supply services.

C. **Projection of Returns—Two Hypothetical Situations**

Two situations likely to characterize minority enterprise are discussed next. The difference between them is mainly one of scale, a function of the capital investment made by the entrepreneur at the outset. In both cases, emphasis has been placed on the high profit side of the industry (garments) and less on the flatwork side.

TABLE 10

Financial Projections
for Representative Businesses of Two Sizes

	Case 1			Case 2	
	Small proprietorship ($50,000 annual gross)			Medium-sized proprietorship ($200,000 annual gross)	
Capacity—lbs. per yr.	250,000 lbs.			1,000,000 lbs.	
lbs. per day	1,000 lbs.			4,000 lbs.	
Equipment Costs:					
Washer extractor	1 (200 lb.)		$ 4,000	1 (400 lb.)	$ 20,000
Spare	1 (50 lb.)		1,000	1 (100 lb.)	3,000
Dryer	1 (100 lb.)		2,000	1 (400 lb.)	4,000
Press	2 (manual)		1,000	1 (automatic)	5,000
Drycleaning machine	1 (small)		5,000	1 (large)	30,000
Heating plant	1		2,000	1	12,000
Installation			1,500		8,000
Other			500		2,000
Vehicles	1		2,000	3	6,000
Total			$19,000		$ 90,000

Annual operating statement

			Case 1		Case 2
Gross receipts			$50,000		$200,000
Operating expenses					
Labor:					
Production	(3)	$16,500		(6)	$42,000
Distribution	(1)	7,500		(3)	26,750
Sales and administration				(2)	17,500
Nonwage benefits	(nonunion)	3,500		(union)	22,000
Total labor costs		$27,500			$108,250
Supplies		1,000			4,000
Equipment maintenance		1,000			5,000
Materials replacement		5,000			35,000
Total operating expense			$34,500		$152,250
Overhead expenses:	(3,000			(10,000	
Rent and Utilities	sq. ft.)	4,000		sq. ft.)	12,000
Equipment depreciation	(10 yr.)	1,900		(10 yr.)	9,000
Total overhead			5,900		21,000
Total expenses			$40,400		$173,250
Net profit before taxes and owner's compensation			$ 9,600		$ 26,750

Certain Assumptions are Made

1. All buildings and real estate are rented, not purchased.

2. Input capacity is determined by the capacity of the washer/extractor machine. All other equipment capacity is geared to this. This is not unreasonable, but in practice other measures of capacity would be necessary also.

3. An assumed revenue of 20 cents per pound of goods processed is used as base (the average of the linen supply industry).

4. Labor needs are calculated as follows:
   a. production—from manufacturers' literature
   b. distribution—it is assumed that the average client has a contract worth $30 and is serviced once a week. From projected net receipts, it can be estimated that Case 1 firm has weekly revenues of about $1,000 and Case 2, of $4,000. The number of contracts this revenue represents is:
      Case 1—$1,000/$30 $=$ 33
      Case 2—$4,000/$30 $=$ 133

Each vehicle can make 10 calls per day, or 50 to 60 per week; Case 1 needs one vehicle and driver, and Case 2 needs three.

IV. GUIDANCE FOR ESTABLISHING THE BUSINESS

A. Approaching the Market

The most opportune situation for both Case 1 and Case 2 might be to purchase an existing business with an established clientele. This may not be possible, however. Marketing is a very important part of the industrial launderers/linen supply industry and can be thought of as two activities:

1. Direct selling to potential customers.
2. Being placed on bidders' lists (for institutional and other larger customers).

Both these activities can be started by subscribing to "contact leads" published by specialist organizations covering the industrial laundries/linen service market locally. A blanket mailing coverage of all establishments in the "customer types" list (LSAA) derived from the local yellow pages of the phone book is another basic approach. The "customer types" list as shown in Table 4 is large and can yield much valuable business.

Minority businessmen will, of course, attempt to contact local minority-owned businesses in the customer-types listing. Direct person-to-person contact with the potential client is more effective than any other means of selling. Initially, it may be that only small clients, who are difficult to service without making a loss, are recruited; however, in the beginning "all business is good business" and small contracts will help. The aim should be to bid effectively on the larger contracts let periodically by larger companies, chains, restaurants, and so on. Public institutions and military agencies welcome potential bidders; other larger organizations must be "sold" more heavily.

Specialization in a particular market that is also a particular product group is an additional possibility. Specialization in servicing gas stations, for instance, might yield high profits as experience grows and knowledge of the "gas station" industry is accumulated. Another profitable area of specialization might be dentists' and doctors' offices, particularly where the latter are grouped together in "medical centers" and have minority representation. Indeed, this latter factor can be a criterion used to search out markets, since minority businesses are most frequently found among gas stations, automotive repairs, food franchise outlets, some areas of retail trade, beauty shops, and bars.

Attempts at getting "guarantees" of business from minority operations have sometimes been successful in other industries and can be applied here, too. Certainly this would be an effective method in larger cities which have a large minority community.

B. Obtaining Financing

Established firms in industrial launderers/linen supply industries make use of bulk credit and of equipment-secured debt to finance operations and expansion. For the newcomer to the industries, financing can be difficult to obtain, and for minority newcomers, even more so.

There are, however, opportunities for minimizing startup capital needs. The use of used machinery and vehicles is an obvious one, as is the purchase of stock and other materials from other companies which are going out of business, or being amalgamated, or spinning off some operations. The trade journals "personals" are an effective market source for this. Leasing premises rather than buying or constructing them is an obvious capital-saver, but less obvious is the possibility of lease/lending machinery from some of the major manufacturers. In times of slow business and poor credit, manufacturers tend to be more open to the possibilities of lease/lend in order to move their stocks of machinery.

The new business will, of course, need some new capital to start and to continue operations. In order to obtain this as cheaply as possible, a sound "financial plan" is essential. Elements of this include knowledge of the Federal, State, and local loans and guarantees programs available for small business. Another listing of non-profit "help" agencies for minority business, some of which have financial resources, is the publication *Private Programs Assisting Minority Business,* issued in 1970 by the Office of Minority Business Enterprise, U.S. Department of Commerce, Washington, D.C. 20230.

FURNITURE STORES

I. RECOMMENDATION

Sustained market demand in the furniture industry offers attractive opportunities for new business development in the furniture retail field. With rising incomes, increasing population, and new housing predicted for the 1970's, furniture store sales are expected to rise throughout the decade.

Key determinants of profitability in the business include the ability to select styles and lines which appeal to customers, ample floor space to display merchandise, adequate storage for inventory, a good sales force, and access to a line of credit with which to finance purchases on relatively favorable terms. Managers must also give close attention to control of key elements of cost, such as inventory, advertising, wages and rent. Undercapitalization and shrinkage of working capital are major causes of failure.

There are many sources of information and help in furniture retailing. Organizations such as the National Home Furnishings Association provide members with assistance in store layout, advertising, sales training, and cost control. There are also many professional buying organizations which can help in the selection of proper merchandise. Thus, an individual who has a flare for retailing, management skills, and a fundamental knowledge of interior decoration should be able to establish and operate a furniture store successfully, provided he has picked his location carefully and is properly financed.

II. DESCRIPTION

A. Identification

Furniture stores Standard Industrial Classification (SIC) 5712 are described as establishments primarily engaged in the retail sale of household furniture. Many such stores also sell floor coverings, major appliances, and such home furnishings as lamps, draperies, decorative art objects, and mirrors. Types of furniture sold include upholstered furniture such as chairs and sofas, wood pieces, bedding, dining room pieces, dinettes, children's furniture, and the like.

B. Dimensions

There are presently about 27,000 furniture stores in the United States and, in addition, a great number of department and discount stores which handle furniture as part of their product line. The industry is a major factor in the economy, with 1967 retail sales amounting to about $6.5 billion and a 1967 payroll of $231 million for the 180,000 furniture retail employees.

Industry sales are expected to rise to $9 billion by 1975, reflecting growing income, increasing use of credit (making possible the financing of additional furniture purchases), and construction of new housing. The family formations which will occur as the members of the baby boom of the early 1950's reach adulthood are expected to bolster furniture demand for much of the decade.

The furniture retail industry is still characterized primarily by the small retailer. About three out of every four stores had fewer than eight employees in 1967, and 94 percent of the stores had fewer than 20 employees. The predominance of the small store is also reflected in sales figures; one out of every five stores does more than $100,000 of business annually and only one out of 20 stores has sales exceeding $500,000 per year.

The trend in the industry, nevertheless, is towards larger stores. Especially in urban areas with adequate markets, furniture stores are expanding product lines so as to better service the total furniture needs of the more affluent customers. This trend can be inferred from the fact that, though the total number of stores has not changed significantly in recent years, the total number of employees has grown considerably.

C. Characteristics

1. The Product and the Customer

A complete furniture store will display and sell living room furniture, including sofas, chairs, recliners, convertibles, credenzas and tables; bedroom furniture, including beds, mattresses, and springs, dressers, and night tables; dining room furniture, including tables, chairs, buffets, and serving tables; dinettes, floor coverings, children's furniture, major appliances, decorative art objects, mirrors, clocks, porch and outdoor furniture, odd chairs, hassocks, desks, card tables, bars, and lamps.

A furniture store sells a way of living and life style to its customers. Most homemakers have great aspirations for fixing up their homes to their hearts' desires. Their homes are not only to be used, but to be displayed. Women take pride in their homes and like to show them to others. To many families, a home symbolizes success and "the good life."

The homemaker usually has plans for a change or for improvement. Items to be purchased are seldom bought on impulse, but are thought about carefully and discussed in the home and with friends. Almost two-thirds of all purchases are made to replace items already owned. Convenience in shopping is a relatively minor factor. Families will make a furniture purchase in the store where they feel they will get the most value in appearance and style for the amount of money they have available.

Most purchases of furniture involve a relatively large commitment of the family funds, and two-thirds of all purchases are made by a husband and wife buying together. Credit is generally involved in the purchase. Many stores finance credit sales themselves and make an additional profit thereby. Others "sell" a portion of their installment "paper" to financial institutions.

The salesman is important to the furniture buyer. She asks his advice on color, texture, groupings. She is often unsure of how a particular piece will fit into her grouping, and she will seek confidence from the salesman that her choice is a good one. A furniture retailer who has sold customers quality merchandise in the past can often depend on his customers returning, particularly if the relationship is maintained on a satisfactory basis while the installment payments are being made.

Almost half of all families in the United States earning over $4,000 annually will make at least one purchase of an item of furniture (including mattresses/bedsprings and floor coverings) a year. About one out of every 10 customers is under 25 years of age, and about 15 percent of the customers are over 55. Well over half of the customers are in the prime 25 to 44 year age bracket. Forty percent of the customers will own their own homes. Eighty-six percent of the purchases will be for homes and the balance for apartment units, although with the rising number of apartment units being built, this ratio should change in the coming years. It should also be kept in mind that these percentages are on a national basis and could be expected to vary in specific areas.

Most customers learn about a store from discussions with family and friends, window shopping, or advertising. Many get specific ideas from furniture ads in magazines, from magazine articles, or from seeing furnishings in other homes.

Most customers do not buy by brand name, and many are unable to quote a brand name. The main reasons for selecting a particular store are store reputation, price, and assortment. Store reputation counts most heavily among shoppers in specialized furniture stores, while price is a more important factor among chain department store shoppers. The average sale in the furniture industry is about $160.

2. Operations

The successful furniture retailer should have these attributes:

a. *Taste and Skill in Selecting and Displaying Merchandise.* The ultimate determinant of whether or not a sale is made is whether the customer is attracted to the product. The owner/manager must see to it that his merchandise will appeal to his market and that it is displayed in a way which will induce his customers to want the merchandise for their homes.

b. *Good Salesmanship.* Retailing is basically selling. An order-taker will not do for a furniture store. The salesman must know his merchandise and how to sell.

c. *Ability To Learn and Keep Abreast of Changes.* The successful furniture retailer must be willing and able to learn from published material on the industry and successful practices in retailing, and he must be sensitive to changes in style and taste.

d. *Hard Work and Attention to Detail.* There are many things which can go wrong in retailing. Deliveries aren't made on time. Credit accounts are not handled properly. Merchandise is damaged. Inventory is shrinking without explanation. Displays need to be changed. Overstock needs to be reduced. Advertising decisions are required. Special promotions are needed. The owner of a retail store must be alert to all these matters. He must watch his cost ratios. He must pay his bills and collect his outstanding accounts. He will have to work long hours and at least 6 days a week.

e. *Ability To Understand and Make Decisions on the Basis of Figures.* A successful merchant must be sensitive to his books and accounts so that he can determine the actions which make money for him and those which are losing propositions. Basically, these decisions can be made on the basis of an analysis of his sales and costs. But the individual who does not easily understand accounts and numbers may find it difficult to understand what is happening to his business.

A good sales force is essential to successful operation of a furniture store. This requires continuous training. A good salesman will like to work with customers and will be appropriately patient while the homemaker ponders her decision. The salesman must know his products thoroughly; he must know the essentials of interior decoration, such as color, texture, form, arrangements, and space requirements; and he must know how to communicate this knowledge to the customer in a helpful and constructive manner which leads to a sale.

There are different arrangements for compensation. Some stores have a commission arrangement for salesmen; others have a straight salary; and others have a combination. Salaries vary considerably from place to place and depend a good deal upon the experience of the salesman. Thus an inexperienced salesperson in a relatively low-wage area might receive $80 to $90 per week, while a topflight experienced salesperson with interior decorating skills in a higher wage area might receive as much as $12,000 to $14,000 annually.

3. Competition

Furniture stores not only compete among themselves, but they also compete with appliance stores, stores specializing in floor coverings, department stores, chain department stores, discount chains, and specialty stores selling homefurnishings of various kinds.

Within inner cities, there is also competition from stores offering purported bargains at inflated prices and high credit rates. These stores may advertise special bargains as an inducement to bring shoppers into the store, but the salesman is generally skillful at steering the shoppers away from the so-called bargain. In many instances, stores of this type sell and resell repossessed merchandise, making their profit on a continuing series of downpayments. Fortunately, this type of operation is gradually being phased out with the increasing knowledge of the inner-city consumer and more stringent controls by authorities.

Highly effective and ethical price competition will be faced from the large chain department stores and mail-order houses. These establishments generally feature relatively high quality merchandise at economy prices. In recent years, they have improved their styling, as well. The furniture retailer must compete with these stores, as he would with department stores and with other furniture retailers, by offering value, style, and efficient service. Maintaining contact with present customers is important, and effective advertising can also be useful in bringing potential customers into a store.

The amount and variety of merchandise displayed by a furniture retailer is important in meeting competition. The opportunity to see a wide variety of furnishings will bring the shopper into the store, and the more choices that can be seen, the greater the possibility that the shopper will find something she likes. Thus, there is a trend toward greater and greater floor space on the part of the independent furniture retailer.

4. Ease of Entry

The individual who has the attributes and skills for success in furniture retailing must nevertheless find the right location and sufficient capital before he can enter the industry.

The right location is a place that will provide the retailer with ample floorspace at a reasonable price in a market which is growing and not overly saturated with competition. The location must also provide parking space if it is in a suburban area. If it is in the inner city, it must be reasonably accessible to the potential market. Before selecting a location, a careful market survey should be made to determine if there is sufficient business to justify the selection.

A new entrant, who is properly capitalized and who knows his business, should not be frightened away from establishing a furniture store simply because there is considerable competition already in the area. Unless he is prepared to hold his own in competition with other retailers and the chains, he should not enter the business. Even if competition is relatively scarce at a particular time, he can always expect newcomers or branch outlets of existing firms.

A major factor affecting ease of entry will be the ability to secure sufficient capital for inventory and to finance credit purchases.

5. Capital Requirements

Capital requirements are usually considerable for a furniture retailer. Capital is required for store inventory and supplies, warehouse backup inventory, fixtures and equipment, decorating and carpeting, and installment accounts. Inventory and leasehold improvements for the average independent full-stock furniture store require an investment of about $5 a square foot, or $50,000 for a 10,000-square-foot store doing an annual volume of about $250,000. A store doing this amount of business would need about $100,000 to $150,000 to finance installment sales, of which perhaps 20 percent would be required as an investment by the store itself, with the balance of the debt sold to a financing institution. This would require a total investment in the neighborhood of $75,000 for a store doing $250,000 worth of business annually.

There is very little trade credit available for this type of investment. Most suppliers require 30- to 60-day payment or faster, particularly for a new entrant in a field where failures are frequent. Some bank financing may be available, although the bank would require additional security, probably in the form of personal guarantees and assignment of personal property and/or a Small Business Administration guarantee.

6. Profitability

In 1966, at the height of an expansionary period, retail furniture stores ranked fourth in rate of failure among 23 types of retail establishments studied by Dun & Bradstreet. However, for those establishments which do succeed, profitability is generally good. In 1969, a relatively average year, profits before taxes averaged about 5 to 6 percent of sales for all sizes of stores.

Gross margin within the industry on sales runs to about 40 percent, with many firms earning an additional 4 to 6 percent on credit operations. However, those firms which sell their installment paper do not earn this extra amount.

7. Dependence on Outside Factors

Besides replacement sales and increases in consumer income, the retail furniture business is dependent upon growth in population, new family formations, and new housing. The long term trends in all these factors are up.

This business is affected by seasonality. Summer is generally slack as are the months of January and February. Most business is accounted for in the last 4 months of the year. Therefore, seasonal factors must be accounted for in normal planning.

Business cycles also affect furniture sales, but these cyclical factors are not as easily planned for. Home furnishing purchases are postponed when people are earning less and boom when pent-up demand is released. Thus it would be wise to postpone new entry into the industry at a time when consumers are worried and holding back on expenditures which can be postponed. Experienced store owners generally try to improve their financial strength during prosperous times in order to withstand recessionary periods.

III. FEASIBILITY ANALYSIS

A. Key Factors

The following are the principal factors which affect performance in retail furniture stores:

1. Management

Management must be alert to customer satisfaction and taste and must take care of all the details of a successful retailing operation, including sales training, credit management, advertising, stock control, display, control of pilferage, cost control, and so on.

2. Capital

Adequate capital is essential for investment in floor displays and ability to offer installment credit.

3. Market Location

The proposed establishment should be situated to serve a growing market, preferably one where consumer disposable income is growing and where new housing is being constructed. While specific location within such a market is not crucial, the store should be situated where it is convenient to and easily noticed by consumers.

4. Floorspace

The volume of business that can be done is closely related to the amount of floorspace available. Newer establishments try to operate from a single floor, but multifloor stores can be successful. A variety of tasteful displays will attract potential customers to the store and provide increased opportunities for salesmen to be successful.

5. Salesmanship

All aspects of salesmanship are important. This includes the possession of a well-trained, capable sales staff, the use of good advertising, and the preparation of good displays.

6. Customer Relations

Established customers are a source of repeat business, and installment payments provide a way to maintain relationships with these customers. Customers must have confidence in the store's integrity. The store must keep up to date on customers' style preferences.

7. Credit

The store must provide for installment credit for purchasers.

B. Problems and Potentials for Minority Ventures

1. Problems

New ventures into retail furniture are apt to run into problems from unethical competitors, legitimate price competition from the large department chains and discount houses, inadequate capital, and unsuitable locations.

Unethical competition can come from the unscrupulous ghetto retailer who preys on unsuspecting customers with overpriced shoddy merchandise, "bait" advertising, and quick repossessions. Fast-talking salesmen and apparent "easy credit" often dupe unsuspecting consumers into unwise purchases.

To the extent that a minority furniture retailer will be looking to the minority community for his prime market, he will be faced with serious competition from the department store chains and discount houses. Minority community shoppers usually have lower than average disposable incomes and are less able to afford more expensive furniture lines. Thus, they have a greater tendency to purchase the economical, budget-priced furniture of the department chains and discount stores.

Minority entrepreneurs have traditionally experienced difficulty securing adequate capital for their ventures, and without adequate financial resources, entry into the retail furniture business should be dismissed as a possibility for a minority entrepreneur. The average time it takes to receive goods from a supplier is 6 to 12 weeks. If a dealer has only a small credit line, his order will not be processed until the line is paid off or brought down to his credit limits. Small dealers without adequate capital are often forced to buy from suppliers whose furniture lines do not provide as much value as those who are more successful and more stringent on credit.

An undercapitalized furniture retailer will not be able to stock sufficient inventory to attract the more affluent customer. He will not be able to deliver merchandise to customers as rapidly as some of his competitors and will lose many sales for this reason. He will have difficulty securing financing for his installment sales, and he will lose customers to more securely financed operations. His equipment and fixtures will deteriorate more readily and detract from the overall appearance of his store. He may not be able to advertise competitively.

The entrepreneur who seeks to serve the inner-city minority market may find it difficult to secure adequate space in a suitable location. Many downtown shopping areas have become seedy and do not provide an appropriate atmosphere for the purchase of home furnishings. Moreover, problems of fire insurance and crime are magnified in a downtown location.

For all these reasons, minority entrepreneurs have not made a significant penetration into the retail furniture industry. In an industry which has over 27,000 establishments, there are less than 100 which are owned by minority entrepreneurs or less than one-half of 1 percent. Only one black-owned furniture store does an annual gross of over $1 million and most do under $200,000 of business annually.

2. Potentials

There is an awakening self-consciousness among minority consumers that could lead to consumer preference toward minority entrepreneurs. Thus, a furniture store offering good value and located within a minority community might be preferred by many minority homemakers over a chain department store, or a large suburban-oriented independent furniture retailer.

Recent improvements in financial packages available for minority entrepreneurs may also improve the potential for a minority business. Various civic groups have been organized in many cities to help minority entrepreneurs, and these may be able to assist the protential new businessman by helping him to do his advance planning and to secure necessary lines of credit. Special sources of capital and business planning assistance are available to businesses in many cities, and these may help an entrepreneur overcome the handicaps of inadequate capitalization. New minority-owned banks are becoming more capable of financing consumer installments and providing lines of credit for retailers.

C. Projections

The following figures represent financial projections which are typical for many furniture retailers. Individual stores may vary widely from these percentages, and each individual situation should be studied carefully on the basis of its own conditions. Two potential situations are projected: one, a smaller store with a volume approximating $200,000 annually; and the other, a moderate-sized store with a volume of about $600,000.

	Situation 1		Situation 2	
	Amount	Percent	Amount	Percent
Gross sales	$208,000	104	$636,000	106
Returns and allowances	8,000	4	36,000	6
Annual volume	200,000	100	600,000	100
Cost of merchandise	120,000	60	348,000	58
Gross margin	80,000	40	252,000	42
Income from credit operations	6,000	3	24,000	4
Operating expenses (total)	70,000	35	240,000	40
Net profit from operations	16,000	8	36,000	6
Deductions from income (interest, bad debts, etc.)	6,000	3	12,000	2
Net profit before taxes	10,000	5	24,000	4
Typical investment	75,000		200,000	
Return on investment		13.3		12

Profits and return on investment from furniture stores vary much more among stores within a certain size range than they do among the averages of different size ranges. This suggests that size, itself, is not a dominant factor in profitability. Other factors such as management, reputation, and location are much more important.

The following are some key indicators for the two sizes of stores:

	Situation 1	Situation 2
Installment sales as a percentage of total sales	84%	80%
Installment accounts receivable as a percentage of installment sales	63%	58%
Bad debts charged off on installment accounts as a percentage of installment sales	1%	1%
Amount of average sale	$140	$180
Dollar sales per square foot of selling space	$ 28	$ 32
Sales per employee	$34,000	$35,000
Sales per salesman	$100,000	$128,000
Sales per handling and delivery employee	$105,000	$107,000
Ratio of assets to liabilities	2.6X	3.0X
Net sales per $ of net worth	$ 1.90	$ 2.00

IV. ESTABLISHING THE NEW BUSINESS

A. Establishing the Market

The first step in starting a new furniture store is to determine the market which the store is intended to serve. The prospective entrepreneur must identify the general type of consumer he proposes to cater to. For example, he may wish to locate in the inner city and make his appeal largely to inner-city minority residents; or he may wish to take a location which is on the fringes so that he can cater not only to the inner-city population, but to some suburban population or inner-city residents moving to the fringes of the city. He may wish to cater to young marrieds starting out in small apartments or he may desire to sell more to established homemakers and residents of single family homes.

Whatever the decision, it will affect where the new store is to be located, how large it should be, what its total market is, and what kind of furniture lines it should carry from the standpoint of both styles and price. For example, young marrieds may want the more modern styles with vivid colors and economical prices; more mature families may prefer Early American and may be willing to pay higher prices for more substantial furniture.

When the character of the market is determined, the entrepreneur should determine its potential size. There are various local statistics available which can be used to clarify how many people with certain characteristics live within shopping range of various potential locations, how much they spend annually on furniture, how their incomes are changing, and the like. Market data may be available from local chambers of commerce, planning commissions, or councils of government. The feasibility of a new store may be glimpsed in the following way. Visit the furniture stores in the same shopping area, as well as the department stores. Determine what types of customers they try to serve. Make a list of each one and estimate how much floorspace each has. Using estimates of sales per square foot, either locally used or industrywide (about $30 of sales per square foot), estimates can be made of total sales volume for each competitor. These can be compared to the estimated total furniture purchases for the market, providing insights into the volume which might be achievable in the store being planned. For example, if the estimated sales volume of all stores based upon square footage is considerably more than the total estimated purchases in the market area, it is likely that the market is oversaturated with furniture stores.

The general procedure to be followed in selecting a store location begins with the identification of several potential locations where space is known to be available, the computation of the number of potential customers within the shopping area of each location, and the determination of the amount of annual expenditures on furniture that each will make. An analysis of competition in each area will suggest where underserved markets exist.

B. Determining Size of Operation

The size of the proposed business will be determined by the size of the market, the amount of competition which can be expected, the available capital resources, and the amount of experience of the proposed management. These should be carefully weighed against each other. For instance, even though a large market is anticipated, the proposed store should not be larger than the capital resources which the individual has available to support it. Moreover, if the proposed entrepreneur is somewhat inexperienced, he may be wiser to make his mistakes learning the business in a smaller operation that is more securely financed, than in a larger operation in a precarious financial position.

C. Securing Capital

A number of cities have organizations which specialize in assisting minority entrepreneurs to secure capital. A prospective entrepreneur should seek out these sources and go over his plans with them.

The local Small Business Administration office or OMBE affiliate may help to put the prospective entrepreneur in touch with sources of capital and to provide the names of banks which have made minority loans. Minority-owned banks may also provide capital.

The Small Business Administration can also be helpful with a lease guarantee. Many landlords are unwilling to lease to an inexperienced and new businessman, because they have no recourse in the event the business fails. The SBA has a program to reassure such landlords by insuring the lease of the small businessman.

D. Starting Operations

The new businessman should seek experienced help in completing negotiations with the landlord. There are a number of variables to the standard lease which many real estate organizations are willing to grant but which are not offered if the tenant does not ask for them. An experienced businessman or lease negotiator can be useful during these negotiations. Help should be requested from a local organization specializing in assisting minority entrepreneurs.

Unless the prospective entrepreneur is very experienced in the trade, he should investigate affiliation with an established buying office. Such an office is worth its cost in advising the businessman on lines to carry and in taking the time to visit the various furniture markets to be on the lookout for good buys. A buying office cannot substitute for the businessman's own knowledge of his customers and their taste, but it can be a valuable and profitable supplementary service, particularly to the small furniture retailer who cannot take the time and expense to visit all the markets.

Every effort should be made to have attractive displays of furniture ready for the opening. There are many articles and books on display and layout, and these should be studied carefully and the recommendations should be adapted to the particular store. It is more important to spend original capital on display inventory, fixtures, and proper displays than on warehouse inventory. In most cases, customers are willing to wait several weeks for merchandise, and shipments from the factory can generally be secured in ample time. Warehouse inventory should be used for special purchases and fast sellers.

If the sales force is inexperienced, careful time and attention should be paid to their training. If the entrepreneur himself has neither the time nor the ability to give this training, outside help should be secured. It is essential that the sales staff be first rate.

The businessman should spend considerable time and money planning for the opening. Special values should be featured. Even special gifts or prizes should be purchased and given to persons coming into the store during the opening days. Advertising which is appropriate to the size of the store and the investment available should be prepared and used. Advertising is extremely important in bringing customers to the store.

V. SUMMARY

Although it is a difficult business, demanding long hours and constant supervision, furniture retailing does offer the individual with an interest in furniture and a talent for selling an opportunity to enter a business which has growth and profit potential. Moreover, to the extent that minority homemakers can be persuaded to give shopping preference to stores which are owned by members of the same minority and located in the same community, such stores would have a competitive advantage to offset traditional disadvantages associated with inadequate capital resources and limited experience in business management.

In summary, sound management, a trained sales force, and adequate financial resources are keys to success in furniture retailing.

SUPERMARKETS

I. RECOMMENDATION

While the operation of a supermarket in the inner city appears on the surface to be a natural type of business venture for a minority entrepreneur or cooperative, it is a highly risky business requiring a very complex organization with sophisticated business methods, highly experienced management, considerable capital, and large scale buying power.

Despite apparent high prices for merchandise, margins are extremely low and competition is intense, largely on the basis of price and intensive promotional schemes. The large chain supermarkets continue to increase their share of the overall business, and the independent grocer is very hard-pressed to compete unless he knows the business thoroughly and can "outmanage" the area chainstore manager.

Inner-city locations are very difficult to operate profitably. Insurance rates are exceptionally high and losses to pilferage, shoplifting, and robbery are considerable, as are the costs of guarding against such occurrences.

The fact remains that the inner city needs supermarkets and that the chainstores are not very eager to open in such locations. This creates an opportunity for the minority entrepreneur or cooperative, but adequate financing and superior management are absolutely necessary, or the venture is certain to fail. For individuals desiring entry into the food business, a more likely prospect would be the convenience store which requires a much smaller investment and less complex managerial skills.

II. Description

A. Identification

The Standard Industrial Classification (SIC) 5411 includes stores which are commonly known as supermarkets, foodstores, or grocery stores. They are primarily engaged in the retail sale of food products for consumption in the home. For purposes of this profile, the supermarket is defined as any foodstore offering primarily self-service which does a business of about $1 million annually, or in the neighborhood of $20,000 per week.

There is a classification of store known as "superette," which is a term used for stores with sales of $150,000 to $1 million annually. Much of what is said in this profile about supermarkets applies to superettes as well. Small grocery stores are those with sales of less than $150,000 annually. These last types are generally of the "mom and pop" variety which are a carryover from earlier years and which exist largely because the owner's family is willing to work long hours for very little "take-home" pay. These stores are on their way out and are not recommended for minority entrepreneur consideration.

Convenience stores are another category which may belong in either the small store or the superette class. These stores are open long hours 7 days a week, and carry a line of food items which cater to the homemaker who has run out of a necessary item.

B. Dimensions of the Industry

The retail food industry in the United States is a multibillion dollar a year business, with total U.S. grocery sales in 1967 of $74.2 billion, up from $38.2 billion in 1958. During this period, the number of all grocery stores declined from 285,000 to 226,000, with average sales per store increasing at a steady rate from $169,000 annually to $328,000. Supermarkets accounted for almost three out of every four sales dollars (72.3 percent) in the retail food industry, but they accounted for only 15.4 percent of all stores.

These basic facts about grocery stores must be kept in mind at all times:

1. There will be continuing growth along with population growth.
2. The trend has been to larger and larger stores.
3. Establishments owned by large chains have continued to grow and currently dominate the industry.

There has been a recent trend toward growth of small stores of the so-called convenience category, but these are special cases and do not pose a threat to the domination of the large chains.

Expenditures for food have grown over the years at a rate faster than the growth of population. This is generally attributed to the increase in convenience foods such as frozen foods, prepackaged meals, special mixes, and the like, which cost more than the basic foods that are prepared at home.

There has been considerable interest in minority penetration into the supermarket field in recent years, due largely to the virtual abandonment of the inner city by many chains and the need to provide a source for food to inner-city residents. In addition, there have been a number of claims that many of the chainstores charge higher prices at their remaining inner-city locations than at their suburban stores. While these charges have been denied, they are widely believed throughout minority communities.

Although a number of minority grocery stores have been established, many of these have experienced difficulties attaining sufficient volume and adequate cost controls for profitable operation. Some have failed. There are, as yet, no outstanding minority-owned successes in the supermarket field although many of those that have started in the past 5 years have shown signs of overcoming their initial difficulties and surviving.

C. Characteristics of the Industry

1. The Product

The average inventory of the modern supermarket consists of some 6,000 to 8,000 items, defined as either individual products or individual brands. Indeed, it is the large inventory which permits the supermarket to capture its volume of sales. Above all, the successful supermarket seeks to be a "one-stop" shopping center, and the larger the inventory, the more realistic is this claim.

The table below shows how many different items are carried in the various departments of one of the largest chains, and the percentage of total sales each department accounts for.

Department	Number of items	Percent of total	Percentage of total sales
Meat	465	7.1	28.3
Produce	241	3.7	7.6
Dairy	281	4.4	11.5
Frozen foods	286	4.5	3.3
Bakery	278	4.3	5.0
Grocery	3,837	59.0	40.5
Nonfoods	1,100	17.0	3.8
Total	6,488	100.0	100.0

The supermarket sells the convenience of one-stop shopping, and the desirability of a large number of items from which to choose. Supermarkets compete with each other on price, quality, store appearance, and location. The tendency in recent years has been to add more and more items, to establish special delicatessen departments, and to increase the number of nonfood items on which markups are higher. The average store in a large chain offered 6,488 items in 1970 as compared to 5,144 in 1957, and nonfood items increased from 654 to 1,100. Meat and produce items also increased greatly.

The quality of produce and meats is an important part of the supermarket product. While most supermarkets carry the same brands of nationally-advertised foods, there may be considerable difference in the quality of meats and produce, and many homemakers choose among supermarkets on the basis of real or fancied differences in the qualities of these items.

Many of the supermarket chains also feature their own brands of groceries. The quality of these private brands is usually high and they often offer considerable savings to the shopper willing to forego the nationally-advertised brand. Private labels are also available to independents, particularly if they deal with a large wholesaler who has established a reputation for his own brands.

Nonfood items generally consist of items such as drugs and cosmetics, small housewares, special buys in soft-goods items such as socks, dishtowels, underwear, children's wear, garden supplies, and stationery. Items such as drugs, cosmetics, and soft-goods items have become increasingly important because there is usually a larger markup on these goods than on food items. In many cases, a service jobber will supply these items and service them on the shelves or on special display fixtures. The supermarket pays only for the items which are sold.

Frozen foods have become increasingly important, and many of the newer supermarkets devote considerable refrigerated space to displays of these items.

Some supermarkets also feature their own bakery products, even to the extent of having a bakery on the premise. This, too, can be an important factor in bringing the customer to the store.

Under some circumstances, bakery, meats, and/or produce departments can be leased to specialists. If such an arrangement is possible, it may prove wise for a new entrepreneur to thus free himself to manage other departments more closely.

2. The Customer

The average urban family of four is apt to spend about $2,000 a year in the grocery store. Most of the purchases are made by women, although men are becoming increasingly important as supermarket shoppers, and many managers have recently been slanting displays of foods toward those which might promote impulse purchases from men.

Many families try to do all their shopping for food once a week, although the typical pattern is to make one trip to the supermarket for the week's shopping on Thursday, Friday, or Saturday, when most specials are featured, with an occasional trip or two during the other days to pick up forgotten items or such perishables as bread, dairy products, meats, and frozen foods.

The weekend specials are a major aspect of supermarket merchandising. However, many supermarkets are trying to change consumer habits into buying early in the week as well, and it is not uncommon to see the major chains advertising in the Monday newspapers, as well as Thursday and Friday.

While the average supermarket shopper comes to the store with a list of purchases to be made, impulse buying is a major factor in building volume. Special displays are valuable features of food merchandising, and food manufacturers often pay for the privilege of featuring their merchandise in these displays.

The new "consumerism" has brought about an increasing demand on the part of articulate consumer "spokesmen" for "unit pricing" and "open dating." Unit pricing provides the customer with a comparison of the price per standard unit for different brands and different size containers, so that she does not have to perform the mathematical computations herself. Thus the prices for a 13-ounce container, a one-pound three-ounce container, and a two-and-a-half pound container will also be shown in terms of the equivalent price per pound for each container. The customer can then see which item actually costs less.

Open dating refers to providing the customer with information on the freshness of items. Most grocery items are stamped with coded numbers which indicate when an item is to be removed from the shelf as no longer fresh. These codes were designed to be deciphered only by stores employees. However, stores have recently begun providing consumers with information with which to understand codes.

Many customers develop loyalties to particular stores based upon convenience of location, preference for the store's private brands, a belief that the store offers better bargains or has better quality meat and/or produce, a desire for the store's greater variety of items, or even friendliness with the clerks. However, such loyalties are fickle, and they change easily. Many of the chains show a considerable shift in their weekly volume, based upon the competitiveness of their weekend specials or their competitive position on special promotions. The wide use of trading stamps and special promotions tends to support the assumption that the average customer finds little to choose between the many chains on the basis of convenience, price, and quality, and therefore makes his decision on the basis of special promotions, weekend specials, and trading stamps.

This being true, it is logical to assume that a minority-owned supermarket which could compete on an equal basis with the chains when it comes to convenience, price, and quality could easily capture the loyalty of enough members of the minority community, based upon a consciousness of race and an identification with the owner of the store, to achieve profitability.

With the average urban family of four spending in the neighborhood of $2,000 a year on retail food purchases, a supermarket could attain a volume of $1 million by securing 500 such families as customers. However, since most families will split their purchases among many different outlets, a minimum-sized supermarket should seek about 2,000 to 3,000 customers.

3. Operations

While the operation of a supermarket may appear on the surface to be a relatively simple job requiring rudimentary skills, such appearances are dangerously deceptive and have led many individuals and groups into bankruptcy. In actual practice, supermarket management is a highly complex skill requiring application of diverse talents and continuous attention to many different aspects of the job.

The appearance of the store is an important feature, requiring a knowledge of point-of-sale merchandising, proper lighting, and appropriate arrangement of merchandise to facilitate shopping and assure that the customer will come back. The width of aisles, for example, is highly important. If they are too wide, they take up valuable space which could be used to stock more merchandise. If they are too narrow, the customer becomes irritated at being unable to maneuver her shopping cart easily. The store must be kept clean at all times, and yet there is a continuing tendency to become cluttered and messy. If the store has a rundown, overly-cluttered, and messy atmosphere, the shopper may conclude that the items being sold are insanitary.

Stocking the various items is another important aspect of management which requires considerable detailed supervision and knowledge. With several thousand items to keep track of, the supermarket manager must determine how much shelf space to allot to each item, and he must carry just enough of each item to turn over his stock rapidly while at the same time making sure that he does not run out of stock and disappoint his customers. Careful inventory control requires constant checking of the sales of the various stock items. Inventory control may well be the most important factor affecting profitability.

The quality of produce and meat offered for sale is yet another aspect of management full of pitfalls for the inexperienced or slipshod manager. Meat suppliers and produce houses cannot be expected to watch the quality of the product they deliver on behalf of the retailer. Just as the housewife examines every cut of meat and every piece of produce carefully, so, too, must the store management see to it that the meat it receives and the produce it buys is of the highest quality. A superior meat and produce department can make an otherwise run-of-the-mill store successful. On the other hand, meat and produce of poor quality can ruin an otherwise well-run store.

Proper purchasing of other items is also a key item for the independent supermarket manager. This means taking advantage of special buys and knowing which wholesaler can help him best. Some independents can make money by speculating on food and buying larger than usual quantities in anticipation of price rises on such high volume staples as sugar and canned goods. This requires exceptional skill and experience and can lead to disaster for the unwary store owner who stocks up on an item before the price goes down.

Careful control over stealing and pilferage is an essential aspect of supermarket management. The freedom with which customers and children roam the aisles and the small size of many items make it inevitable that many items will be slipped into pockets. Stock clerks and warehouse clerks are also prone to help themselves to merchandise freely. Sloppy checkout procedures can lead to undercharges which cheat the management and overcharges which cheat the customer and undermine the store's reputation. Cashiers who fail to ring up items for customers whom they know can also result in losses. Bad checks are another loss problem for supermarkets.

There are some established security services which provide agents and investigative services to assist the store manager in protecting against loss. It is also possible to minimize pilferage by lowering shelves, placing registers so that a better view of the store can be maintained, and using closed circuit TV.

The supermarket manager must also master the techniques of advertising, and he must play and win the game of competitive pricing of specials. This means he must know when and how to put certain items on special price and thus attract customers into the store. He will be competing with the chains, and he must study their moves and make countermoves in a constant strategic battle. Some of the larger food retailers actually make money on advertising because brand name manufacturers pay the retailer for the privilege of having their brands listed in his advertising. However, advertising in a competitive market takes an extreme amount of time, often out of proportion to other aspects of management.

An independent supermarket owner should give serious consideration to joining a retailer's cooperative or affiliating with a wholesaler who sponsors joint advertising and features independent brand merchandise. There are a number of these associations in and around the larger metropolitan areas. They offer many advantages. First of all, there is identification through advertising with a number of other stores. Second, the retailer receives the advantage of special promotions and purchases. Third, advice on store operation is generally available. Someone who is thinking of starting a new store should check with wholesalers and independents who have joined in cooperatives in order to compare the advantages offered by such groups.

Labor requirements, of course, vary with the size of the supermarket to be operated. Nevertheless, there are several critical positions which must be filled regardless of store size. The following list identifies the positions and indicates their criticality:

Clerk
Assistant department heads
   *Produce
   *Meat
   Delicatessen
   Grocery
Department heads
   (same as above)
Assistant store manager
   (usually only in larger stores and serves as grocery department head)
*Store manager

---

*Critical jobs.

Wage scales vary according to the geographic area in which the supermarket is located as they are dependent primarily on the strength of the employees' union. For example, wage scales in Washington, D.C., and Los Angeles are high, while in Jackson, Mississippi, where the union is relatively ineffective, wages are much lower.

	Washington, D. C., wages (Weekly)	Mississippi wages (Weekly)
Clerks	$130–$155	$ 45–$ 75
Assistant department heads	$175–$190	$90
Department heads	$220–$230	$100–$115
Assistant store manager	$220–$230	$100–$115
Store manager	$250+	$125–$150

Nonwage benefits differ according to area also. Typical Washington, D.C., benefits, for example cover medical, dental, hospital, and vacation expenses, while those in Mississippi include only vacation. Wages and benefits do not vary according to the size of the store, as they are controlled by the union. Therefore, wages and benefits in a certain area would be the same despite store size and capacity.

4. Competition

The independent supermarket operating in the inner city will be doing business in one of the most competitive industries in the Nation. The size of the market in any one area and the relative ease of entry virtually assure competition in any location where there is sufficient population to assure a reasonable market.

Within the industry, a 1-mile radius is usually accepted as the primary trading area for a supermarket. In 1968, the typical new supermarket had to compete with two other supermarkets with an average combined sales area of 27,000 feet and weekly sales in excess of $50,000.

The supermarket operator is subjected to many different kinds of competition. The convenience store or neighborhood delicatessen competes by being open longer hours and more days. There is also competition from special frozen food stores, bakeries, dairy stores, and in some cases butcher shops. Drugstores and discount department stores sell competitive food and nonfood items. During appropriate seasons produce vendors can be found on street corners or operating out of trucks. But the largest source of competition is the big supermarket chain which competes by heavy advertising, by lower prices, by offering a large variety of items from which to choose, and by employing a wide range of promotional "gimmicks" to get people into the stores.

However, it is possible for an ably-managed independent to compete with the chainstores. By exercising closer supervision over his store the independent can see to it that operation is cleaner and neater. He can take more trouble to know his customers and to develop a cheery and friendly atmosphere. He can be more flexible in his pricing of "specials" and from time to time make special buys which permit him to undercut chainstore prices. With a little care and attention he can offer better produce and better meats than the chains. By identifying himself with the neighborhood and the institutions of the community he can gather a large amount of goodwill which can translate into steady customers. There should be no underestimation of the difficulty of competing in the supermarket industry. But it is possible for a new entrant to do so, if he has sufficient capital, understands food merchandising, and can become an effective manager.

5. Ease of Entry

Given sufficient capital, it is very easy to enter the supermarket business. There are existing businesses which can be purchased, although this should be done with care to make certain that the business being purchased can be operated at a profit. There are also vacant buildings in the inner city, many of them formerly occupied by supermarkets, which have been closed, and these are generally available for the establishment of a business.

Superficially, it might be said that all it really takes to enter the supermarket business is to find a location, equip it with some shelves, checkout counters, and other equipment, order up the stock, and open the doors. However, the potential supermarket operator should not follow this route. Careful planning should take place to establish the right location. Arrangements should be completed for the best possible deal on equipment. Store layout is a complex problem. Stock should be carefully ordered. Personnel should be employed and trained. And considerable time and expense should be given to the opening announcement and the special inducements to get customers into the store during the first week.

With proper planning and advance arrangements, there is no reason why a supermarket cannot begin to break even within the first 3 months after opening. However, considering that mistakes will be made in determining the best inventory arrangement, it may take several more months before inventories are adjusted and regulated to enable the business to reach a break-even point.

6. Financing

Adequate capitalization and financing is one of the keys to successful operation of a supermarket. In most cases, capital is not required for land and building, because an existing building can be leased or arrangements can be made to have a building constructed by someone else and leased by the supermarket operator. Prospective operators of supermarkets in inner-city areas should be alert to leasing commercial space in new housing developments. It is almost always better to lease than to build since less capital is required and a certain flexibility is maintained. Virtually all of the chainstores follow this method.

Some capital will be required for equipment. Equipment can be expensive. For example, a supermarket with 15,000 square feet of selling area could require a minimum of 75 feet of frozen food shelving, about 100 feet of produce shelving (cooled), about 30 feet of dairy shelving and 30 feet of cooled beverage shelving, and a minimum of 50 feet for the meat section. At least six checkout stands and registers would also be required. While the total investment for such equipment is considerable, there is a strong possibility that used equipment can be picked up for some purposes and other equipment leased. However, even with leased equipment there may be considerable investment involved in installing the necessary plumbing and in meeting local building and food-handling codes.

A rough estimate of inventory investment would be about $5 to $10 per square foot of selling space or between two and four times the weekly estimated volume. However, much of this inventory can be secured on credit, depending on the relationship established with a supplier and his confidence in the store management.

Even with maximum use of lease arrangements, financing of equipment, and purchase of inventory on credit, startup costs of a new market will nevertheless be considerable, and it is recommended that $50,000 to $100,000 be available for a store with about 10,000 square feet of selling space, which anticipates a minimum volume of about $20,000 per week. Some of this may not necessarily have to be in cash, but may be in the form of a line of credit available from a bank. For a larger store of 15,000 square feet of selling space, the initial investment would be closer to the $100,000 to $200,000 range.

7. Profitability

The average gross profit among supermarkets (net sales less cost of goods sold) is about 20 percent of net sales, with net profit on sales averaging between 1 percent and 2 percent. An average net profit of 1½ percent on gross volume of $1 million would yield an annual net profit of $15,000. If this were achieved on an investment of $50,000, it would bring about 30-percent return.

The average small food retailer does not make this type of profit, while the large chains often show higher profits on those individual stores that are successful.

The key to profitability in supermarket operation is high volume and inventory control. Managers who can turn over stock rapidly while keeping costs within bounds can show a reasonable profit despite the intense competition within the industry.

Smaller stores such as superettes are characterized by lower profitability. These stores generally do not show the profit of the larger, higher volume stores and are usually justified on the basis of the opportunity afforded to the owner and his family to work in their own store. Thus, while the owner (and his family) may draw a decent living from the store, profits tend to be quite low.

The owner of a superette operating in a protected location or as a convenience store can sell at a higher gross margin and earn a somewhat better profit than a superette attempting to compete with chain-stores in the same trading area.

8. Dependence on Outside Factors

The retail food business is considered a somewhat "depression proof" business in that people always have to eat, and even in times of depression they will spend their welfare allowances, unemployment compensation, and food stamps in the grocery store. Thus, almost more than any other business, the supermarket is dependent for success on the ability of management in selecting the right location, treating the customers well, and controlling costs.

Supermarket operators planning to open in the inner city may find their location and market affected by urban renewal and highway-building programs. These can often change neighborhoods and relocate customers out of the trading area. A wise step before settling on a specific location would be to check with the city planning office to determine what plans are being considered that would change the character of the neighborhood or affect the number of people living in the trading area.

III. FEASIBILITY

A. Factors Influencing Feasibility

The major factors influencing feasibility are: location, management, volume, inventory control, store appearance, price, quality control, and merchandising.

1. Location

Ideally, the location should be within a primary trading area (radius of 1 mile) that has ample population to support the volume of sales desired and where competition is not overly intense. The cost of operating in the location (that is, rent and other charges such as utilities and maintenance) should be appropriate to the quality of the building and within reasonable limits for the volume expected.

2. Management

A supermarket operation is very complex. The average supermarket manager for a chainstore is not only carefully trained, but he receives backup services from a host of experts in merchandising, advertising, store layout, buying, personnel supervision, equipment maintenance, quality control, inventory control, and the like. The independent supermarket operator must often become his own expert in all these fields. The individual desiring to operate his own supermarket should have several years' experience as manager of another store. Without such experience, he would be well advised to seek employment first with a chainstore for several years, using the opportunity to study carefully their methods of operation.

3. Volume

The retail food business is primarily a volume business, particularly for supermarkets. The store must produce the volume required to support its overhead, or it will inevitably lose money.

4. Inventory Control

It is extremely important to maintain the proper balance between inventory and sales volume. On the one hand, the successful supermarket manager wants to keep enough inventory on hand so that his customers can always find what they want; but on the other, he does not want to tie up his money and his shelf space in items which do not sell rapidly. Moreover, many food items will spoil if not sold quickly. The problem is not simple. Some items do not turn over quickly, but they must be kept on hand because customers will be lost without them. The big chainstores have computers and special analysts to help in making these decisions. The independent supermarket operator must make them on his own, although affiliation with an association or a cooperative can provide some help.

Another aspect of inventory control is inventory shrinkage resulting from stealing by the staff, shoplifting by customers, or just plain carelessness. Where profit margins are so small, profits can quickly disappear unless inventory shrinkage is controlled.

5. Store Appearance

The big supermarket chains spend hundreds of thousands of dollars fixing up their stores so that they will be attractive places in which to shop. The independent operator may not have the capital to make this kind of investment, and he will have to be ingenious in his ability to decorate and to lay out fixtures, and diligent in seeing to it that his store is clean, neat, and appealing.

6. Price

Food shoppers are kept constantly aware of the comparative prices of food items by heavy advertising on the part of food retailers. Moreover, many standard items are exactly the same, and it is easy for the shopper to make price comparisons. The homemaker is more apt to be concerned about the price of food than other items since it is the largest single item in the family budget. For all these reasons, the supermarket operator must compete on the basis of price. This can be done in several ways. Sometimes a manager will deliberately cut his inventory so that he can cut prices, reduce his gross margin, and still show a profit. Sometimes price competition is more apparent than real, and the operator reduces a few weekend specials while maintaining adequate markups on the bulk of his merchandise. Again, the big chains have an advantage because they can use their huge purchasing power to secure volume discounts. The independent operator will have to be aggressive and alert to good buys in order to match their basic advantage.

7. Quality Control

There are many opportunities to compete on the basis of quality control in food retailing, particularly in the quality of produce and meats. Baked goods and dairy products also have quality control problems. Careful attention needs to be paid to frozen foods. When these are allowed to thaw and then are refrozen, they lose their flavor. Although there are alarm services to warn the owner when the refrigeration fails, careless handling can cause losses when frozen foods are allowed to stand outside their cases for too long a period.

8. Merchandising

The successful supermarket manager must be a good merchandiser. He must know how to advertise, how to set up good displays, what kinds of special promotions to feature, and how to treat his customers to give them the feeling that they enjoy shopping in his store. The use of trading stamps and special premiums is an important part of food retailing. There are many arguments for and against such merchandising techniques, and these must be understood by the successful operator so that he can use those which are most appropriate to his competitive position.

B. Special Problems and Potentials for Minority Entrepreneurs

1. Problems

The problems faced by a minority entrepreneur trying to establish a food supermarket will be the same as those of any independent attempting to enter a business which is dominated by big, aggressive, and amply financed chainstores, plus special factors created by racial discrimination and environmental problems.

It would be extremely difficult for an inexperienced and unaffiliated minority entrepreneur to go into the suburban shopping centers to compete with the chains on their home ground. In the first place, most shopping center operators would turn up their noses at an independent, inexperienced supermarket operator. They need one of the high volume chain operations to pull customers into their center. This limits the minority entrepreneur to the inner city or its less desirable fringes, where the chains, by and large, do not want to go. While such locations may offer less competition from the chains, they have problems of their own stemming from the character of the neighborhood, the increased cost of insurance, and excessive costs from vandalism, shoplifting, and theft.

Moreover, size is essential to success, and in the supermarket industry, size requires investment. Most minority entrepreneurs do not have access to the kinds of investment required for a supermarket of the size required for profitability, and conventional sources of financing will hardly be available when the proposal is to establish a store in a difficult area. Food retailing accounts for a major portion of minority-owned businesses. However, very few of these businesses are adequate in size, and most subsist without profit, enabling an owner to draw a minimum amount for personal income.

2. Potentials

Nevertheless, there appears to be a shortage of retail food outlets in some inner-city areas where minorities live, and thus there is an opportunity for an individual or a group with the willingness to work hard at the business, the skill to solve the many problems presented, and an access to special sources of capital for minority ventures. If plans can be carefully drawn and effective management secured, there are reasonable chances that sufficient capital can be forthcoming.

Most groups which have been established to help with the economic development of the inner city are interested in establishing retail food operations. The lack of such facilities is a hardship to the residents of the areas in question, and this factor adds a special urgency to the need for providing financing. However, a number of ventures have already been financed in many areas, and a significant proportion of these have experienced severe financial difficulties. This has made lenders somewhat more cautious than they might otherwise be.

New housing projects for the inner city offer an opportunity for the establishment of food supermarkets. These projects will bring a concentration of new families into the area, and many of them will either provide for commercial space or be located close to sites which can be developed for commercial use. In almost all cases, it will be desirable to establish a new supermarket operation in these locations. Minority entrepreneurs seeking to become supermarket operators should carefully investigate such opportunities in connection with new inner city housing projects.

C. Operating Projections

Shown below are hypothetical operating projections for two sizes of supermarkets. The first is a minimal operation, reflecting the very lowest feasible volume of $1 million annually in about 10,000 square feet of selling space (15,000 square feet overall). The second example is designed to show what might be a more typical operation for an average supermarket having 20,000 square feet of selling space and an annual volume of $2,300,000.

These figures are used as typical examples. Individual operations may vary considerably from these examples depending upon local and special circumstances.

Item	Minimal Amount	%	Average Amount	%
Annual sales	$1,000,000	100.0	$2,300,000	100.0
Cost of goods sold	805,000	80.5	1,851,500	80.5
Gross margin		19.5		19.5
Operating expenses:				
Labor (including fringe benefits) $92,000		9.2	207,000	9.0
Purchased services 16,000		1.6	36,800	1.6
Promotion and advertising 11,000		1.1	23,000	1.0
Rental of premises and equipment 21,000		2.1	43,700	1.9
Supplies 10,000		1.0	20,700	0.9
Taxes, licenses, and insurance 14,000		1.4	32,200	1.4
Utilities 9,000		0.9	18,400	0.8
Maintenance and Repairs 7,000		0.7	13,800	0.6
Depreciation and amortization 10,000		1.0	20,700	0.9
Total	190,000	19.0	416,300	18.1
Operating profit	$ 5,000	0.5	$ 32,200	1.4
Other income (discounts earned, advertising allowances, etc.)	4,000	0.4	13,800	0.6
Total income	$ 9,000	0.9	$ 46,000	2.0
Capital investment	$ 75,000		$ 150,000	
Return on investment		12.0		30.7

Typical operating ratios for supermarkets in 1969 are shown below:

Gross profit with warehouse 21.1%
Gross profit without warehouse 19.3%
Net operating profit ratio before taxes 1.5%
Sales by department:
   Grocery 67.5%
   Meat 25.2%
   Produce 7.4%
Average hourly labor cost .... $ 2.77
Grocery inventory turnover rate .... 19.4 times per year
Typical sales per man-hour $34.69
Typical sales per customer .... $ 6.02
Typical sales per square foot of
   selling area (weekly) .... $ 4.15

IV. STARTING THE NEW STORE

A. The Location

The first step in starting a new supermarket is to select the right location. Assuming that the potential new entrepreneur or cooperative already knows the general area in which the supermarket is to be located, a search must be made for an appropriate location. A thorough investigation must be made of all potential locations. These could be: (1) a store presently being operated which is available for purchase; (2) a store which was formerly occupied by a supermarket, but which is now vacant; (3) other vacant commercial space which could be adapted for supermarket operation; (4) newly-constructed commercial space in a proposed shopping center or in the commercial portion of a new housing project; (5) vacant land on which a foodstore could be constructed.

A careful study should be made of all potential locations on the following basis:

1. The Total Market

An estimate should be made of the total market for retail food purchases within the primary trading area of the store. While a rough rule of thumb is a 1-mile radius for the primary trading area of a suburban-type supermarket with ample parking space, a smaller radius should be used to identify the primary trading area in the inner city where many of the customers will have to walk in order to shop. The number of people in the trading area should be determined and their average income estimated. From these data, it is a relatively simple matter to determine their annual food purchases. The advertising departments of local newspapers or radio stations can provide this information. Each prospective location should be analyzed on this basis to see which offers access to the largest market.

2. Competition

The largest market may not necessarily be the best due to competitive factors. Thus, an analysis should be made of the competition serving the same markets and the amount of business each of the competitors does. (This latter estimate can be judged roughly on the basis of the square footage of selling space—which can be paced off by the individual making the study.) After judging the portion of the market potential competitors are taking, an estimate can be made of the potential share of the market that the proposed new supermarket might expect in each location. When this potential is applied to each prospective location, a judgment can be made on which location offers the best opportunity to build volume.

3. Amount and Quality of Space

A comparison should be made of the amount of space available in each of the locations and whether or not the space is sufficient to provide a selling area large enough to support the volume desired. In determining the desirability of space, consideration should be given to its cost and its condition. Thus, one location may have less space available than another, but it may cost less per square foot and be in better condition. It is also important to look at the shape of the space and any posts or other structural characteristics which would handicap use as a foodstore. Moreover, in determining cost, consideration should be given not only to the monthly rent, but also to the cost of renovation, maintenance, and other payments which the tenant is expected to pay.

Sufficient parking space will have to be available along with the store space, if significant business is to be expected from customers who will shop by automobile. A small supermarket depending almost wholly on customers who come by automobile would probably want about 3 square feet of parking space for every square foot of selling space. Thus, a store with 10,000 square feet of selling space would require 30,000 square feet of parking. However, if it expects to do a high volume in that selling space, it may require more parking space. If a significant proportion of customers will come to the store on foot, smaller parking spaces will be sufficient. Obviously, in a city where land costs are high, the supermarket operator generally tries to make do on less space for parking than in the suburbs where land costs are less and all customers come by automobile.

4. Special Factors

There are special factors influencing location to be considered. The quality of the neighborhood is one factor. The potential operator should determine whether the proposed location is becoming a better neighborhood in which to do business or worse. Are there large projects being planned which will relocate customers out of the area? Are new housing projects being planned on vacant land? What kind of neighboring commercial establishments are in the area? Obviously, it is better to be located in a progressive shopping area tenanted by good merchants than to be in an area where seedy bars and grills predominate.

The potential entrepreneur should array all these factors carefully and study them to determine which location is the most advantageous for his purposes. The importance of this kind of locational study cannot be overestimated. It is essential to the establishment of a new supermarket. The average chain spends close to $5,000 on research before selecting a new location. The new entrepreneur may not be able to afford that kind of investment, but he can spend his own time gathering the facts and looking over potential sites carefully. If funds are available, it may be wise to hire an expert economic research firm to help choose the best location.

B. Operational Planning

After the location has been secured, careful plans must be drawn which can be shown to financial backers and others. A determination must be made of what is needed to get the store started, including: renovation of the proposed location; purchase or leasing of equipment; amount of startup inventory; and startup expenses for promotion and training of personnel. A statement should be prepared indicating the cost of all these items and how they are to be financed. A pro forma operating statement should be prepared showing anticipated annual volume and costs.

C. Arranging for Equipment

Visits should be made to local grocery store equipment suppliers for information and prices on refrigerated equipment, special produce counters, shelves, cash registers and the like. A determination should be made of what can be purchased secondhand and what can be leased. Care should be taken to make sure the refrigeration equipment will work. Faulty operation of refrigerating devices can result in considerable loss.

D. Preliminary Lease Negotiations

Preliminary discussions should be held with the owner of the land or building to determine the nature of the lease and the cost. It is generally desirable to have an experienced lease negotiator assist with these discussions. The new operator should try to get a relatively short lease with options to renew at an agreeable rate. The owner of the property will try to get a long lease and some type of guarantee, so that if the operator is unable to continue operations, the lease commitments will be met. Finding an acceptable middle ground between these two points of view is the purpose of negotiations and should be determined by how badly the owner needs to find a tenant and how desirable the proposed building is compared to other possibilities.

A common lease arrangement calls for a fixed minimum payment with additional payments as volume increases, thus enabling the owner to share in the store's success. The supermarket operator should be careful to avoid giving away all his potential profits to the owner of the building, but if he can get a lower minimum by agreeing to a larger share of increased volume, it may lessen the risk of potential failure.

E. Arranging for Inventory

Preliminary discussions should be held with a grocery wholesaler to determine the basis on which an opening inventory can be secured. Generally, the grocery business requires payment in 7 days; while the product business requires payment on receipt of goods. Consideration should be given to the reputability of the wholesaler, his prices, and his willingness to supply credit. It is also advantageous to affiliate with a wholesaler who provides group advertising and brand names, thus giving the new supermarket an established identification in the minds of the consumer. There are many such arrangements in metropolitan areas throughout the country. In the Baltimore area, there is a cooperative arrangement for black-owned grocery stores called Jet Stores; in the Miami area, there is an organization for minority foodstore operators called Farm Stores International, Inc.

F. Arranging for Capital

After the location has been determined, operational planning finished, and preliminary negotiations held with the landlord, equipment suppliers, and grocery suppliers, the new entrepreneur will need to arrange additional financing. Presumably, he will have some idea of where he can secure financial backing for a feasible plan prior to starting the whole process. Such financing can come from a number of sources: (1) the potential new owner or group of owners may have financial resources of their own which can be used or pledged as collateral for a bank loan; (2) if a cooperative, shares may be sold throughout the community to members; (3) there may be special sources of financing from local organizations established to help minority entrepreneurs, such as agencies funded under Title I-D of the Economic Opportunity Act, the Urban Coalition, or a local Minority Enterprise Small Business Investment Corporation (MESBIC); (4) a local bank under a loan guaranteed by the Small Business Administration. The potential new operator should take his plans to the appropriate source of financing and complete the arrangements.

G. Securing a Work Force

A competent work force should be trained and ready for the opening day. While potential employees may be secured from the public employment office or a local employment training program, every effort should be made to secure a nucleus of experienced personnel. If necessary, it would be wiser to pay a premium to lure experienced employees away from some of the supermarkets. Under no circumstances should the new operation start with a completely inexperienced work force.

It is particularly important to try to get experienced personnel for the produce department and the meat department. These are specialized functions which require considerable background.

The work force will need considerable training on such items as checkout counters, customer courtesy, stocking merchandise, display, preparation, and handling of meat and produce, and similar items. If the new management does not have the ability and time to undertake such training, arrangements should be made to employ someone to do so. A check should be made with the local manpower development and training office or concentrated employment program to determine whether such training can be arranged and paid for out of public manpower training funds.

H. Opening Day

The opening day of a new supermarket operation should be carefully planned. Prizes and premiums should be secured to induce customers to come in and see the store. The store, itself, must be spotless and in attractive condition. Opening week special prices should be prominently featured in advertising and store displays. A good impression on opening day can mean early attainment of break-even volume, and this achievement can result in lower startup costs.

Many of the above procedures can be abbreviated where an existing business is being purchased. But the prospective purchaser should be certain of what he is purchasing in all these areas and make sure that he is not simply buying another person's problems.

V. SUMMARY

A food supermarket is one of the most competitive businesses in our economy. Operating margins are very small and leave virtually no room for inefficiency or mistakes. Large, highly organized chainstores provide intense competition for the newcomer to the field. Capital requirements are larger than they are for most retail operations. Management is extremely complex.

Supermarkets do not offer an attractive opportunity for inexperienced, undercapitalized entrepreneurs. However, because there is a need for more quality food outlets to serve consumers in the inner city, it may be desirable actively to encourage new supermarkets for the inner city and to provide considerable extra assistance to entrepreneurial ventures of this type, or to the formation of cooperatives. If so, extreme care should be taken in planning the new operation and every effort should be exerted to make certain that it will be capably managed and adequately financed.

BOWLING ALLEYS

I. RECOMMENDATION

The high rate of failure of bowling establishments in the past decade—due primarily to a combination of overreaction to a rising market, underfinancing, and inexperienced management—suggests that a prospective entrepreneur should enter this industry with caution. Individuals should perform thorough market and financial analyses and consult with industry sources (particularly the two large national suppliers of bowling equipment and the association of bowling proprietors) before venturing into the industry.

The key to the success of a bowling operation is the ability of the management to attract and maintain a full schedule of league bowling. Almost 75 percent of all games are rolled during the course of league play. Thus league attraction and league creation are critical to success. Consequently a strategy for league formation at the proposed center should be worked out in advance of facility planning.

Initial capital investment is relatively high. Good management is considered essential, although other labor force requirements are easily met. Sites with high accessibility and large parking areas are highly desirable. Potentially attractive market areas will vary greatly from locale to locale, depending on such factors as popularity of the sport with the target community, availability of competing facilities, alternative forms of recreation and entertainment available, and the potential of a marketing strategy to increase the local demand.

Increasing popularity of the sport among minority groups provides a growing base upon which minority ventures—relatively rare to date—may establish themselves and achieve a profitable level of operations.

II. DESCRIPTION OF THE INDUSTRY

A. Identification

The traditional bowling alleys of the 1940's and 1950's have evolved into the bowling centers of the 1960's and 1970's, which include all the facilities of the earlier establishments plus additional amusements and subsidiary services. Thus, a bowling center is likely to include, in addition to the basic requirements of the sport (alleys, balls, and shoe rental), food and beverage service, bar service, amusement machines (pinball, children's rides, etc.), pool tables, and other miscellaneous recreation (model car racetracks, indoor miniature golf, etc.). The service offered may also extend beyond service and maintenance functions associated with the game of bowling itself to include operation of the above-mentioned recreation and service activities, bowling clinics, meeting halls, child care facilities, and shops for sportswear and bowling balls and accessories. Many of these services may be operated on a lease basis by individuals other than the bowling proprietor.

Establishments whose principal function is to provide facilities for the sport of bowling are classified for statistical purposes as Standard Industrial Classification (SIC) 7933. Four types of bowling are included: tenpin (the oldest, most popular, and nationally played), duckpin, rubberband duckpin, and candlepin bowling. The latter three types of bowling utilize smaller pins and balls and are popular only in a few areas of the country (notably New England, Pennsylvania, and Washington, D.C.). About 95 percent of the bowling done in the United States is tenpin bowling.

In this profile, cost and revenue estimates and corresponding user statistics are based upon tenpin bowling centers. The cost differentials between tenpin bowling establishments and the three less common forms of bowling establishments can be obtained from equipment suppliers. Special market analysis would need to be performed to determine if the area under consideration was suitable for smaller pin bowling enterprises.

B. Dimensions

The popularity of the sport of bowling (as measured by the total number of bowlers sanctioned by the American Bowling Congress) has increased steadily during the past 2 decades. Most rapid growth occurred almost immediately after the introduction of the automatic pinsetter machine by the American Machine and Foundry Company

(AMF) in 1955 and by the Brunswick Corporation in 1957. The number of sanctioned bowlers (that is, bowlers with membership cards in the American Bowling Congress—generally required of all league bowlers) increased from 2½ million in 1955 to 5½ million in 1960 and to over 8 million by 1963.

In response to this rapid rise in popularity, a great surge took place in the number of bowling establishments that were opened to meet the growing demand. The number of certified bowling lanes increased during this same period from 58,200 in 1955 to 108,000 in 1960 and to over 150,000 lanes by 1963. Well over 1,000 new bowling centers opened during this period. While the number of new lanes thus kept pace with the growth in the number of sanctioned bowlers, the new bowlers turned out to be less ardent than their predecessors (as exhibited by a rapid decline in the number of games bowled per lane per day). Hence, there was clear evidence of overbuilding by 1963. This was reflected in a sharp decline in profits throughout the industry after the surge in the late 1950's.

The decline in profits was not due solely to overbuilding, although this was the principal cause. Other factors of importance were poor management and undercapitalization. Many people invested in bowling and became proprietors because they had been bowlers for several years, liked the game, and assumed profits came automatically. They were inexperienced in running these operations and, in the case of absentee ownership, selected other bowling associates— with similarly weak management—to operate the alleys for them. An accompanying problem was that these new entrepreneurs had not fully worked out all the costs of operating a bowling establishment and had based revenue projections on experiences of early years when the smaller number of establishments then in operation were always crowded. Consequently, they lacked the funds necessary to support the operation during the slack period of the middle 1960's.

There are good indications that the bowling industry has now stabilized and that opportunities for profitable ventures are possible with well-planned marketing and operating strategies. The total number of bowling establishments in the United States is now estimated at around 9,000. The Atlantic and North-Central regions of the country continue to have the strongest concentration of establishments, with New York, Ohio, Illinois, and Pennsylvania as the four leading States in this regard. The Mountain and Pacific regions (and particularly California, Washington, Oregon, and Colorado) also have active bowling populations with participation rates above the national average.

C. Characteristics

1. Nature of the Product

While bowling centers offer a wide variety of services in addition to providing facilities for the sport itself, revenues from bowling are by far the chief source of income, accounting for at least half and usually as high as 70 to 80 percent of all revenues generated. In turn, the major source of bowling revenues results from league bowling. A 1968 survey conducted by the Bowling Proprietors' Association of America indicated that 73 percent of all games bowled across the country were by league bowlers (including practice games apart from league action).

This same survey indicated that of the 38 million persons who had bowled at least once in 1967–1968, 30 million were casual bowlers (did not belong to leagues) and 8 million were active bowlers. Of the 1.7 billion annual games rolled, only 27 percent or 0.5 billion were by casual bowlers—the remaining 1.2 billion games were rolled by the 8 million active bowlers. Thus the average casual bowler rolled roughly 15 games per year, while the league bowlers averaged 150 games annually.

The reasons given by survey respondents for starting to bowl did not differ significantly between casual and active bowlers. The dominant reasons given were (1) seeking fun and recreation and (2) encouraged to try sport with friends or family. The reasons for continuing to bowl also did not differ greatly among casual and active bowlers, and were dominated by (1) healthy exercise, (2) challenging activity, (3) fun and relaxation, and (4) a good form of social activity.

The cost of bowling, typically between 50 to 75 cents per game rolled, has not been found to be a serious factor in limiting the market. League bowlers are accustomed to paying considerably more per game, not only to cover their bowling, but also to contribute to cash funds for end-of-the-season league dinners and for cash prizes and trophies. Casual bowlers are likewise relatively insensitive to bowling prices; their participation is probably more limited by the unavailability of alleys at prime time (nonsummer evenings) due to scheduled league bowling than by the cost of the sport.

2. Nature of the Customer

This same 1968 survey indicated that, of persons in the United States 11 years of age and over, some 58 percent had bowled tenpins at least once in their lives and an additional 5 percent had bowled smaller pins. Some 26 percent—of which 6 percent were active league bowlers—had bowled at least once in the past year.

While a greater percentage of metropolitan area residents had tried bowling than nonmetropolitan area residents (62 compared with 47 percent), among those who had tried bowling, the percentage of presently active bowlers was similar in the metropolitan and nonmetropolitan areas (10 compared with 9 percent).

An analysis by age of population reflected the surge in popularity of bowling in its "golden years," 1955 to 1962. While only 34 percent of the population sampled over age 50 had ever bowled, the percent rose markedly to 68 percent from ages 40 to 49, 76 percent from ages 30 to 39, and 79 percent from ages 20 to 29. In the youngest age group, 11 to 19, a total of 67 percent had bowled at least once. Of active league bowlers, the 30 to 39 and 40 to 49 age groups each had 9 percent of their populations represented, while 7 percent of the total population from 20 to 29 were league bowlers.

Statistics broken down by sex revealed that 36 percent of the males sampled had never bowled compared with 45 percent of the females sampled. However, among those who had tried bowling, 10 percent of the males and 9 percent of the females were now regular league bowlers.

As a general rule of thumb, industry sources recommend that a population of at least 1,000 persons per lane is needed to support a bowling center. This figure needs to be adjusted, however, to account for such factors as recent population growth (10 percent growth for the 1960–1970 period is considered a good gauge of increasing market size and potential), proximity to competing bowling centers, neighborhood bowling history (blue-collar areas traditionally have been thought to be better sources of bowlers than white collar areas, although this may be more stereotypical than factual); racial composition (minority community members have only recently begun taking up the sport in significant numbers); accessibility (high-traffic areas—such as shopping centers—are prime locations); and climate (warmer climates favor competing outdoor recreation such as golf and boating). On the basis of these factors, it is clear that each city —and, in fact, each neighborhood within it—must be analyzed separately; there are no simple rules of thumb to pinpoint with certainty a favorable location or to define the local population size needed to support a lane or center.

3. Staffing Needs

As indicated above, one of the major causes of failure in the bowling industry has been the absence of sound managerial skills. Accordingly, manufacturers of bowling alley equipment, Brunswick and AMF, have set up management clinics that cover such areas as marketing and public relations, business management, human relations, advertising, and instruction on how to teach bowling to beginners. In addition, they provide assistance in planning of the center as well as in financing equipment and other facilities. The Bowling Proprietors' Association of America (BPAA) periodically organizes conferences and seminars and also publishes a monthly journal, Bowling Proprietor, containing management articles and advice.

Because leagues are the backbone of any successful operation, an owner or manager must be able to work well with league representatives, present his bowling center in its best light, and be able to coordinate the league activities throughout the season. In this regard, managers with intimate knowledge of the sport have a slight competitive edge on managers without bowling background. However, since leagues are always looking around for new arrangements—especially those leagues with bad past season experience—an ability to negotiate skillfully is essential.

The number of employees needed to run the center will depend upon the size of the center and the variety of subsidiary services offered. A rule-of-thumb figure is one full-time employee for every four lanes; these employees may include a manager, an assistant manager, a counter control man (who assigns alleys and collects fees), an alley maintenance mechanic and an assistant mechanic, janitorial staff, and clerical staff. Other employees—depending on the presence of the service—may include a bartender, waitresses, snackbar personnel, a nursery attendant, playroom supervisors, bowling instructors, pro shop attendant, and billiard room manager. Clearly, these latter employees may be paid and supervised by a lessee of the facilities in which they work.

Typical 1970 wage and salary ranges for bowling employees were managers—$8,000 to $16,000 per year, plus percentage of profits; assistant managers—$6,500 to $12,000 per year, mechanics—$7,000 to $12,000 per year, counter control man—$2.50 to $3.50 per hour, and janitors—$2 to $3 per hour. The snackbar and playroom attendants generally earn between $2 and $2.50 per hour. In total, bowling centers spend between 15 percent and 30 percent of their gross income for employee wages. The ratio of male to female employees in the industry is approximately 3 to 1.

4. Competition and Marketing

A bowling establishment faces two levels of competition: (1) competition from other bowling establishments in the area and (2) competition from other recreation and entertainment alternatives.

Competition among bowling establishments for their share of the local bowling market focuses largely on attracting leagues to their respective establishments. Since the basic service offered (reserved lanes, balls, and shoe rental) are rather standard throughout the industry, the proprietors tend to emphasize the availability of adequate parking, the complement of secondary services available (primarily snackbar and bar), and the overall cordial and friendly environment of their respective establishments. Of critical importance is the ability of the establishment to insure that (1) lanes are available on time, (2) equipment failure is minimized, and (3) the facilities are clean at all times. Price-cutting is rare, although some establishments offer reduced rates continually for children and at offpeak hours (weekdays and weekend afternoons) for adults. The establishments often award trophies free of charge to league winners as an inducement for patronage of their alleys. Other promotional features, such as awards for bowling perfect "300" games and rolling a strike when a specially marked pin is in the head position, are sometimes offered at offpeak hours as well. Free group instruction, special group rates at offpeak hours, and introductory promotional games at reduced prices through community Welcome Wagon operations are also used to attract new bowlers. Finally, the sponsoring of prestigious local or national tournaments or special match games with outstanding bowlers is employed to publicize establishments.

In order to increase the overall bowling market, both Brunswick and AMF and the Bowling Proprietors' Association of America conduct nationwide advertising campaigns and provide assistance to local establishments in organizing individual or group advertising efforts. The weekly exposure of large segments of the public to professional bowling tournaments through the television media ("The Pro Bowlers Tour") also stimulates interest in the sport. More subtly, the bowling industry encourages the use of bowling in advertisements for unrelated product lines (such as the use of amateur bowlers in a prime time commercial for life insurance).

5. Ease of New Firm Entry

The relatively high capital requirements needed to start bowling centers have not acted as a major deterrent to the establishment of new bowling facilities. The large number of bowling center failures in the mid-1960's, however, reduced the appeal of the industry as a business opportunity from its earlier high levels. Both the Bowling Proprietors' Association of America and the two national suppliers of equipment encourage new entry, but they are careful to warn the prospective entrepreneur of the risks involved and the need for well-conceived marketing studies and for well-planned and managed facilities.

There is no institutionalized bias against minority firm entry, although the number of minority proprietors is small due to the large initial investment required and the historic absence of minority bowlers. As bowling continues to grow in popularity with minority groups, the need for establishments serving minority neighborhoods should become more pronounced.

The initial capital investment to start a bowling center is considerable. For example, the investment required for a fully equipped 32-lane center with billiard room, restaurant, and lounge can run as high as $1.5 million. Bowling equipment is expensive, although leasing terms are available. AMF and Brunswick both help their customers with financing, but a substantial downpayment is usually required. These two firms will provide continuing assistance to establishments that have bought or leased their equipment.

Finding staff to operate the center is not considered a serious problem, since most required skill levels are low. For the more skilled employees—managers and mechanics—adequate training programs and materials are made available by the BPAA and by AMF and Brunswick.

The breakeven point in the case of a new bowling center is directly linked to its ability to book leagues for the two evening slots (7 to 9, 9 to 11) each week night. Proprietors opening new centers are often surprised at the number of leagues looking for lanes. The newness of the center is a highly marketable feature, as leagues are continually searching for more modern, better equipped centers. A center that can attract leagues away from older establishments and that also conducts a well-conceived program to establish new leagues can become prcfitable within the first season of operation. More often, centers will not achieve profitable operations until their second or possibly third season of operation.

6. Bowling Center Physical and Capital Requirements

The average bowling establishment contains 15 lanes, although this average is biased downward by the large number of very small bowling facilities at universities, military bases, and clubs with less than 10 alleys. The optimum size recommended by the industry for a full service bowling center is 36 lanes. As indicated above, such a facility together with billiard room, restaurant, and lounge, can require an initial investment of up to $1.5 million.

In general, lanes and automatic pinsetters will cost between $12,000 and $15,000 per lane, excluding installation. Other related basic costs include metal storage lockers ($10 to $14 each), custom seating ($250 per lane), pin finders to indicate pins left standing

($150 per lane), elevator bowling ball returns ($800 per lane), automatic ball cleaners and polishers ($1,500 each), and automatic scorers ($3,000 per lane). Considerable smaller item costs are required for balls, shoes, cleaner, lane duster, pins, scoresheets, spectator seating, and a variety of other supplies and equipment.

The indoor area requirements for a bowling center average about 1,000 square feet per lane. This figure includes additional space for auxiliary facilities, such as snackbars, lounge, playrooms, offices, pro shops, and locker and restrooms. An outside parking requirement of seven spaces (or at least 2,000 square feet) per lane is considered desirable.

Construction costs will vary according to design specifications. A good quality building which includes auxiliary facilities will range from $11 to $15 per square foot. This would include architectural fees. In most buildings, the bowling alley should be soundproofed and the building completely heated and air-conditioned. Approximately one-fourth of the building goes to auxiliary facilities and three-fourths goes to the lanes. The auxiliary rooms and services are:

Pro Shops

The average pro shop produces a little over 5 percent of the gross income. Inventories include the following: bowling balls, priced from $19.95 to $50 (proprietors state the average price for women's bowling balls are $24.95 and for men $27.95); shoes, priced from $5.95 to $14.95, with an average selling price at $9.95; bowling bags priced from $3.95 to $14.95, with an average selling price of $9.95. The markup on items is approximately 40 percent. Most proprietors plan inventory stock according to the economic structure of their communities. An average inventory will range from $2,000 to $3,000.

Rental Shoes and Bowling Balls

Shoe rentals are not highly profitable, but they are very essential. An average of 1 to 2 percent of the gross income is from shoe rental; ball use is included in linage (game) fees. Most bowling shoes are purchased by the operator at approximately $6 per pair. A charge to the customer for shoe rental is 25 cents. Shoes are depreciated over a 2-year period. Balls cost proprietors $15 each, and there are usually five per lane. They depreciate in about a 5-year period.

Cocktail Lounge and Bars

A successful cocktail lounge and bar operation can make as much profit as linage receipts. For a successful operation, liquor costs should not exceed 25 percent of gross receipts from the bar. The key to success is careful cost control. The State controls operations at bowling centers by licensing procedures. This license usually designates the eating areas of the center as a bona fide public eating place, which allows cocktail-waitresses to serve drinks to customers on the lanes. Some proprietors indicate that as much as 79 percent of their bar business is done on the lanes. In order to qualify for this type of licensing the center must have a complete restaurant facility, including a kitchen. This means that there must be service of full meals rather than, or in addition to, an exclusive sandwich operation. This license also allows minors (anyone under 21 years of age) to be on the premises. Other types of licenses may be available, depending on the regulations of the State Department of Alcoholic Beverage Control.

Snackbar-Restaurant

Vending machines for food service can lessen operation cost, but many owners insist upon manual snackbars, and some prefer operated restaurants. The amount of commission to the proprietor from vending machines depends upon the volume and amount of servicing. Items that are not perishable and will last more than a week are possibilities for higher commissions.

Vending machines are advantageous because there are no labor costs, no inventories, no kitchen to equip and supply, and no personnel problems. However, totally automated food service will restrict the type of liquor license available. Full information may be received from the State Department of Alcoholic Beverage Control.

The proprietor who desires a manual operation should spend no more than 40 percent of gross income for operating and food costs. There should be an entrance that is separate from the center in order to attract additional business to the restaurant.

Playroom

Many bowling establishment owners find that supervised playroom service for toddlers and young children will attract women to morning and afternoon league play. No direct income can be earned. Equipment such as cribs, tables and chairs, and a few toys should be estimated at $7 to $10 per lane. Older women in the surrounding neighborhood are often ideal employees for this service because they can work short hours (9 to 12 a.m. or 2 to 4 p.m.) on a part-time basis.

Because of the high initial investment, both Brunswick and AMF offer financial packages for the purchase of basic equipment. A typical schedule requires repayment in 8 years, at an annual interest rate of 5 to 6½ percent on the unpaid balance. Usually, a 15 to 30 percent down payment of the total equipment cost is required.

The payments are usually scheduled to coincide with the peak bowling season. Usually no payments are required during the summer season (June to September), and eight equal monthly payments are required during the peak bowling period.

Accessory equipment may be purchased or leased. For example, the new automatic scorers can be purchased for $11,500 per four lanes outright or financed with 5-year notes. Alternatively, the scorers can be leased for 10 years at a cost of 3 to 5 cents per game rolled depending on volume of usage.

Maintenance of bowling facilities can be estimated at around $500 per lane per year. Equipment is depreciated over a 10-year period in accordance with Federal Government regulations.

7. Profitability

The two major sources of income to bowling centers result from bowling fees and from sales of food and liquor. The larger the center, the greater will be the share of total receipts credited to the latter activity. Thus, for example, a typical establishment with an annual business volume of $65,000 is likely to have generated over 80 percent of this income from bowling fees. On the other hand, a typical establishment with annual volume of $475,000 will have generated only 40 percent to 50 percent of this income from bowling fees. Consequently, the profits of larger centers in particular are related to successful bar and restaurant operations as well as to sound bowling business.

Typical profitable bowling centers show net profits of between 4 percent and 7 percent of sales, after owners' salaries of up to 9 percent. Unprofitable centers may show net losses of similar proportions. Trade sources indicate that slightly over half of all centers fall into the "profitable" category.

8. Market Fluctuation

As suggested by the analysis above, the bowling industry has experienced both a boom period and a subsequent slowdown in the past decade. While there are more bowlers today than ever before, the average active bowler is apparently not as dedicated to the sport as in past decades. Other recreational sports (notably golf, tennis, and boating and fishing) and other leisure activities (notably television and cardplaying) offer strong competition to bowling. Bowling is unlikely to experience another "golden age" like the 1958 to 1962 period. It should, however, be able to continue to compete for its share of the growing recreation market.

III. ANALYSIS OF BUSINESS FEASIBILITY

A. Review of Key Factors

The following factors are essential to successful development of a profitable bowling center:

1. Market

League bowling is the "bread and butter" part of the industry; those centers that can attract leagues to the evening time slots (7 to 9 and 9 to 11 on Monday through Friday and on Sunday) will generally show an annual profit; other centers usually will not.

A general rule is that 1,000 persons without ready access to existing bowling establishments are required to support a lane. This standard must be adjusted to the socioeconomic characteristics of the population, the historic popularity of the sport in the region, and the availability of competing forms of recreation and entertainment.

2. Location

Given the appropriate market, a center should be located in a commercially zoned area with high accessiblity and visibility. A large shopping center complex, for example, is cited by the industry as an ideal location. Highway sites are also popular choices.

3. Site Requirements

The center should be located in a structure providing at least 1,000 square feet per lane. Outside parking in the order of at least seven spaces per lane (2,000 square feet per lane) is also suggested. While second-floor locations are feasible, ground-floor locations are desirable.

4. Complementary Services

At a minimum, a bowling center must provide alleys, balls, shoe rental, service desk, bowler and spectator sitting areas, and restrooms. Some form of refreshment service (vending machines, snackbar, lounge, or restaurant) is considered mandatory. Other services, such as pro shops, child care areas, billiard and/or other game rooms, are considered desirable to enhance the attractiveness of the center to potential clientele.

5. Equipment

Bowling equipment is available from two large national suppliers: Brunswick and AMF. Both have wide ranges of equipment and supplies and are available to assist in planning the center to insure that all needs are met. Several forms of financing are available, although initial capital requirements are still relatively high.

6. Management

A manager of a bowling center should have both familiarity with the sport itself and a good background in bowling center management. Training programs are offered by the two bowling suppliers and by the Bowling Proprietors' Association of America. However, it is considered prudent to receive some additional training in an existing center before undertaking the management of a new center.

7. Work Force

In addition to the management staff, a number of less skilled workers are required to maintain and operate the facilities. Roughly one full-time employee per four lanes is required to run a bowling center. There are certain economies of scale associated with the bowling operation itself (that is, fewer additional employees are required as extra lanes are introduced), but larger centers usually offer additional services as well and hence require more diverse staff positions to operate the center efficiently.

B. Projections of Attainable Returns on Investment

Representative projections are furnished for three typical levels of operation: A center with $65,000 annual volume of business (10 lanes), a center with $150,000 annual volume of business (20 lanes), and a center with $250,000 annual volume of business (32 lanes). It is assumed that as the number of lanes increases, an appropriate level of secondary services is offered at the center in addition to the bowling facilities. Proprietorships are assumed in all cases, and the amount of profit shown has not been reduced by the amount of owner's compensation.

Those bowling establishments achieving a smaller level of gross receipts are generally characterized as being less successful in attracting leagues than the profitable centers. The less profitable centers can be characterized as having higher rental and employee costs and greater maintenance costs. Thus, a combination of inability to attract league bowling and less efficient management generally accounts for reduced profits or net losses.

1. 10-Lane Bowling Alley

Revenues

Bowling income (8-month season)	$ 46,000	
Bowling income (summer)	5,500	
Food and bar sales	11,000	
Other revenue	2,500	
Total revenues	$ 65,000	100%

Operating expenses

Employee wages (excluding owner/manager)	$ 10,000	
Supplies and maintenance	4,300	
Rental space, including utilities	10,000	
Food and bar costs	8,000	
Other expenses (advertising, licenses and fees, insurance)	7,000	
Total operating expenses	$ 39,300	60.5%
Gross operating profit	$ 25,700	39.5%
Other expenses (equipment, interest, and depreciation)	$ 15,700	
Net profit before owner's draw and tax	$ 10,000	15.4%

2. 20-Lane Bowling Center

Revenues

Bowling income (8-month season)	$ 97,500	
Bowling income (summer)	14,400	
Food and bar sales	31,500	
Other revenues	6,600	
Total revenues	$150,000	100%

Operating expenses

Employee wages (excluding owner/manager)	$ 30,000	
Supplies and maintenance	9,000	
Rental space, including utilities	24,000	
Food and bar costs	20,400	
Other expenses	14,600	
Total operating expenses	$ 98,000	65.3%
Gross operating profit	$ 52,000	34.7%
Other expenses	$ 34,500	
Net profit before owner's draw and tax	$ 17,500	11.7%

3. 32-Lane Bowling Center

Revenues

Bowling income (8-month season)	$125,000	
Bowling income (summer)	23,500	
Food and bar sales	92,000	
Other revenues	9,500	
Total revenues	$250,000	100%

Operating expenses

Employee wages (includes nonowner manager)	$ 62,500	
Supplies and maintenance	14,500	
Rental space, including utilities	37,000	
Food and bar costs	40,000	
Other expenses	22,000	
Total operating expenses	$176,000	70.4%
Gross operating profit	$ 74,000	29.6%
Other expenses	$ 50,000	
Net profit before owner's draw and tax	$ 24,000	9.6%

IV. ESTABLISHING THE BUSINESS

A. Approaching the Market

A well-conceived market analysis study of the intended locale of the bowling center is highly recommended before commitment to begin construction. Emphasis should be placed on studying existing bowling patterns of the intended client community to determine their present level of interest in the sport and to identify other bowling centers in the area that will provide the major competition to the proposed facility. Estimates should then be made of the extent to which: (1) existing active bowlers can be drawn away from these centers to the proposed center, (2) casual bowlers in the area can be converted to active bowlers, and (3) nonbowlers can be encouraged to take up the sport. Estimates of other possible revenue flows (bar, restaurant, billiards, etc.) should also be made. These figures could then be reviewed with AMF and Brunswick and with other bowling proprietors in the city or region to check and revise as necessary.

While special attractions (introductory discounts, free drawings for prizes, free games for rolling strikes when a specially marked head pin is set up, opening week tournaments, and special match games between regional professionals) will serve to introduce the new center to the target community, the critical factor will be the ability to schedule league bowling. Consequently, the market strategy adopted should have this goal as the top priority item. Existing league representatives should be approached. Potential groups (such as plants in the vicinity, military bases, and community organizations) should be contacted and attempts made to establish a league on a trial basis.

B. Facility Requirements

Both of the national suppliers, AMF and Brunswick, will be more than willing to provide the entrepreneur with alternative plans for designing and equipping the facility. A variety of alternatives are available to suit virtually any type of bowling establishment.

As indicated above, roughly 3,000 square feet per lane of indoor and outdoor space will be required, with two-thirds of it for outside parking. Thus, a 10-lane bowling alley will require a ¾-acre site; a 20-lane bowling center will require a 1½-acre site; and a 32-lane bowling center will require a 2½-acre site. A single-floor structure is ideal, although use of converted first- or second-floor space in an existing multistory building is feasible. The intended area must be properly zoned, both for the bowling activity and for the sale of food and beverages.

Both AMF and Brunswick offer financial packages for purchase of equipment and supplies. A typical schedule requires repayment in 8 years.

C. Financing

Bank loans may also be available. However, in view of the high rate of failure in the industry in the mid-1960's—due primarily to an overreaction on the supply side of the market to an increasing market demand—banks may be hesitant about authorizing loans for bowling center ventures.

In some locales, franchise arrangements may be possible. The franchisee will pay as much as half of the original investment. Usually a franchise fee is based upon a monthly royalty per lane plus an initial cost for the franchise.

D. Labor Force

As indicated above, a full-time labor force of roughly one person per four lanes is considered desirable. As the number of lanes increases, certain economies of scale exist in the labor force needed to maintain the lanes.

A labor force breakdown for a 20-lane bowling operation might include the following.

Owner/manager 1	
Assistant manager 1	
Mechanic 1	Staff costs: $45,000
Maintenance 1	
Food service 1	
5	

A labor force breakdown for a 32-lane bowling operation might include the following:

Manager 1	
Assistant manager 1	
Mechanic 2	Staff costs: $62,500
Maintenance 2	
Food service 2	
8	

The managers can receive training from their bowling equipment supplier or from the Bowling Proprietors' Association of America. The monthly trade journal, The Bowling Proprietor, also provides valuable management information. Mechanics will receive training from the equipment supplier. The maintenance and food service staff will be drawn from the unskilled labor force.

The food service operation and the secondary services (pro shop, gamerooms, etc.) can be leased to concessionaires, if desired.

DRY CLEANING

I. RECOMMENDATION

A sustained demand for dry cleaning services offers attractive opportunities for new business development in the field. Industry leaders expect that a growing population and rising incomes will enable the dry cleaner to expand his services, his sales levels, and his total profits throughout the coming decade.

The most important factors affecting profitability in the dry cleaning industry, assuming adequate capability in the plant, include the manager's ability to market the services of the establishment to his potential clientele and to train and manage his labor force effectively. Labor expenses can account for about 50 percent of total operating costs, and the manager who can obtain maximum performance from his employees is the one most likely to earn a profit from a given sales level.

Both the introduction of fabrics which require little or no dry cleaning and the establishment of coin-operated dry cleaning machines will affect the potential markets open to the professional dry cleaner in the years ahead. The prevailing opinion about this competition is that it will change the nature of the dry cleaner's work somewhat but will not cause a decline in business. The need for careful cleaning of the better or more prized garments in the wardrobe will certainly not diminish, and the effect of such technological changes is likely to be a focusing of the dry cleaning business on those garments and cleaning activities which return higher margins to the cleaner. A dry cleaning establishment that is well placed in its chosen market area, is marketed with flair and careful attention to the needs of its customers, and is diligently managed by a cost-conscious operator is likely to capitalize on the generally favorable trends in the industry.

II. DESCRIPTION OF THE INDUSTRY

A. Identification

Standard Industry Classification (SIC) 7216 includes businesses primarily engaged in dry cleaning and in the dyeing of apparel and household fabrics. Collecting and distributing units (branch outlets) that are owned and operated by cleaning and dyeing plants are considered part of the businesses owning them and are not treated as separate establishments.

B. Dimensions of the Industry

Dry cleaning industry statistics indicate that the industry is in a period of growth and concentration. Despite a decrease in the number of establishments from 1963 to 1967 (31,722 and 30,625 respectively), the value of total receipts has increased from $1.437 billion to $1.938 billion during the same period. The number of industry employees has similarly increased during the same period from 211,664 to 246,348.

The size distribution of dry cleaning establishments indicates the degree to which small businesses share in the total market. An industry survey conducted in 1966 revealed that the average dry cleaning establishment had an annual sales volume of $48,000 and that approximately 60 percent of all plants have sales volumes of under $50,000 per year.

Annual sales	Number of plants	Percentage of total
Less than $25,000	10,440	29
$25,000 to $50,000	11,160	31
$50,000 to $100,000	7,560	21
$100,000 to $200,000	3,610	10
More than $200,000	3,240	9

Though the averages have risen since that time, industry experts indicate that the composition of the dry cleaning industry has not changed considerably since 1966.

One of the factors explaining the growth in the total receipts of the dry cleaning industry is the diversification by the dry cleaner into other cleaning fields. The dry cleaner has increasingly branched out into the more profitable aspects of the traditional laundry business, and the expansion into such activities as shirt cleaning and laundering is likely to be continued. An important reason for this trend is the increasingly convenience-oriented customers' desire for one-stop cleaning/laundering service. The attraction of new labor-saving machinery and the consequent desire to increase business to support the use of such capital equipment is another trend explaining industry concentration at the higher volume end of the industry.

C. Characteristics of the Industry

1. The Customer

There are three basic markets for dry cleaning establishments. The first market is the luxury group. This group is more likely to require pickup and delivery service of the dry cleaner, although such service is becoming less and less important. This group will also require more hand processing and care with garments. Because the volume of a business that caters only to the luxury group would be relatively low, such establishments should locate only in large metropolitan areas where the luxury group is of sufficient size to support them.

A second market is the middle income group. The service required here must meet acceptable standards but can be considered as aiming at the mass market. Pickup and delivery service is not a requirement in this market, and a location convenient to a large number of convenience shoppers is important. This is a market most newer businesses aim to serve, and many older plants have had to adjust to it to survive.

The third market is the lower income market. This market is usually served by three kinds of service outlets: chainstore operations with highly efficient central plants and their own small stores; small neighborhood tailor shops with dry cleaning done by a wholesale plant, and "mom and pop" operations. Inevitably, this is a small margin field. Prices must be lower than standard, and profit must come through either high volume and maximum efficiency or a minimal cost structure. A heavy burden is placed on good management in this part of the dry cleaning industry.

2. Types of Services

The dry cleaners' recent interest in diversification has led to the offering of more types of service to the customer.

Approximately 70 percent of all dry cleaners now provide shirt service for their own customers. At least 50 percent of these do the work on their own premises, while others farm out the shirt service to a wholesale laundry. The advantages of providing shirt service usually outweigh the disadvantages. The typical dry cleaning customer, for example, is a monthly customer. But with shirt service available, the customer tends to bring in work on a weekly basis, and this usually means more dry cleaning as well. Also, shirt service is dependable in terms of volume, particularly among luxury and middle-income groups who usually use five shirts per week per male in the family.

To add in-house shirt service to a dry cleaning establishment does, of course, add to initial investment costs. Handling a weekly volume of $500 to $600 in shirt work would require additional space (at least 15 by 20 feet), additional equipment (a washer, an extractor, and a shirt finishing unit at a cost of approximately $7,500) and the employment of at least one full-time shirt operator. Low-income environments provide fewer shirt customers and smaller bundles, and are, therefore, not as likely to justify such an investment.

Other services that might be included by the expanding dry cleaner include alterations (paid repairs and reweaving), storage, and shoe repair. These usually involve minimal additional costs (for alterations, for example, the sewing machine is already installed), and may allow for more efficient use of existing assets and clientele.

3. Pricing Policies

The pricing policies of any particular dry cleaning establishment will necessarily reflect the market policies of the business. Those cleaning establishments catering to the upper income market normally charge up to 50 percent more than the standard charge for any given piece of work, while those serving the lower income market may reduce charges by as much as 20 percent. Within these broad ranges, the individual dry cleaning establishment will price its work so as to be competitive with others in its general class.

4. Types of Business Organization

Legal forms of organization within the dry cleaning industry have shown very little variation over the past 15 years. Approximately 62 percent of all plants operate as individual proprietorships. Of the remaining 38 percent, the number of partnerships has declined slightly to 16 percent, and the number of corporations has risen to almost 22 percent during this period.

Franchises have, however, begun to play an increasingly important role in the dry cleaning trade. These organizations offer the individual some of the advantages of the larger business (layout, equipment selection, advertising and promotion, training and financing) but allow him to retain a degree of independence.

5. Space and Equipment Needs

An individual expecting to achieve a sales volume of up to $50,000 a year would need a minimum of 800 square feet of space, including a cleaning plant and a possible call office or pickup and delivery store. No more than 10 percent of the total space should be allocated to the call office. The call office usually is located in a different location than the actual dry cleaning plant (this could be the optimal arrangement if the call office is located in a high-rent district). For dry cleaning establishments located on the main arteries that lead to shopping centers, parking space must be provided or available. This space could be for as few as four automobiles, although on the average, a dry cleaning establishment provides space for six automobiles. If the call office is located in a downtown business area with a market composed mainly of transients and professionals who live and work in the immediate neighborhood, no parking space is required. For dry cleaning establishments located in shopping centers, there is, of course, no problem with parking. No outdoor workspace is required for a dry cleaning establishment.

The following is a list of minimum equipment requirements:
Boiler
Air compressor
Spotting board
Prespotting tank
Dry cleaning unit, including integral or separate filter, still, extractor, tumbler, solvent reclaimer, and solvent storage tank
Utility press
Ironing board with steam electric iron
Water spray gun per finisher
Legger and topper press
Puff irons
Steam air forms
Sewing machine
Baskets, carts, and tables

Optional but desirable are the following:

Wet cleaning washer and table	Bagger
Small extractor	Tag holder
Compact dry cabinet	Efficiency table
Conveyor	Invoice holder
Mushroom press	Pants stand
Silk offset press	Pants holder

Equipment manufacturers, who may be located either through the local telephone director or through advertisements in trade journals such as Textile Services Management or the American Dry Cleaner, will provide free advice on equipment needs, plant planning, and layout. Two good sources for equipment manufacturers are *Coinamatic Age Annual Buyers Guide: Purchasing Directory for the Laundry and Dry Cleaning Industry* and *McRae's Blue Book Annual*, an alphabetic directory of manufacturers and their local distributors.

6. Manpower Requirements

For establishments with $25,000 or less in annual sales, only two or three full-time workers can usually be supported. For full service establishments with annual sales in the $25,000 to $50,000 range, four or five people are usually required for effective operation.

About one-third of all dry cleaning establishments are unionized. In metropolitan areas, the number is higher and stood at 41 percent in 1967. The following job descriptions are indicative of the various types of employees needed in the dry cleaning trade:

a. *Assembler* (Matcher, Sorter, Assorter, Distributor). Sorts or assembles the various dry cleaned garments and other items of each customer's order; and matches the articles according to description and identifying number as shown by plant records.

b. *Clerk, Retail Receiving.* Receives work from routemen or from customers over the counter in the receiving office of a dry cleaning establishment. Work involves *most of the following:* maintaining a record of articles or bundles received; returning completed work to customers who call for it; collecting payment and maintaining simple records of money received; and, in establishments where dry cleaning is done in-plant, fastening an identifying marker to each article, examining an article for defects such as holes, stains, tears, and making a record of the identification symbol assigned to each article with a brief description of the article and of any defects noted. Store managers are excluded in this description.

c. *Finisher, Flatwork, Machine.* Performs flatwork finishing operations by machine. work involves *one or more of the following:* shaking out the creases in semidry washing to prepare it for the flatwork ironing machine; feeding clean, damp flatwork pieces into the flatwork ironing machine by placing the articles on the feeder rollers; and catching or receiving articles as they emerge from the machine and partially folding them.

d. *Presser, Hand.* Presses dry cleaned or wet cleaned garments with a hand iron, (usually dresses and other articles that cannot be satisfactorily or completely finished on a steam pressing machine) or pleats garments by hand.

e. *Presser, Machine.* Smooths the surfaces of garments, slipcovers, drapes and other shaped-fabric articles with a pressing machine to shape the articles, remove wrinkles, and flatten seams. May operate two presses, loading one while the other is closed.

Average earnings within the industry were $2.32 per hour in 1971, with the average employee receiving a weekly wage of $81.90.

7. Capital Requirements—1971

The initial investment for a small establishment with an annual sales volume of $25,000 would be approximately $14,000.

    a. Downpayment on fixtures
       and equipment   — $ 4,000 (total cost of $20,000)
    b. Supplies   — $ 1,000
    c. Rent deposit   — $ 1,400 (leased at $350 a month)
    d. Utility deposit   — $ 500
    e. Initial promotion   — $ 1,000
    f. Operating capital   — $ 6,000

III. BUSINESS FEASIBILITY

A. Major Factors

1. Market Location

Dry cleaning stores must be where the customers are. Like other services, there are three major areas that have proved successful for dry cleaning establishments: in shopping centers, on the right hand side of main arteries that lead to shopping centers, or, in some circumstances, downtown business areas. A general rule of thumb with regard to competition within the market area is to expect one establishment for every 1,500 families.

There are several reasons why a shopping center is a good location for a dry cleaning store:

a. The center will draw customers from a wide area—customers who might otherwise not be reached because of their proximity to other establishments.

b. In a study of consumer attitudes toward dry cleaning establishments conducted by the National Institute of Dry Cleaners, 74 percent of the consumers questioned said that they bring their dry cleaning to the cleaning establishment and pick it up. (These consumers represented a wide range of income levels.) In 62 percent of these families, the wife usually has the pickup and delivery job, and, more often than not, she combines it with other shopping. A shopping center with a supermarket is, therefore, a good location for a dry cleaning establishment. Arteries on the way to shopping centers are also convenient for the same reasons.

Downtown business areas of large cities are generally not good locations. Rents are extremely high, and unless the owner has an advertising gimmick of some sort, the establishment is not likely to be successful. Downtown markets are limited to transients and commuters, but the latter market is also served by lower priced establishments on commuter routes leading to and from residential areas. In small cities of under 100,000 population, where the downtown area is also the major shopping area, such locations are often feasible and profitable.

2. Marketing and Promotion

The dry cleaning industry is selling a service, and growth takes place by extending the range of service. This takes a great deal of skill and persuasiveness in advertising techniques, and competition is sometimes severe. The following promotional techniques have proved of value to many dry cleaning establishments:

a. *Newspaper Advertising*—Generally, newspapers reach more prospects than any other medium. Care should be taken to place ads in a newspaper that reaches the most women (women do most family shopping) on days when there are large numbers of supermarket sale ads. If the market to be served is only a segment of a large city, a community newspaper might be better than a large citywide daily.

b. *Direct-Mail Advertising*—If the mailing lists are carefully selected by income levels or geographic sections, direct-mail advertising can be most effective. It can also be lowest in cost because, theoretically, there is no waste circulation.

c. *Cut-Price Specials*—Specials are extremely good ways to attract new customers. But they should be varied and timed for promotional advantage. "Back to School" specials, "Spring Housecleaning" specials, or "Mother's Day" specials have proved particularly useful.

d. *The Yellow Pages*—Advertising in the classified section of the telephone directory is an unbeatable way to reach a prospect precisely when he is ready to buy. Advertisements in the Yellow Pages should be explicit regarding services offered and plant location.

Other useful promotional techniques include extending open hours to early morning and late evening times on weekdays and having radio and television specials.

B. The Minority Entrepreneur

A recent study by the National Business League of black entrepreneurship in seven urban areas (Atlanta, Cleveland, Durham, Jackson, Los Angeles, Norfolk, and Richmond) reveals that laundries and dry cleaners account for 38.6 percent of the black public service businesses surveyed in those areas.

C. Projection of Returns—Two Hypothetical Business Situations

The following hypothetical financial projections for two common sizes of dry cleaning businesses are based on industry averages for successful establishments. Projections for individual stores may vary widely from these.

Annual Operating Statement

Net receipts	$50,000	$100,000
Operating expenses		
Labor:		
Production	16,500	29,000
Sales and distribution	6,000	15,000
Administration	2,500	8,000
Total labor costs	$25,000	$ 52,000
Supplies and materials	4,500	8,500
Equipment maintenance	2,000	4,000
Total operating expenses	$31,500	$ 64,500
Overhead expenses		
Rent and utilities	$ 5,000	$ 8,000
Equipment depreciation	1,500	3,500
Indirect overhead	3,000	8,000
Total overhead	$ 9,500	$ 19,500
Total expenses	$41,000	$ 84,000
Net profit before tax, including owner's or manager's compensation	$ 9,000	$ 16,000

IV. ESTABLISHING THE NEW BUSINESS

A. Approaching the Market

The first step in starting a new dry cleaning business is to determine the market which the store is intended to serve. The prospective entrepreneur must identify the general type of consumer he proposes to cater to. For example, he may wish to cater to lower income inner-city residents or to the residents of a suburban fringe area with a particular income and ethnic character.

Whatever the decision, it will affect the location of the new store, how large it will be, and the services it will provide. In lower income areas, for example, a wide range of services is not needed, prices must be lower than standard, and profit must come through large volume and maximum efficiency.

The general procedure to be followed in selecting a store location begins with the identification of several potential locations where space is known to be available, the computation of the number of potential customers within the area of each location, and the determination of the amount of monthly expenditures each customer will make on dry cleaning. An analysis of competition in each area (by checking price structures, quality of service, packaging, types of advertising, etc.) will also suggest where underserved markets exist.

B. Securing Capital

A number of cities have organizations which specialize in assisting minority entrepreneurs to secure capital. A prospective entrepreneur should seek out these sources and go over his plans with them.

The local Small Business Administration (SBA) office or Office of Minority Business Enterprise (OMBE) affiliate may help put the prospective entrepreneur in touch with sources of capital and provide the names of banks which have made loans to minority individuals. Minority-owned banks may also be sources of debt financing.

The Small Business Administration can also help with a lease guarantee. Many landlords are unwilling to lease to a new and inexperienced businessman because they have no recourse in the event the business fails. The SBA has a program to reassure such landlords by insuring the lease of the small businessman.

C. Starting Operations

There are many legal details which must be attended to prior to starting a business. The prospective entrepreneur must get a license or permit to do business and will probably need to have a boiler permit as well. Some States (California, as an example) require that the cleaner, spotter, and finisher be certified as qualified technicians. The entrepreneur must investigate these and other requirements before starting operations.

Insurance is also a major factor to be considered. Basic insurance needs include fire, theft, and vandalism coverage. Because the dry cleaner is responsible for customers' costly garments while they are entrusted to his care, bailee insurance is a requirement. Also, since customers, salesmen, and visitors enter the store, public liability protection is important.

If the plant employees are inexperienced, careful time and attention should be paid to their training. If the entrepreneur himself has neither the time nor the ability to give this training, outside help should be secured. It is essential that all employees be adequately trained and productive.

CONTRACT DRESS MANUFACTURING

I. RECOMMENDATION

Entry into contract dress manufacturing involves relatively little investment, but considerable knowledge of the industry. The principal managerial requirements are production planning and supervision and contacts within the trade to secure business. The availability and productivity of the labor force are the key variables affecting profitability.

Investment requirements are limited because dress manufacturing contractors can generally lease the required machines or purchase them on credit. Manufacturing plant requirements are minimal, and plants can be established in almost any type of vacant building which has heat, light, and plumbing. Since the materials being processed are owned by others, no investment in inventory is required.

The cost of labor is the major cost of doing business, and success or failure will be determined by the ability to achieve a high rate of labor productivity relative to the cost of wages. This can be accomplished by successful recruitment and training of the work force, good labor relations, and highly effective production planning and supervision. Care should be taken to make certain that foremen and supervisors are experienced and capable, since attempts to establish production with inexperienced management, inexperienced supervision, and inexperienced labor have been disastrous. There is, however, no reason why contract dress manufacturing should not be suitable for the minority entrepreneur with some experience in production planning and supervision.

II. DESCRIPTION OF THE INDUSTRY

A. Identification

Women's and misses' outerwear is a segment of a major manufacturing group known as Major Group 23, Apparel and Related Products, a group sometimes known as the needle trades. Women's and Misses' Dresses are classified as Standard Industrial Classification (SIC) 2335, the code which covers establishments primarily engaged in the manufacture of women's, misses' and juniors' dresses, including ensemble dresses, whether sold by the piece or by the dozen. There are further subclassifications by fabric (i.e., cotton, wool, and manmade fabrics) and by price.

The apparel production industry is characterized by three major types of establishments: (1) regular factories known as "manufacturers"; (2) apparel jobbers; and (3) contractors. The manufacturer purchases fabric, employs production workers to cut and sew garments, and sells the finished product. The apparel jobber buys the raw materials, designs samples, and markets the finished product, but he does not manufacture the garments. Instead he arranges with outside factories (contractors) to perform the manufacturing operations. The apparel contractor employs production workers in his own establishment to process materials owned by others (either jobber or manufacturer), makes products to specification, and does not become involved in the sale of the finished garment. In many instances, the jobber will employ his own cutters, and thus the contractor need only sew the various pieces together. In other instances, the contractor will perform both the cutting and sewing operations.

B. Dimensions of the Industry

The needle trades are the second largest employer in nondurable goods manufacturing, surpassed only by the food manufacturing industry. In 1967, more than 1,357,000 persons were employed by the industry. Value added by manufacturing was over $10 billion. There were more than 26,000 establishments, 48 percent of which had over 20 employees.

Women's and misses' dresses are the largest single type of employer within the Apparel and Related Products Group, with 5,225 establishments in 1967, of which 59 percent had over 20 employees. The total number of employees was 209,900, with value added by manufacturing exceeding $1.5 billion. The industry has been constantly growing as it keeps pace with the growth in population and the general rise in the national standard of living. Value added increased at a rate of approximately 6 percent annually between 1963 and 1967, and at a rate of over 4 percent annually between 1958 and 1967. Employment has also increased steadily, but at a somewhat slower rate of about 1.5 percent annually between 1958 and 1967.

Within the women's and misses' dresses group, contractors are the most numerous type of employer, having 2,642 establishments in the United States, of which over 77 percent have more than 20 employees. They also account for the largest segment of value added, $588 million compared to $523 million for manufacturers. Contractors are not growing at as fast a rate as manufacturers, however, with the value of their product having grown at a rate of only 2 percent annually in the 1963–67 period compared to a manufacturers' value-added growth rate of more than 15 percent annually during the same period.

Most dress manufacturing contractors are located in the New York area, with significant numbers in Pennsylvania, New Jersey, and California. North and South Carolina, Georgia, Florida, Illinois, Texas, Massachusetts, and Connecticut also have noticeable concentrations in the industry. There is a trend in location of contractors toward the

South and West. In 1963, 75 percent of all contractors were in the three States in the Mid-Atlantic Region (New York, Pennsylvania, and New Jersey). In 1967 this percentage had dropped to 69 percent. Concentrations of contractors are increasing in and around metropolitan areas such as Dallas, Los Angeles, St. Louis, and Miami.

C. Characteristics of the Industry

1. Organization

The dress manufacturing contractor performs a relatively simple function. He receives textile goods from a jobber or occasionally a manufacturer. This fabric may or may not have already been cut to the desired patterns. He then proceeds to sew the sections together to make a finished garment, presses it, and ships it back to the jobber. The contractor performs a useful function because styling and fashion play such an important part in the overall industry and are so volatile and unpredictable that flexibility in manufacturing is highly desirable. Thus, the jobber traditionally employs a designer to design a seasonal "line" for him. He then makes samples and displays them to the trade. Certain items will turn out to be popular, while others will be ignored. He then must purchase the goods and get relatively quick production of certain numbers of large quantities. Access to a number of contractors greatly increases the jobber's ability to expand or contract his deliveries to meet changing markets.

While there has been a trend among many segments of the industry to go into integrated manufacturing on a larger scale, the traditional roles of jobber and contractor are still highly important, and are expected to remain that way, particularly for higher-priced dresses, where production runs are small and style is all-important.

The jobber pays the contractor for each dress produced. The contractor develops his cost on the basis of his piecework and hourly rates for labor, his overhead, trucking costs, and his profit.

2. Labor

Apparel manufacturing is highly labor intensive; for the contractor, his operations are almost totally labor intensive, with the wages of production workers accounting for almost two-thirds of the total value of contractors' shipments in 1967.

About one-half of all production workers are sewing machine operators, and women represent more than 95 percent of the sewing machine operators. There are two types of systems used in production: (1) the singlehand system of sewing in which the operator performs all or most of the operations needed to produce a finished garment, and (2) the section system, in which each operator performs only one or two of the operations required to complete the garment. As might be expected, singlehand operators get paid more and are usually employed on more expensive garments. Slightly more than half of the sewing machine operators are employed on the singlehand system of sewing.

Other production workers are hand and machine pressers, hand sewers, cutters and markers, final inspectors, thread trimmers, and work distributors.

For all jobs, the ratio of women to men workers varies among areas. For example, women outnumber men 10 to 1 in Miami and in the Wilkes-Barre-Hazleton area in Pennsylvania, while the proportion is only 3 to 1 in New York City.

About 60 percent of the production workers are paid on a piece-work basis. Sewing machine operators and pressers are typically paid on this type of incentive program. Time rates usually apply to cutters and markers, inspectors, thread trimmers, and work distributors.

Most workers in the industry are unionized, and nearly all agreements are with the International Ladies Garment Workers' Union. However, there are considerable variations. For example, only one-eighth are unionized in the Los Angeles area and less than one-tenth in Miami and Dallas. However, in New York and Pennsylvania, virtually every shop is unionized.

Average hourly earnings in 1968 ranged from $3.27 an hour in New York City to $1.90 an hour in Miami. However, there are a great many variations within areas, because so many of the workers are on incentive plans, with the faster and more skilled operators earning considerably more than those who are slower. Most of the shops in the higher-paying areas use the singlehand system, while most of the shops in the lower-paying areas use the section system.

Most shops work a 35-hour week except in the Los Angeles, Dallas, and Miami areas, where the schedule is 40 hours a week. Paid holidays are common, and employees receive health, welfare, and vacation benefits.

3. Competition

Competition is very intense, as might be expected where entry into the industry is relatively easy and where there are many firms producing an undifferentiated product.

The major form of competition is in pricing and a difference between competitors of a few cents on the cost of processing can result in the loss of business. Contractors are always trying to cut costs, and the more profitable operators are highly sensitive to cost items.

Contractors are also selected on the basis of quality and service. The jobber wants his contractor to be reasonably convenient and able to produce acceptable work on a reliable basis. During the rush seasons, it is relatively easy for a contractor to get work, because all of the jobbers are hard put to find enough contractors to fill their orders. During the slack season, the jobber will look around very carefully for the best price.

4. Ease of Entry

As indicated above, there are no special licensing requirements or other restrictions barring entry into the business. The individual desiring to establish himself as a contractor need only find some space, order some machines on time, line up some business, and employ a work force. If sufficient business has been lined up in advance, and the manager is capable of producing the work within the quoted price, there is no reason why a new firm should not be profitable from the start.

When starting a plant in an area where the labor force is not experienced, allowance should be made for an additional startup cost to train the labor force. If local job-training resources are not available to assist in training, an average of about $1,000 per worker should be allowed for training inexperienced employees.

5. Capital Requirements

Capital requirements for a contract dress manufacturing business are relatively small. Listed below are the basic machinery and capital requirements for the smallest size business feasible, as well as for an average shop.

	Smallest	Average
Weekly production	800 medium-priced dresses	2,500 medium-priced dresses
Building size	2,500 square feet	7,000 square feet
Single-needle regular machines	20	55
Special machines	4-6	15
Pressing irons	2	5
Steam boiler	1	1
Racks	6	12

If cutting is done internally, the plant will require a cutting table, spreading machine, two cutting machines, and one drill.

Payments on equipment and fixtures	$5,000	$12,000
Rent deposit	300	1,100
Operating capital	4,000	10,000
Miscellaneous supplies	100	200
	$9,400	$23,300

Most equipment is purchased from a machinery dealer or from the factory. To start an operation, the best method is to purchase rebuilt machines on a time payment plan. Other capital will have to be secured from personal resources or from a financial institution.

The factory space is usually leased. In some cases, where operations are being started in areas where no factory buildings are available, local development corporations will construct factory buildings and lease them to a manufacturer. This situation is more likely when the proposed tenant is an established business, not a new entry.

6. Profitability

Profitability on sales is very low due to the intense competition and the very keen pressure to keep costs down. Mounting imports are also keeping a downward pressure on prices. The intense unionization of the industry tends to make it difficult for individual entrepreneurs to reap profit from low wage rates. Whatever advantages accrue to businesses in low wage areas are often counterbalanced by high shipping costs, high training costs, or simply increased competition from other new factories established in the low wage areas.

On the other hand, the low capital investment permits a relatively high return on investment. The 1964 profit ratios for all dress manufacturers are shown as follows:

	Upper Quartile	Median	Lower Quartile
	%	%	%
On sales	1.74	0.76	0.16
On total net worth	20.64	11.03	2.33
On net working capital	23.76	12.15	3.20

7. Dependence on Outside Factors

The individual contractor is dependent to a considerable degree on the seasonal factors. Business is at its best from January to May, while fall styles are being produced, and from June to October, while spring clothes are being made. There is relatively little activity during the other months. The seasonal aspect should be kept in mind when starting a new business, so that entry into the business can coincide with heavy seasonal activity and the opportunity to secure orders from busy jobbers.

To a certain extent, the contractor is also dependent upon how well his jobbers are doing. If he limits his work to a few jobbers, he may find himself without orders if the jobbers happen to guess wrong on styles for a particular season. The likelihood that such an event will happen can be reduced by keeping contract with a large number of jobbers.

The women's dress industry itself tends to fluctuate with styling changes. Although there has been a steady growth over the years, there are rather heavy variations in business from season to season or year to year depending in part on how well new styles are going over in the trade and on the state of the economy in general. These factors are largely out of the control of the contractor, and he must provide for them by conserving his profits during the good seasons to keep him solvent during the poor seasons.

III. BUSINESS OPPORTUNITIES IN THE INDUSTRY
A. Important Factors Affecting Opportunities

1. Labor Supply

The most important factor in locating a factory and insuring its successful operation is the availability of a good labor supply in relationship to its cost. The test of whether a labor supply is good is the ability of the labor force to turn out acceptable quality at a competitive cost. This can sometimes be accomplished with a work force that is relatively low-wage but of only average efficiency, or it can be accomplished with a highly efficient work force receiving higher wages. If the relationship between the skill of the work force and what it costs is favorable, many other factors of operation, such as distance from markets, rent, even in some cases inefficient management, can be overcome.

2. Production Management

The management of production is related to the efficiency of the labor supply, and thus becomes highly important. Key factors are the layout of the plant, production scheduling, training of the labor force, supervision of the work force, and labor relations.

3. Sales and Cost Estimating

The successful contractor must have good contacts within the industry, particularly among jobbers who have confidence in his ability to turn out acceptable quality when promised. The jobber cannot afford to take a chance on unknown firms, because if the goods are unacceptable or are not delivered on time, the entire sale may be lost because the season is missed. Equally important is the ability to do good cost estimating. A price which is too low will result in a loss on the sale. An overestimated price may lose the sale.

4. Overall Management

The management of a successful dress contractor requires not only the skills of production management, sales ability, and good estimating, but general business skills and care. Management must know how and when to borrow money at the lowest cost and must insure proper maintenance of his machines so that malfunctions do not interrupt production schedules.

5. Cutting Operations

A typical consideration which management must take into account is the decision about whether or not to have a cutting operation. This will depend to some extent on whether his jobbers want to do their own cutting or not. There are a number of advantages to having a capacity to perform the cutting operation: it is somewhat more profitable; the contractor can have better control over quality; and as material can be saved, the contractor can cut extra dresses to sell on his own.

6. Contractors' Associations

Another consideration is whether or not to join a contractors' association. It is generally deemed advisable to do so. These associations are located in all regions of the country, and they can help in obtaining business from jobbers. However, one of their prime functions is to conduct negotiations with the unions on behalf of all contractors.

7. Location

It is best for a contractor to be located at least within overnight trucking distance of the garment center where his customer-jobbers are located. This factor is more important with regard to medium and higher-priced dresses. Lower-priced dresses are not quite as subject to sudden shifts in style, and the savings in labor costs which can be achieved by moving further away from the garment center become more important as the overall price of the garment drops, assuming an adequate supply of labor remains available.

B. Problems and Potentials for Minority Entrepreneurs

1. Problems

A minority entrepreneur should not experience any special problems in the dress manufacturing industry, except in the sense that social contact with jobbers and within the industry may be limited. There are not very many minority jobbers, and the opportunity to develop sales contacts through mutual friendships and at social gatherings will be somewhat limited. This could be a serious handicap, since so many of the people within the industry already know each other. Many contractors have worked previously as cutters or foremen for other contractors and manufacturers; others have been salesmen within the industry and they have a wide range of contacts. The entrepreneur who does not have access to the "trade" in this respect will have some problems, and these should be carefully considered in advance. One way to overcome them is to get some assurances in advance that help will be forthcoming from someone who is widely regarded in the industry and who can be helpful in opening doors and setting up opportunities to bid on work.

Training the labor force can be a serious problem and one requiring extra capital. Unfortunately, virtually all Federal manpower training programs are unavailable for training operators in apparel manufacturing. Some years ago, the unions successfully convinced the Federal Government that such training programs would give new manufacturers an unfair advantage over those already in existence. While it is possible in some instances to secure State and local help in training a labor force, this type of help tends to be more prevalent in the Southern and rural areas where local development authorities are interested in persuading existing manufacturers to relocate. The prospective new entrepreneur should check carefully with local authorities to see whether or not some assistance would be available with training costs. Lacking such assistance, it may be wiser to rely on using already skilled operators who are available within the local labor force. This will require some preliminary study on the extent of their availability and on their willingness to become employed within the proposed new firm. A high rate of wastage or unacceptable work can be caused by inexperienced operators. This would clearly be detrimental to the new entrepreneur and might be the cause of a business failure.

2. Potentials

On the other hand, the extent to which a minority entrepreneur can develop rapport with the available labor force and secure good productivity from them can be an advantage, particularly in urban areas. Black and Spanish-speaking Americans constitute a highly underemployed labor force in most American cities. A minority entrepreneur who can recruit, train, motivate, and properly supervise a good labor force within the city will have certain advantages in the dress contracting business. It is possible to overestimate this factor, since attaining a productive labor force is more likely to be a function of good managerial skills than it is a function of the racial affinity between the manager and the work force. Nevertheless, it may be reasonable to assume that a given level of competence within management may produce better results with a labor force whose value-systems it understands and can identify with.

A minority entrepreneur may also have access at present to sources of capital and other assistance which might not be available to other entrepreneurs with equally limited means. For example, the Singer Company is committed to trying to help minority entrepreneurs get a start in the apparel industry, and, under certain conditions, it has made machines available on highly favorable terms and assisted in securing business. Bank loans may be available under guarantees from the Small Business Administration, which is committed to helping in the establishment of minority businesses.

C. Hypothetical Projections

Hypothetical operating projections for the smallest-sized operation considered feasible and for an average operation are shown below. Considerable care should be utilized in using the figures shown in these examples, since individual operations may vary considerably on the basis of local and special factors. The examples shown below should be used as rough guides in formulating projections for a specific project.

	Smallest	Average
Annual sales	$125,000	$375,000
Number of employees	30	80
Investment (no cutting)	$ 7,500	$ 20,000
Production wages and benefits	79,000	237,000
Materials, containers, trucking, etc.	7,900	23,700
Utilities	1,500	4,000
Rent	3,600	7,000
Overhead, owner's salary, office expenses	20,000	65,000
Interest and depreciation	4,000	8,000
Total expenses	$123,500	$364,700
Profit before tax	$ 1,500	$ 10,300
Profit percentage on sales	1.2%	2.7%

IV. GUIDANCE IN STARTING A NEW BUSINESS

A prospective entrepreneur who has no experience in the dress contracting business should discard any notions of entering until such experience has been attained. It would be wise to seek employment with an existing contractor or jobber as a production employee or supervisor, or as a salesman to the trade. While the apparel trades are not particularly complex, there are a great many aspects of the business that are really known only to insiders or to those who have had considerable exposure to its operations. A minority individual or group seeking to establish a dress manufacturing business as an economic development project for the inner city would be well advised to find a manager for the new business from among the supervisory or administrative employees of existing firms.

The first step in planning the new business is to determine the general area of location and to visit jobbers in the vicinity to determine the extent to which a new dress contractor would be able to count on business after establishment. While it is recognized that no commitments are possible in advance, the operator of the new business ought to have some feel for whether or not his services will be welcome among jobbers. Moreover, it is not enough to rely on vague assurances given in an effort to "get rid of a salesman." The potential new entrepreneur should have some feel for the amount of work which might be available, the conditions under which it will become available with regard to cost and time, and other special considerations affecting the market.

In discussions with jobbers, it may be advisable to determine exactly what segment of the business the new firm might specialize in. All other things being equal, if available labor is experienced and the proposed location is in an urban area or within 100 miles of one, specialization in higher quality dresses (above $10.75 to $16.75

wholesale) is desirable, since margins are slightly better at this level. However, if the labor force will not be experienced, lower-priced lines should be sought.

After an appraisal of the market and a preliminary examination of the types of financial resources which would be available, a visit should be made to a machinery manufacturer or jobber to determine what machines are available and at what cost. As indicated above, one of the major machinery manufacturers in the country has a program to help minority enterprises, and the availability of this help should be checked. A representative of the chosen machinery manufacturer may also be helpful in determining the amount of space needed and the plant layout.

Steps should next be taken to ascertain the type of factory space available on a lease basis. Most city locations have vacant factory space available, and a trip to an industrial realtor can save time. Considerations to be taken into account in arranging for space include the following:

1. Convenience to labor force; if it is too far from public transportation, many potential workers will not be interested.
2. Truck loading space.
3. Light and heat.
4. Safety and convenience for employees.
5. Total space.
6. Cost.

Arrangements need to be made for an efficient production force. This must include middle-level production supervisors, as well as overall production control. Where the owner is competent in these fields, he can settle for less-experienced help, but if the owner is not going to be able to spend time on the floor supervising production, it is essential that he be able to employ a reliable and experienced person who can.

A decision must be made about the extent to which training will be required for the work force. All other things being equal, it is better for an inexperienced entrepreneur to plan for an experienced labor force. The pitfalls which await the inexperienced entrant into a new business who must deal with an inexperienced work force will guarantee bankruptcy unless sufficient funds are available to compensate for the mistakes. Where an experienced labor force is not available, the inexperienced entrepreneur should start in as small a way as possible and gradually build his own experienced labor force.

The potential entrepreneur should consult with local employment officials and those responsible for local manpower programs to determine the extent of assistance available for training. If a wholly experienced work force cannot be employed and if training subsidies are not available, it would be wise to include sufficient funds for training in the initial startup costs.

The main purpose of training is to give piecework operators sufficient experience with the machines to gain proficiency. If they are too slow, management must generally make up the difference in order to give them the minimum wage. Moreover, careless or inexperienced operators can ruin material, and the contractor will have to compensate the jobber for the loss.

If the proposed new business is to be located in an area where union shops predominate, it would be wise for the new entrant to contact the union for advice on the labor force, methods of recruitment, and leads to experienced supervisors. The International Ladies Garment Workers Union is well-established and has a large array of experts in many facets of the business. The local contractors' association should also be visited and assistance secured as appropriate.

Other assistance can be secured from local organizations offering special programs to help potential minority entrepreneurs. In many cities these organizations are affiliated with the Office of Minority Business Enterprise, U.S. Department of Commerce. Some of these organizations may be able to put the potential entrepreneur in touch with a retired dress manufacturer who is interested in public service. If such a person is available, he can generally be extremely helpful in contacts with jobbers and in production control methods.

A final step prior to operations will be securing capital. If preliminary investigations have been complete, the prospective new entrepreneur should be able to prepare some simple projections indicating the amount of business he expects to do the first year, the amount of equipment he will need, what his costs of operation will be, and how much money he will need to get through the first year.

When capital needs have been estimated and supporting documents carefully prepared, a visit should be made to a local bank which is interested in helping minority businesses or to the local office of the Small Business Administration.

V. SUMMARY

Dress manufacturing on a contract basis is a volatile business that is highly competitive and labor-intensive. While it is readily entered with comparatively little capital investment, management should have contacts and experience in the field.

Key factors in determining profitability are the productivity of the labor force in relationship to its cost, the production planning and supervision ability of management, and the ability of management to secure business from jobbers.

BUILDING SERVICE CONTRACTING

I. RECOMMENDATION

Building maintenance service is one of the fastest growing industries in the United States today. The growth of the service sector of the economy, the increasing urban concentration, and an ever-growing tendency for office building owners to "contract out" their office building cleaning needs combine to support a current industry growth rate of 15 percent. The attractiveness of this market and its relative ease of entry have caused a high level of competition among building maintenance contractors. Firms obtain business largely on the basis of price competition in bidding, though an established reputation for reliability is also important. These industry characteristics, along with the labor intensive nature of building maintenance services, underscore the importance of managerial skills to success.

The building maintenance industry employs a large number of minority workers, and there exists a growing number of such persons with experience in supervisory positions. An experienced maintenance crew supervisor, who acquires independently or through franchiser training practical skill in cost estimating, bidding, and employee management, can earn a moderate return on his time and invested capital in the building maintenance service business.

II. DESCRIPTION OF THE INDUSTRY

A. Identification

Building maintenance services are included in Standard Industrial Classification (SIC) 7349, Miscellaneous Services to Dwellings and other Buildings, described as:

> Establishments primarily engaged in furnishing, to dwellings and other buildings, specialized services not elsewhere classified, such as janitorial services, floor waxing, office cleaning.

Building maintenance contracting is a service-oriented activity providing janitorial and related services to homes, small businesses, commercial office buildings, hospitals, apartment houses, government offices, factories, hotels, motels, schools, etc. Services provided include such things as:

- Dusting, dustmopping of floor areas.
- Other floor cleaning, including vacuuming, floor waxing and buffing, wet mopping, and stripping and machine scrubbing.
- Toilet room cleaning.
- Cleaning of stairways and landings, as necessary.
- Cleaning of walls, woodwork and partitions.
- Cleaning of building exterior.
- Window washing, as necessary.

Sample building maintenance specifications, detailing the required services, are attached as appendix A of this report.

In addition to those services listed above, a building maintenance contractor may provide what is known as the "total maintenance concept." This includes the provision of heating, air conditioning, and electrical engineers, painters, carpenters, yardmen, and garage personnel. Other operations handled under such a contract might include elevator operators and dispatchers, guards and lobby dispatchers, and specialized personnel who might be required by the particular building or institution.

There is a decided trend toward this total concept form of building maintenance. If a building services contractor is not himself equipped to handle all the above-mentioned services, he may contract with the building owner to provide them, then subcontract those services which he himself is not equipped to perform. This tends to make the building maintenance contractor more attractive to his prospective client. A building owner or manager is interested in receiving the best maintenance at the lowest possible cost with the least visibility. This is best provided by the one contractor who renders *all* the services required by the building. In the total concept plan, the contractor in effect serves as the "middle man," presenting the building owner with a completed product—a clean and efficiently run building.

B. Dimensions

There were some 9,675 businesses with payrolls in 1967 which provided general building maintenance and janitorial services on a contract basis, according to the 1967 Census of Business of the U. S. Department of Commerce. These businesses earned gross receipts of $884 million and paid wages amounting to over $555 million during 1967. These figures indicate that there has been significant growth in the industry since 1963, when there were 6,949 businesses, $500 million in receipts, and payrolls totaled $317 million.

It is currently estimated that over half of all building maintenance service firms are unaccounted for by these statistics, as they report no payroll in census data. Current figures are unavailable, but, in 1963, 9,414 firms provided contract building maintenance service with no employees in addition to the proprietor and perhaps members of his family. This large number of one-man firms account for only a small fraction of total industry earnings, however. These 9,414 proprietors reported only about $38½ million in receipts in 1963, the last year in which data were collected for these nonpayroll firms.

The structure of the industry is suggested by the accompanying breakdown of all the 1963 reporting firms by size in terms of receipts.

TABLE 1

Dimensions of the Industry—1963

Size of establishment (By receipts)	Establishments (Number)	Receipts ($000)	Payroll entire year ($000)
Total, all establishments	16,363	538,523	316,893
Establishments operated entire year, total	14,074	508,005	301,422
With annual receipts of:			
$500,000 or more	175	N.A.	N.A.
$300,000 to $500,000	140	N.A.	N.A.
$100,000 to $300,000	554	90,554	56,157
$ 50,000 to $100,000	625	43,362	24,040
$ 30,000 to $ 50,000	721	27,178	13,077
$ 20,000 to $ 30,000	852	20,426	8,272
$ 15,000 to $ 20,000	715	12,096	4,218
$ 10,000 to $ 15,000	1,250	14,969	4,195
$ 5,000 to $ 10,000	3,101	20,483	2,980
$ 3,000 to $ 5,000	2,358	8,051	634
$ 2,000 to $ 3,000	2,063	4,126	326
Less than $ 2,000	1,490	1,490	182
New establishments in business at end of year	2,289	$ 20,085	$ 9,940

The current market for building services is over $1 billion. It is estimated by Building Services Contractor (the leading trade publication in the field) that by 1976, more than $2 billion a year will be spent on commercial, institutional, and industrial cleaning services. The same source estimates that over 30 percent of the Nation's office buildings and factories were cleaned by outside contractors in 1968, compared with 15 percent only 5 years before. Combining this growing share of the office building market with the rapid rise in industrial and commercial construction affords a glimpse of the growth potential of this industry.

The trend today is toward greater concentration within the industry. That is, while there are still a great many small establishments, larger establishments are accounting for an ever greater portion of the gross receipts. Most of the building maintenance service establishments are located in urban areas for the obvious reasons. The cities provide the concentration of business, commercial, and government buildings to be serviced, as well as employee availability. In particular, the contractor will find his clients among predominantly urban facilities (in addition to commercial office space), such as railroad stations, department stores, sports stadia, airports, etc. New York City, for example, where over 95 percent of all the large office buildings are cleaned and maintained by service establishments, accounts for one of the largest concentrations of building service contractors in the Nation.

Minority entrepreneurship in this field is relatively scarce. According to industry sources, only about 5 percent of the establishments grossing from $100,000 to $1 million annually are minority owned. However, this figure is above the national average for all businesses of this size. Because a major portion of the work force in this field is now made up of minority group members, there exists a growing pool of minority individuals with some experience in a supervisory capacity who might be able to make the transition from labor into management of building maintenance establishments.

C. Characteristics

1. Nature of the Product

The building maintenance contractor serves building owners and/or managers. He provides these clients with a continuing service—a clean and well run building. The reliability of the building service contractor is being purchased as well as his cleaning ability—the assurance that the work will, in fact, be performed. Thus, the product can actually be broken down into two components: quantity and quality of cleaning and other building maintenance functions and the assurance that those functions will, in fact, be performed.

Building maintenance services are usually provided to building owners and managers on a contract basis. Contracts are generally for 1 year, with either party entitled to terminate upon 30 days' notice. Since building maintenance and janitorial services are performed on a continuing basis, the contractual system is the most efficient manner to insure the provision of these services. A sample Professional Building Maintenance Agreement is attached as appendix B.

2. Nature of the Customer

The customer of a building services contractor is the building owner or manager. As discussed above, the client *must* have the services provided by the building contractor—that is, he must have a clean, serviceable building. However, in order to achieve this goal, he may have the option of: (1) doing his own janitorial and other maintenance work; or (2) contracting such work to the building services. Which of these options will be chosen depends upon the size and complexity of the building to be maintained and the costs of performing the maintenance work with in-house staff compared to contracting out the work.

Building owners are finding—to a greater and greater degree—that it is more economical for them to contract out their janitorial and building maintenance functions. A firm devoted to maintenance work can afford to use the more advanced equipment being developed and can rely more heavily on specialization of labor. The result is that the contracting firm can usually do a better job for less money. Thus, a building owner will generally include the cost of a building maintenance contractor when computing the overall cost of the building. On an average, if a commercial office building rents space at $6.50 per square foot, it will assume that maintenance costs will be $.50 per square foot per year.

The customer will choose a building services contractor on the following basis:

a) the contractor's ability to provide quality service;

b) the contractor's reliability to assure that such services will, in fact, be provided; and

c) the cost which will be required for these services.

On the other hand, how does the building services contractor decide for whose work he will bid? In undertaking market analysis of potential customers, the building services contractor will take into account such things as: the number of commercial, government, or other serviceable buildings or businesses in his market area; the amount, types, and degree of completion of new construction; the amount of potential business already accounted for; the possibility of providing services to those buildings already accounted for at a less expensive rate (due to the new contractor's lower overhead, lower salary requirement, or greater efficiency), etc.

The number and types of customers of a building services contractor will also depend upon certain characteristics of his own operation. These might include: number of employees on the payroll at a given time; number of potential employees in the market areas; amount of equipment on hand or available; capital required for expansion and possibility of obtaining it.

Major locational determinants include the location of potential customers in relation to the dwellings of the contractor's employees and the location of the customer with respect to the contractor's place of business and storage supply. The contractor must decide if a building is, for example, so distant from the location of the cleaning equipment and the employees needed to do the cleaning that it is impractical for him to service it.

All of these factors are included in the contractor's estimating calculations. Cost estimating is one of the major skills required of the building services entrepreneur. He must accurately measure the above-listed factors, decide what weight to give each, and translate these decisions into a price which will be competitive and which will at the same time provide him with an acceptable profit level. These estimating procedures are discussed in greater detail below. An example of one possible estimating procedure is attached as appendix C of this report.

3. Technology

Building services contracting has traditionally been a labor intensive business. The main expense item of any contractor is his payroll. In a sense, the contractor is merely a "labor broker" who handles personnel problems for the building owner.

The new or prospective entrepreneur is likely to need a wide range of skills, preferably gained by experience as he develops an enterprise in the building maintenance field. He will probably do much (if not all) of the actual cleaning work at first, as well as the estimating of new jobs and the selling of his services. When the operation expands, the entrepreneur, while still cleaning, estimating, and selling, will have to train his new employees. In addition, growth will bring problems of accounting, inventory control, purchasing procedures. He will have to have a relatively high degree of proficiency to operate a successful establishment.

Once a business has become established, the entrepreneur of a building maintenance service can usually take out as profit 5 percent of the net receipts of the business, according to informed industry sources. The percentage will vary, of course, depending on:

a) the accuracy of entrepreneur's estimating procedures. If the entrepreneur does not estimate properly, profits built into business contracts will be consumed by costs overrun.

b) the extent of the competition on the contract. In some instances the entrepreneur will cut profit margins in an effort to win contracts.

c) the amount the entrepreneur wishes to reinvest in the establishment. This in turn will depend on the desired rate of growth.

The employees of a building services contractor are, for the most part, unskilled. (The major exceptions to this are window cleaners and any engineers provided.) Any training received is usually on-the-job, although some larger contractors are beginning to use classes to supplement this training.

Most employees used by the building services contractor are women, who are used for all but the heavy work. The majority of the employees in this field, particularly in the larger urban areas, are minority group members. Since most of building contract work is accomplished during the nighttime hours, it provides an excellent "moonlighting" job and a source of income for those with little formal training or education.

Wage rates for employees hover around the minimum wage rates applicable. In larger urban areas, wages are usually somewhat higher. In Washington, D.C., for example, with a minimum wage of $1.65 per hour, the wages of building service employees range from $1.75 to $2 per hour, with $1.90 per hour the average rate. Window cleaners' wages are higher, often ranging from $4 to $4.50 per hour and up.

In some locations, wage rates and availability of labor may be somewhat affected by unionization. (The building services industry is covered by the Building Service Employee Union, as well as others for the more specialized employees.) This is mainly true in highly industrialized towns which are in any case predominantly union. Elsewhere, the moonlighting nature of the jobs and rapid turnover among the employees have prevented unionization from taking hold.

One of the main problems of a building services contractor is the high turnover rate among his employees. Industry sources indicate that most remain on the job for a period of 2 to 6 months. This is an annual turnover rate of from 200 to 600 percent. This situation, again due to the moonlighting nature of the job, has caused a premium to be placed on reliability by the building services employer.

The high turnover rate has also led to increasing the screening procedures for potential employees of the building services company. Many job application forms now contain rather pointed questions involving: the reason the applicant desires work; whether or not he is buying a home; how long he has been on his present job, etc. The whole object of such screening is for the contractor to acquire a "solid" employee who will have an interest in working and who will stay on the job.

Equipment required in the building services contractor field has been relatively basic in the past. A sample inventory of equipment is reproduced below:

Sweeper
Buffer
Brushes
Floor pads
Extension cords
Mop bucket—round—oval
Wringer
Mop
Dust mop handle
Dustpan
Trash containers
Water pails
Pushbroom
Strawbroom
Rubber gloves
Uniforms
Smocks
Shirts
Ammonia
Bowl cleaner
Cleanser
Disinfectant
Furniture polish
Liquid detergent
Floor finish
Plastic bags
Sanitary napkins
Toilet seat covers } occasional
Paper towels

Recently, technological advances and greater sophistication have affected the equipment used by the building services contractor. In addition to the list of basic items reproduced above, such machines as institutional vacuums, high pressure cleaners, and power sweepers with centrifugal clutch are now available. These technological advances have affected profitability positively and have somewhat reduced labor requirements in the industry.

One major piece of equipment used by the building services contractor is a truck. The new entrepreneur may at first transport machines and supplies in a car or station wagon. Usually, however, the enterprise will develop to the point where one or more trucks are needed. In a survey performed by Building Services Contractor, the average number of trucks in operation per firm surveyed was 4.3.

The same survey noted that 92 percent of building services contractors keep a warehouse of expendable cleaning supplies, with the average firm keeping 54 days of normal consumption on hand. Being able to keep such stock on hand is a problem to be dealt with by any new entrepreneur.

There are definite economies of scale accruing to a building services contractor. These usually begin at annual gross revenues of $500,000 and include savings on supplies, which can then be purchased directly from the manufacturer rather than from the distributor, savings on machines (with fewer having to be purchased for each additional $100,000 of income), and easing of credit binds for the growing business.

4. Competition

The largest form of competition the building services contractor has to face outside of his own industry is in the form of buildings which do their own in-house maintenance. This alternative is becoming more and more rare, however, as building administrators realize the advantage of contracting with a maintenance company. The building administrator is relieved of the worry of hiring and firing of maintenance employees, can rely on the contractor's use of more specialized labor, obtains the use of more advanced and complex equipment, and has no inventory problems in this area.

The growing market for the building maintenance services industry does not insure high margins and ease in securing work. However, a great many small contractors in this field assure intensive bidding competition, with the emphasis on shaving prices. Cost of maintenance is a primary determining factor in the choice of a building services contractor, and the building owner will, reputation for quality and reliability being equal, choose the contractor who comes in with the lowest bid for the job required. In this type of price competition, the large contractor has some advantages, the small contractor others. The large contractor may be able to provide equipment and supplies at a less costly rate than his smaller competitor because of economies of scale; the cost of "gearing up" to do a job, especially a large one, may be lower for him. On the other hand, the small contractor may have lower overhead, due to lower direct expenses and less equipment, and may be willing to have a smaller profit margin for the sake of getting the job and developing his reputation.

The problem of estimating must again be stressed. The small contractor, and especially the new entrepreneur, must be particularly careful in his estimating procedures. A net deficit is likely to result from inaccurate decisions about costs and personnel requirements, and although a contractor may be willing to reduce his profit margin, maintaining a loss is hardly a sound business practice.

5. Ease of Entry

The ease of entry into building services contracting is attested to by the large number of firms beginning operation each year. There are no licensing requirements in this industry, and many contractors begin with no more than experience in the cleaning field, determination, and a small amount of capital. Because many businesses begin with no more than the owner and operator (and perhaps one other part-time employee), qualified employees do not present an immediate problem for the prospective entrepreneur. At this stage, no office or storage space is required, and a new enterprise can be operated from the entrepreneur's home. Between $1,200 and $1,500 monthly contracts may be sufficient to begin an operation if accurate cost estimation and time allocations have been made. The failure rate of building services contractors is, according to industry sources, higher than the combined rate for all businesses. Some of the reasons for failure cited by trade authorities include: overextension, resulting in inability to complete jobs properly and to the satisfaction of the client; poor estimating procedures, resulting in cost overruns and unprofitable contracts; lack of managerial experience, resulting in higher than usual labor turnover; competitive weakness because of lack of established reputation; and general administrative difficulties.

In addition, industry sources indicate that experience in the building maintenance field is almost essential to the success of an enterprise. The majority of contractors interviewed stated that they had worked for 6 months to 2 years in the field before attempting to branch out into independent operation, and many noted that it was this early experience that helped to insure their success.

6. Financing

It is difficult to estimate the capital requirements of a new or prospective building services contractor. Industry sources indicate that a rough rule of thumb is: have available capital in the amount of three times the expected first month's gross income. For example, an entrepreneur who has secured a contract that will produce monthly gross receipts of $1,500 will be able to begin operations with $4,500. This amount will cover the cost of supplies, salary for the entrepreneur and any employees he might require, and working capital requirements needed to carry him through the timelag in payment for past services.

There are no special programs or sources of capital for establishing a building services contractor. The Small Business Administration, however, has been quite active in providing regular business and economic opportunity loans in this field, a large portion of which have been to minority entrepreneurs. The breakdown of these loans is presented below.

TABLE 2
SBA Regular Business and Economic Opportunity Loans:
Building Maintenance and Janitorial Services

Number total	White and others	Percent	Black	Percent	Other nonwhite	Percent
60	33	55	23	38.3	4	6.7

Volume total	White and others	Percent	Black	Percent	Other nonwhite	Percent
$750,250	$522,300	69.6	$186,950	24.9	$41,000	5.5

Another form of organization and source of capitalization that is becoming increasingly popular in this field is the franchise arrangement. One of the largest franchise operations provides such assistance as training programs, managerial assistance, continuing counseling support, working equipment, supplies, advertising and promotions for a nominal fixed fee.

7. Profitability

As noted above, the reasonably successful building service contractor can expect an average of about 5 percent profit on net receipts. The industry can be expected to grow at about 15 percent per annum.

Factors tending to decrease profitability are: inaccurate cost estimation; the high labor turnover, with resultant costs; frequent theft of equipment and supplies; and overextension of operation.

8. Dependence on Outside Factors

The field of business maintenance contracting is less subject to the effects of economic conditions than are many industries or types of business. Building cleaning and maintenance needs exist irrespective of business cycles, and purchasers of these services usually think of them as fixed costs. One effect of the business cycle, however, is the decrease in construction during times of recession, in turn causing a decrease (or, more accurately, a less rapid increase) in the contractor's potential business. The availability of credit would most likely affect the building services contractor less than other areas of the economy.

III. FEASIBILITY ANALYSIS

A. Review of Key Factors

The following factors bear on the feasibility of establishing a building service contracting business:

1. *Management*

The new entrepreneur requires experience in the field of cleaning or building maintenance. At least 1 year working for an established firm will enable him to acquire the technique of accurate cost estimating which is essential to his success. Because personnel management is also vital, the new entrepreneur will need experience or potential in this field as well. If the prospective manager has shown some knack for selling, accounting, and ability to handle inventory, he is enhancing his chances for success.

2. *Market*

The market for his services will determine the new contractor's success. Such a market can be analyzed in part by the following:

a) concentration of office buildings in the area;

b) new construction, noting state of completion;

c) competition;

d) the contractor's own reputation.

3. *Location*

While not crucial at the early stages of operation, the contractor's offices and warehouses should be convenient both to his prospective clients and, if possible, to the homes of his employees.

4. *Labor*

Although availability of labor is usually not a problem, retention and management of this labor can be problems. Employee benefits, profit-sharing and other such methods are often used to hold employees, and careful screening of applicants and training of employees are used to ease the management problem. The building services contractor may benefit from the activities of government-funded manpower programs which screen jobseekers and which provide basic education and pre-vocational training to them. Such programs as JOB 70, the Work Incentive Program (WIN), and on-the-job training under the Manpower Development and Training Act (MDTA O-J-T) would provide a ready source of potential employees in most urban areas. An analysis of the quantity and quality of the work force is essential in assuming the potential feasibility of the enterprise.

B. Special Factors for New Minority Ventures

The largest market for a building services contractor is in the urban areas. It is in urban areas, too, that there exists a reservoir of potential employees, many of them minority members. Thus, location and labor will serve as assets to the prospective minority entrepreneur who can also benefit from a continually growing market and the increasing acceptance of minority entrepreneurship.

C. Projections of Attainable Returns in Industry

Projections follow for two different types of operations. The first is for a starting independent operation, with three part-time employees. The second is for a new franchise operation for professional building maintenance.

1. *Small, One-Man Operation*

The projections here are based on the following assumptions:

a. A one-man operation, with the prospective entrepreneur having had some experience in the building maintenance field.

b. Three part-time workers, each available for approximately 17 hours per week of employment at $1.65 per hour.

c. An initial investment by the manager of $4,500.

d. A 40-hour work week for the owner, who does both selling and supervising of the operation as well as some actual building maintenance work.

e. Operation out of the home of the manager during at least the first year of operation, using the personal vehicle (car, station wagon, or small truck) for the business.

f. A relatively high cash requirement, since the owner will be unable, as a new operator, to secure his supplies and equipment on credit and will require initial cash outlays.

As the following operating statements shows, such an operation, grossing $18,000 per annum, might provide a net profit of about $9,600. This figure is deceptively high, however. It does not take into account the owner's draw for salary and any amounts to be reinvested in the business.

Gross Annual Revenue		$18,000
Investment	$4,500	
Area served and customer type	7 to 12 buildings	
	4,000 to 6,000 sq. ft. each	
	36,000 sq. ft. total	
Production hours	74 hours per week	
Operating location	Works from own home	
Vehicles	Car, station wagon or	
	used truck	
Equipment and material	$3,000	
Distribution of labor		
Owner's function	Management, sales, and cleaning	
Number and type of employees	Owner, 3 part-time employees	
	for cleaning	
Fixed costs		
Vehicle depreciation	$ 500	
Equipment depreciation	750	
Telephone and yellow pages	50	
Rent, office help, supervisory, outside services	0	
Total fixed costs		$ 1,300
Variable costs		
Labor	$4,500	
Advertising, selling expenses	700	
Payroll tax, employee fringes	600	
Vehicle operating cost	1,000	
Liability insurance	300	
Total variable costs		$ 7,100
Net profit before tax and		
owner's compensation		$ 9,600

If the entrepreneur has had adequate experience in the field, if he is able to sell his services, if his cost-estimating procedures are accurate, and if he provides quality service, a 1st-year operation of this size is feasible. However, unless all of these characteristics are present, as well as a willingness by the new entrepreneur to forego present profits and reinvest heavily in his business, an establishment such as this cannot be maintained for any length of time.

2. Franchise Operation

The owner of a typical, but hypothetical, franchise must initially invest $5,000. Of this amount, $1,500 is paid to the franchiser for goods and services, including:

- The licensed use of the franchiser's trademark and training— $900.
- Professional products, business forms, supplies and tools, sales promotion aids, and technical manuals—$500.
- Equipment—$100.

The training provided by the franchiser is particularly geared to servicing buildings, offices, and plants under contract. Because of such possible benefits as the established name of the franchiser, cost-cutting centralized purchase of supplies, advertising provided by the franchiser, and continuous consultation and advice, the franchisee may possess advantages over the independent operator. In addition, special financing is occasionally provided by the franchiser, making it easier for an individual to begin a business.

New operation—Husband and wife or part-timer

Investment	$5,000	
Area serviced and customer type	22,000 square feet	
	4 to 10 commercial buildings	
	4,000 to 6,000 square feet each	

Operating location—works from home
Vehicles—one truck, probably used
Equipment—primarily supplied by franchiser

Distribution of labor
 Owner's functions—housekeeping, sales and management
 Number and type of employees—owner and wife, with
  one part-time employee

Gross Annual Revenue		$15,000
Fixed costs		
Vehicle depreciation	$ 500	
Equipment depreciation	50	
Telephone and yellow pages	100	
Rent, office help, outside services	50	
Manager's administrative salary	1,000	
Total fixed costs		$ 1,700
Variable costs		
Manager's production salary	$7,500	
Labor (part-time)	1,750	
Sales expense (advertising—paid by franchiser)	- 0 -	
Vehicle operating cost	1,200	
Franchising fee (percentage of gross income—here, 7 percent)	1,050	
Liability insurance (paid by franchiser)	- 0 -	
Total variable costs		$11,500
Total costs		$13,200
Profit before tax		$ 1,800
Net to owner		
Manager's administrative salary	$1,000	
Manager's production salary	7,500	
Profit before tax	1,800	
Net to owner before taxes		$10,300

IV. ESTABLISHING THE BUSINESS

A. Approaching the Market

If he is planning an independent, one-man operation, the prospective building services contractor should have his market fairly well defined. In addition, he should have already secured contracts assuring him of $1,500 monthly gross revenue. These agreements are made through previous contacts while working in the field. Ability to secure these contracts will indicate to the entrepreneur that his bidding has been price competitive, and if his performance is of acceptable quality, he should be able to maintain an independent operation at this level for at least 1 year.

The franchisee, on the other hand, does not require an initial knowledge of the cleaning industry. The franchiser trains him to be an expert professional cleaner. The franchiser also generally provides the new owner with an advertising and sales promotion program, other assorted sales aids, and instructions on their use. These benefits, added to the use of the franchise brand name and the advantage of its reputation, will ease the franchisee's approach to the market.

B. Plant Requirements

The small, one-man operation requires minimum space and can comfortably be operated from the entrepreneur's home. The only room needed is a storage room for equipment and supplies; a garage or basement area will certainly suffice for the 1st year of operation at this level. The same is true for the beginning franchise.

Growth of the establishment will require office space and more storage space than can be adequately provided in the home. At this point, the entrepreneur will seek a location close to the buildings which he is servicing and as close as possible to the location of his employees. Office space may range from about 1,000 square feet for an establishment with 15 to 40 full- and part-time employees, to 22,000 square feet of office space for a 900-man operation. In addition, storage space may run 500 to 13,000 square feet, accordingly.

C. Financing

The basic investment involved in building services contracting is the purchase of equipment and supplies. Although some financing arrangements may be made with equipment suppliers, expendable items such as chemicals, cleaning agents, and paper products will require a cash outlay. In addition, enough capital must be kept on hand to meet 1 month's payroll requirements, supplies, and rent.

(This is necessary because of the timelag between contractual agreement and actual payment.)

Because the initial capital requirement is relatively low, the building services contractor can often begin operation with his own savings or other private sources. If a franchise operation is contemplated, the franchiser is often willing to provide special financing arrangements. And it may be possible to secure a loan from the Small Business Administration. Unless the individual entrepreneur has an independently stable credit reputation, it may be difficult to secure conventional bank financing for this type of operation.

D. Labor Force

The labor force used by a building services contractor is, for the most part, unskilled. Although the wages are low, recruitment of employees is rarely a problem. The new entrepreneur, probably needing only two or possibly three part-time employees, will be able to recruit them through his previous business contacts or through the standard advertising methods.

As the enterprise develops, however, maintaining a reliable and efficient labor force will require special effort. Such an effort might include such things as profit sharing, bonuses for outstanding work, and other employee benefits. Raising the wage rate as much above the minimum wage as possible is probably the best method of securing and maintaining personnel.

APPENDIX A – *Typical Specifications for Custodial Services*

1. ## Waste Paper—Ash Trays—Daily

   Waste baskets and ash trays shall be emptied daily. Ash trays shall be wiped clean. Trash generated by normal daily office routine shall be emptied into trash containers. Trash removal shall be provided by the *contractor or building owner.* If by contractor, he generally subcontracts.

2. ## Dusting—Daily

   All furniture, file cabinets, and horizontal surfaces which can be reached while standing on the floor shall be dusted daily with a chemically treated cloth.

3. ## Dust Mopping—Floors—Daily

   All noncarpeted floors shall be dust mopped with a treated yarn dust mop daily with special attention being given to areas under desks and furniture to prevent the accumulation of dust and dirt. Dust mopping shall be done after furniture has been dusted.

4. ## Toilet Rooms—Daily
   a. Wash all mirrors.
   b. Wash hand basins and hardware.
   c. Wash urinals.
   d. Wash toilet seats using disinfectant in water.
   e. Wash toilet bowls.
   f. Damp mop floor using disinfectant in water.
   g. Damp wipe, clean, and disinfect all tile and other surfaces. Spot wipe and clean where necessary. Walls and partitions are to be free of handprints and dust.
   h. Replenish hand soap, towels, and tissue. These expendable items shall be furnished by the building owner or contractor. In 90 percent of contracts, provided by the contractor.
   i. Toilet bowl brush shall be used on toilet bowls, and care shall be given to clean flush holes under rim of bowl and passage trap.
   j. Bowl cleaner shall be used at least once each month or more often if necessary.

5. *Stairways and Landings—Daily—As Necessary*

All stairways and landings shall be dust mopped with a treated yarn dust mop daily. Railings, ledges, and equipment shall be dusted daily. Spot cleaning of doors and walls shall be done as necessary. These floor areas shall be damp mopped, scrubbed, waxed, and buffed as necessary.

6. *Vacuuming—Daily*

All rugs in office areas and public spaces shall be vacuum cleaned daily. Hard-to-get spots and corners shall be cleaned with necessary tools.

7. *Floor Waxing & Buffing—Daily and As Necessary*

All noncarpeted resilient floors shall be waxed with Underwriter Laboratory approved materials. The frequency of the waxing shall be governed by the amount of wear due to weather and other conditions. The floors and traffic areas shall be waxed so as to maintain a uniform appearance throughout the entire building. Corridors and elevator floors shall be buffed daily.

8. *Wet Mopping—Daily and As Needed*

All waxed floors shall be damp mopped when dirt can not be swept or dusted, and spots shall be removed daily.

9. *Stripping and Machine Scrubbing—As Needed*

This operation shall be accomplished as frequently as necessary, depending on the need to remove dirt-embedded finishes, stains, spillages, and wax buildup.

10. *Water Coolers—Daily*

All water coolers shall be cleaned and polished daily.

11. *Spot Cleaning—Daily*

Walls, doors, painted woodworks, and interior glass shall be kept free from handprints and smudges which can be removed with cloth and neutral cleaner. The type of cleaner to be used shall be appropriate for the wall material.

12. *Ash Receivers—Daily*

Ash receivers shall be cleaned and sanitized as necessary.

13. *Lighting Fixtures—Semiannually—Annually*

   All lighting fixtures shall be dusted every 6 months and washed annually.

14. *High Dusting—Quarterly*

   Pipes, ledges, mouldings, etc., shall be dusted every 3 months·

15. *Venetian Blinds—Daily*

   A sufficient number of venetian blinds shall be dusted or damp wiped daily so that all blinds shall be dusted every 90 days. Draperies shall be straightened and vacuumed.

16. *Walls, Woodwork, and Partitions—Quarterly*

   All walls shall be brushed down every 3 months with approved wall duster or a vacuum cleaner.

17. *Glass Partitions and Doors—Monthly*

   All glass partitions and doors shall be damp cleaned monthly.

18. *Window Washing—Quarterly*

   All windows shall be washed inside and outside once every three months. [Often contracted out, because of high insurance risks, labor skills required, etc.]

19. *Air-Conditioning Grills—Monthly*

   All areas around air-conditioning and return air grills shall be cleaned once each month.

20. *Elevators—Daily*

   The interior surfaces and fixtures of the elevators and the elevator lobby doors shall be dusted daily and damp wiped as necessary.

21. *Polishing—Daily—Monthly*

   All doorplates, kick plates, brass and metal fixtures within the building shall be wiped daily and polished monthly.

22. *Toilet Rooms—Daily* [This involves day laborers.]

   Maid and/or porter shall make periodic checks of toilet and rest rooms, and shall replenish supplies, clean fixtures as necessary, empty waste cans, etc.

23. *Policing Floors—Daily* [This involves day laborers.]

    Corridors, lobbies, and other public areas shall be kept free of wastepapers, cigarette butts, matches, etc.

24. *Entrance Lobby—Daily*

    Entrance lobby shall be serviced daily. Lobby glass shall be washed and cleaned as necessary. Particular attention shall be given floor and glass doors during inclement weather.

25. *Building Exterior—Daily*

    Entrance shall be swept clean of litter. Sidewalk shall be kept clean and free of snow and ice. Salt or other ice-melting material shall be furnished by the building management.

26. *General—As Necessary*

    a. Employees of contractor shall report to the building superintendent any conditions such as leaky faucets, stopped toilets and drains, broken fixtures, etc., or any other unusual happenings in buildings.

    b. Employees of contractor shall check windows and turn off all lights when night cleaning is finished.

    c. Employees of contractor shall have proper identification during hours of employment.

    d. Employees of contractor shall not disturb papers on desk, open drawers or cabinets, use telephones, televisions, radios, drink, or gamble while on duty. They shall report any open safes and cabinets to the building guard force or building management.

    e. Day employees shall be under supervision of the building superintendent. The duties and work schedule shall be agreed upon by contractor and building management.

    f. Daytime employees of contractor will wear uniforms. They will be neat and clean in appearance.

    g. No cleaning services shall be provided on legal holidays.

APPENDIX B — Sample Professional Building Maintenance Agreement

AGREEMENT made on _____[date]_____ between ___[contractor]___ and ____[client]____

NOW THEREFORE, the parties agree as follows:

1. Beginning on _____[date]_____, Contractor will provide and perform for the Client the services described in the work schedule [see appendix A], in the buildings and areas to be serviced therein set forth.

2. All personnel furnished by the Contractor will be employees of the Contractor, and the Contractor will pay all salaries and expenses of, and all Federal social security taxes, Federal and State unemployment taxes, and any similar payroll taxes relating to such employees, and will carry workmen's compensation insurance for such employees. The Contractor will be considered for all purposes an independent contractor, and will not at any time directly or indirectly act as an agent, servant, or employee of the Client.

3. The Contractor will provide all proper safeguards and shall assume all risks incurred in performing its services hereunder.

4. The Contractor shall provide the insurance coverage agreed upon, include comprehensive liability coverage and workmen's compensation coverage.

5. Without limiting the responsibility of the Contractor for the proper conduct of its personnel and the cleaning of the areas to be serviced hereunder, the conduct of the cleaning personnel hereunder is to be guided by rules and regulations as agreed upon from time to time between the Client and the Contractor, and such additional special written instructions as may be issued by the Client to the Contractor from time to time through its designated agent.

6. The Contractor is responsible for the direct supervision of its personnel through its designated representative, and such representative will, in turn, be available at all reasonable times to report and confer with the designated agents of the Client with respect to services rendered.

7. The Contractor agrees that the cleaning services to be provided hereunder shall be performed by qualified, careful, and efficient employees in strict conformity with the best practices and highest applicable standards. The Contractor further agrees that upon the request of its Client, it will remove from services hereunder any of its employees who in the opinion of the Client are guilty of improper conduct or are not qualified to perform the work assigned to them.

8. It shall be understood and agreed that during the term of this agreement and for ninety (90) days thereafter, the Client will not, directly or indirectly, hire any person employed by the Contractor.

9. In exchange for performance of services hereunder, the Client shall make payment to the Contractor for services rendered hereunder at the rate of _____ per month. The Contractor will give the Client at least thirty (30) days notice of any price change for services rendered hereunder, and the Client will notify the Contractor of any changes in the use of the areas covered by this agreement and any additions to or changes in the furnishings or floor, wall, or ceiling surfaces forming a part of the Client's premises.

10. The Contractor will perform all services required hereunder, except when prevented by strike, lockout, act of God, accident, or other circumstances beyond its control.

11. This agreement shall continue in effect for 1 year from the date services are to begin, but may be terminated by either party by giving thirty (30) days written notice by registered mail addressed to the other party.

APPENDIX C — *Estimating a Single Job**

Assume that the building maintenance contractor is pricing the maintenance of 50,000 square feet of office space. The work is to be done each weekday evening after employees leave at 5 p.m. Calculations indicate that three men and a supervisor will be needed on a regular 40-hour week. The estimate should look like this:

MATERIALS AND EQUIPMENT
(Approximately 15% of total labor costs)

Materials (per month)	$ 160.00	
Prorated equipment depreciation	60.00	
Equipment repairs and maintenance	10.00	
		$ 230.00

LABOR COSTS

Number of men	Monthly hours	Wage rate	Monthly payroll	
3	480	$2.25	$1,080.00	
1 supervisor	160	$2.60	416.00	
			$1,496.00	
Vacation, sickleave, overtime factor, etc.—10%			149.60	
				$ 1,645.60

TAXES AND INSURANCE

**Social Security—5.2% of monthly payroll $1,496.00	$ 77.79	
State and Federal employment taxes 2% of monthly billing	30.71	
Insurance cost (prorated for total monthly billings on all accounts serviced by firm)	30.00	$ 138.50
SUBTOTAL (70% of bid price)		$ 2,014.10

To arrive at total price, divide subtotal by 70%

$2,014.10 ÷ 70% = $2,877.28

15% of monthly contract for overhead =	$ 431.59	
15% of monthly contract for profit =	431.59	$ 863.18
TOTAL MONTHLY CONTRACT		$ 2,877.28
TOTAL YEARLY CONTRACT		$34,527.36
PER SQUARE FOOT PER YEAR		69¢

(National average ranges from 50¢ to 80¢ per square foot for maintenance)

*Adapted from Building Services Contractor for April 1968.
**As of July 1971.

CONVENIENCE STORES

I. Recommendation

The convenience store is a fast-growing segment of the retail food business which provides an attractive opportunity for independent business ownership and management. The industry is relatively easy to enter, and with some training and experience in foodstores, an individual has adequate opportunities to achieve business success. Although certain aspects of the business are complex, a new store owner or manager can secure help in buying and in resolving managerial problems through franchise operation, membership in a cooperative, or affiliation with a voluntary wholesale organization. While convenience stores have expanded rapidly throughout many suburban areas, their growth has not been as great within the inner city, and appropriate locations in these areas offer minority entrepreneurs a favorable opportunity to establish themselves in the industry.

II. Description of the Industry

The National Association of Convenience Stores describes the convenience store as a shop oriented towards convenience goods, located to serve a neighborhood, occupying 1,000 to 3,000 square feet, and with space to park five to 15 cars. Most convenience stores operate for long hours—usually from 7 a.m. to 11 p.m.—and some stores operate 24 hours per day. Convenience stores provide a service supplemental to other types of retail firms, such as supermarkets and discount centers specializing in fill-in items. Convenience stores stock only those frequently demanded items needed by the housewife between major supermarket shopping trips. However, convenience stores are classified as retail grocery stores, Standard Industrial Classification (SIC) 5411.

Table 1 gives some of the characteristics of the convenience store:

TABLE 1
Convenience Store Characteristics, 1967

Characteristics	Mean	Range
Gross area of building (square feet)	2,400	2,000 to 4,000
Investment (excluding inventory)	$50,000	$40,000 to $120,000
Inventory (number of items)	2,500	1,500 to 3,000
Employees	2.5	2 to 7
Hours open per day (7 days per week)	15	12 to 24
Parking spaces available	11	5 to 15
Sales per customer	$1.25	
Average customer shopping time	4 minutes	2 to 12 minutes
Customer trips per week	4 to 5	2 to 6
Percent of customers living within half a mile	50%	30 to 75%
Percent of customers living more than 1 mile away	20%	0 to 40%
Percent of customers who drive to store	85%	
Weekly sales	$3,000	$1,700 to $5,000
Gross margin	25%	20 to 30%
Income before tax	3.5%	2 to 6%

A brief glance at the table indicates that the convenience store is a very small scale operation, requiring only minimal investment. While operating with sophisticated sales and stocking techniques, the store is, in fact, based on a rather simple concept and can be adequately controlled by one person with some training. Some businessmen have seen the convenience store as a return to the "mom and pop" days of food shopping. However, this is not the case, since the only resemblance is in size. In all other characteristics the convenience store now closely resembles the supermarket, although there are important differences. It will be noted that the inventory is on the average only one-fifth the size of that of a supermarket. Weekly sales are being compared to the smallest supermarkets, but gross margins and income are higher (income as much as two to three times higher). This may be attributed to the charging of higher prices for the high degree of convenience offered by the long business hours and the elimination of waiting time. Convenience stores are usually more personal, friendly, and neighborly than supermarkets. Employees are usually recruited from the neighborhood served by the shop. On the average, 50 percent of the customers live within half a mile of the shop and pass it three or four times per day on other trips. Above all, the convenience store is convenient.

III. Industry Growth

The convenience store is undoubtedly filling a wide gap in the retail food market, and the growth has been spectacular. Industry statistics indicate that the number of convenience stores increased 600 percent in the 1960's.

TABLE 2

Growth of Convenience Stores in the U. S., 1957-70

Year	Number of shops	Total sales	Average sales	Percent of U.S. grocery sales
1957	500	$ 75,000,000	$150,000	.2
1960	2,500	375,000,000	150,000	.7
1962	3,500	525,000,000	150,000	.9
1965	5,000	750,000,000	150,000	1.1
1967	8,000	1,300,000,000	151,000	1.7
1968	9,600	1,625,000,000	169,000	2.1
1970	13,600	2,673,000,000	196,500	3.0

The convenience store started its growth in the late 1950's in Florida and Georgia as a drive-in store with an open front. Since then, the phenomenon has spread to all regions of the United States as convenience store chains have developed and thrived.

The enormous gap in average customer shopping time between the supermarket (22 minutes) and the convenience store (4 minutes) is the key to the success of the convenience store. The higher prices, margins, and income available to the convenience store are, therefore, a function of this changing trade-off between time and money. In addition, the convenience stores are discovering new opportunities for selling to the male customer when he shops for cigarettes or beer or is running a one-item errand for his wife to supply the missing ingredient in the dinner she is cooking at the time. (It has been estimated that two-thirds of the items bought in convenience stores are used within 2 hours, and 50 percent of the customers are male.)

IV. Location

Convenience stores are oriented towards single-item or fill-in merchandise with a very short trip time. They are, therefore, highly neighborhood-oriented, even in the suburbs, and can often be found on single-store sites, on street corners, or in small convenience-type shopping centers in company with a barbershop, a drycleaning outlet, and a carryout. In the urban areas, convenience stores have not flourished as much as they have in the suburbs, largely because there tend to be convenient places in which to shop already located in urban neighborhoods. These are the small "mom and pop" grocery stores which stay open 7 days a week, long hours each day, and have no waiting line. Moreover, there are the difficult problems of urban areas associated with rundown neighborhoods, high insurance costs, high crime rates, and the like. Inner-city convenience stores experience two or even three times the pilferage rates of the suburban store, for instance, and net profit margins are necessarily affected. Nevertheless, as the traditional small grocery store phases out of the city, and as new neighborhoods are created through urban development and low income housing, opportunities are presented for minority entrepreneurs to establish convenience stores. Almost any city neighborhood of 10,000 to 15,000 people not having a convenience store or a convenience store substitute could be a potentially good location. An existing supermarket need not be a problem, but care should be taken to make sure there is no significant competition from chain drugstores selling beer, cigarettes, and some food items.

V. Investment

The total investment needed for a convenience store is small relative to that required for a supermarket or grocery store. Total investment required will depend heavily on the cost of the facilities, if an established business, or of the land and building, if a new venture. Land may cost $40,000 to $50,000 in an urbanized location, and the building investment will probably be between $35,000 and $40,000. New equipment costs usually range from $10,000 to $20,000. If the building is already built and equipment can be leased, building and plant costs can be markedly reduced. The cost of the 2,500 items of inventory considered to be about average for a convenience store would range from $12,000 to $15,000. Operating licenses cost about $500, and cash needs may be $2,500 at the commencement of business. If the new owner/manager decides to become a franchisee of one of the larger national chains, the initial investment would be raised by about $10,000. A common financing plan for the new independent convenience store uses about $40,000 of owner's equity investment to secure a bank loan of from $60,000 to $100,000 of long term debt.

Inventory constitutes a large proportion of total investment (15 to 20 percent), and the choice of items is, therefore, very important both in terms of getting the best investment for one's dollar and in terms of the future operating ratios of the store—in particular its profitability.

Nationally advertised brand name items predominate. Because the store is small and is catering to convenience, the operator must adhere to a policy of stocking only the most frequently demanded items of the family grocery budget, with the constraint that the items have a speedy turnover and a high unit margin. Surveys of some of the chains show the proportion of items carried in each subcategory.

TABLE 3
Types of Items Carried

Convenience Store (Typical)

Total	2,000 to 3,000 items
Grocery	48 to 53%
Nonfoods	19 to 23%
HaBa *	12 to 15%
Baked goods	2 to 4%
Dairy	3 to 5%
Meat	1 to 3%
Frozen goods	1 to 3%
Produce	1 to 2%

* HaBa = Health and beauty aids.

TABLE 4
What Convenience Stores Sell

Product	% Handling	Product	% Handling
Bread	100%	Ladies' hosiery	75%
Butter	100	Soft goods	70
Cheese	100	Ice cubes	60
Eggs	100	Radio tubes	60
Milk	100	TV tubes	60
Soft drinks	100	Pet rack	60
Lunch meats, pkg.	100	Greeting cards	60
Health and beauty aids	100	Produce, packaged	55
Tobacco	100	Garden supplies	45
Frozen foods	98	Gourmet foods	45
Light bulbs	98	Records	40
Stationery	95	Fresh poultry, pkg.	35
Beer	90	Wine	27
Baked foods	90	Fresh red meats, pkg.	25
Produce, bulk	87	Liquor	18
Toys	87	Fresh seafood, pkg.	15
Frozen seafood, pkg.	85	Small appliances	15
Housewares	82	Fresh poultry, service	4
Frozen poultry, pkg.	75	Fresh red meats, service	4
Frozen red meats, pkg.	75	Fresh seafood, service	4
Candy, boxed	75		

Over 80 percent of the items are in the following categories: "grocery," "nonfoods," and "HaBa." Most of these items are delivered to the store prepackaged, and goods handling and preparing is cut down to a minimum in order to save on labor costs. This is the basic reason why so few produce, meat, baked and frozen items are carried in convenience stores. Perishables involve higher costs both in labor and equipment, and profit contribution is generally not worth the extra cost involved in carrying them. Even when perishables are carried, they are usually prepackaged at the warehouse or central distributing plant.

On the average, a supermarket has four to five times as many items as a convenience store, the quantity varying in difference from as much as 15 times more in the produce section to one to five times as much in the nonfoods section. Thus, the choice of inventory is a critical one for the convenience store and one which requires much skill and judgment, both in terms of the item's contribution to net profit and as it relates to the tastes and values of the neighborhood customers.

The details of contribution of items to total weekly sales are interesting. A 1967 study published in Progressive Grocer reveals the figures in Table 5 and Table 6. The grocery department contributes over 60 percent of the sales dollar for only 50 percent of total items, while the dairy department, with 12 percent of total sales, makes up only 5 percent of total items.

TABLE 5
Contribution to Total Sales (Weekly)

Total Store (Average)	$3,292.5	100.0%
Grocery	$1,995.9	60.7%
Dairy	385.6	11.7%
Baked goods	272.0	8.3%
Meat	178.5	5.4%
Produce	29.0	.9%

However, it should be kept in mind that soft drinks are included in the dairy department, and there is no breakdown of grocery items, which includes beer and nonfoods, for instance. The actual "Top 10" best sellers, contributing 64 percent of total sales, were as follows:

TABLE 6
"Top 10" Best Sellers

Beer (all brands)	$ 561	
Cigarettes	399	
Soft drinks	206	
HaBa	175	
Milk	160	
Candy	159	
Bread	153	
Snacks	135	
Ice cream (etc.)	107	
Sandwiches	73	
Total	$2,128	64% (80% of total profit)

VI. Operating Information

Convenience stores operate on more generous margins than do supermarkets, largely because they can charge higher prices for the convenience component of their sales; while the range of margins on products in supermarkets is 5.5 percent to 34.8 percent, the range in convenience stores is 23.8 percent to 42 percent. The price differentials between convenience stores and supermarkets are varied but, if prices differ, they are almost always greater in convenience stores. The range is as follows:

TABLE 7
Range of Price Differentials—Convenience Stores and Supermarkets

	Convenience stores	Supermarkets	Differentials
Coffee (regular) (lb.)	99¢	79¢	20¢
Ice cream (gal.)	—	—	10¢
Ice cream (qt.)	—	—	10¢
Cola (6-pack, 10 oz.)	59¢	49¢	10¢
Flour (2 lb.)	43¢	31¢	12¢
Baked beans (16 oz.)	25¢	19¢	6¢
Cigarettes (king, filter)	35¢	30¢	5¢
Bread (regular)	29¢	27¢	2¢
Milk (qt.)	31¢	31¢	—

Margin comparisons reveal quite startling differences. Table 8 shows these in terms of "penny profits" per dollar ($) of sales, per item sold by major departments:

TABLE 8
Penny Profit Differentials

	Convenience stores	Supermarkets	Differentials
Frozen foods	17.0¢	9.7¢	+7.3¢
Dairy	10.9¢	6.1¢	+4.8¢
Nonfoods	13.2¢	17.3¢	−4.1¢
Produce	9.4¢	5.4¢	+4.0¢
Baked goods	7.1¢	5.4¢	+1.7¢
Meat	16.6¢	15.1¢	+1.5¢
Grocery	7.8¢	6.3¢	+1.5¢
Average	8.9¢	7.4¢	+1.5¢

The operating ratios for a typical convenience store are thus some-what different than for the supermarket. These data are derived from Progressive Grocer's 1968 Annual Retail Survey. The survey shows the following:

TABLE 9
Operating Ratios for Convenience Stores

	(Averages)	
Total annual sales	$150,000	
Average gross margin	25.4%	
Operating expenses (costs)	−20.2%	
Other overhead	− 1.5%	
Net other income	+ .3%	
Total income before taxes	= 4.0%	
Taxes	1.8%	
Net income	= 2.2%	($3,300)

Measures of productivity are less important in these small scale op-erations than in supermarkets. In general, labor productivity is low because of the long business hours involved. The typical store re-quires at least 250 man hours per week to operate; sales per man-hour are seldom more than $4. Sales per square foot average between $1 and $2, again much lower than in the supermarket industry. Sales per transaction average about $0.90 to $1.25, again a low figure com-pared to supermarket averages. An interesting comparison, however, is in terms of sales per customer shopping time in the store. For supermarkets the average time is 22 minutes, and average purchases equal $5.75, 26 cents per minute. For convenience stores the average time is 4 minutes and $1.07, an average of 27 cents per minute, al-most identical to the supermarket.

VII. Ownership and Franchising

Of the approximately 14,000 convenience stores now in operation, about 15 percent are owned by individual small companies (with less than 10 stores each), 65 percent by corporations (mostly large chains) and 20 percent are franchised. Because of reduced risk and higher profitability, the trend is towards franchise and away from corporate ownership; almost all the large chains are turning toward the fran-chising method.

One typical chain is corporation-owned, highly neighborhood-oriented, with stores of fairly large size (up to 6,000 square ft.) which are open 7 days per week for 16 hours per day. The average manager is 36 years old. He has between three and six employees. Supervision by the corporation is exercised by intensive training of the manager, a target of "profitability after 1 year," and a long-range goal of $250,000 sales per year. Monthly goals are also set. Strict productivity orientation is typical.

A major franchising operation features store sizes of 50 feet by 50 feet with 12 parking spaces. The stores carry an inventory of 3,000 nationally advertised items. These stores are open from 7 a.m. to 12 midnight and return an average profit of 3½ percent (net before taxes). The firm reports that a typical franchisee makes $17,000 per year from his operation. Total franchisee investment is about $25,000 (though only one quarter of this has to be in the form of a cash down-payment). The franchising costs after the initial investment are:

> 1% of gross sales for royalties;
>
> 2% of gross sales for services (legal, accounting, supervision, business training and help);
>
> 1% of gross sales for advertising (including a grand opening and the distribution of 2,000 hand-bills per week in the neighborhood).

Another franchising operation operates on a similar basis. However, in this case, the typical franchisee investment is $13,400, which is broken down as follows:

Inventory	$11,000
Deposit	1,600
Cash register	200
Supplies	400
License	200
Total	$13,400

In this case the company does not supply the equipment, which must be provided by the franchisee.

Experience in food retailing is a valuable ingredient in the profitable convenience store. A new entrepreneur may find that, for $3,000 to $10,000 in basic franchise fees, he can enter in partnership with a successful food retailing operation. It is strongly recommended, however, that the prospective entrepreneur obtain actual store management experience before entering into a franchise agreement or acquiring a store of his own.

VIII. Starting a New Operation

The individual attempting to start a new convenience store operation in the inner city should attempt to find an appropriate location first. An elaborate statistical survey is not absolutely necessary, but inspection of the proposed neighborhood should be made to learn:

a. The number of people within a short walking distance of the proposed location;

b. The amount of competition, particularly from stores that will be selling the same kinds of items during the same hours of operation;

c. The quality of the competition, in terms of number of items carried, appearance of store, number of hours open, etc.

Small commercial space which might be available in connection with new housing in the inner city may be ideal for the establishment of a convenience store.

The potential businessman should investigate the various franchising, cooperative, and voluntary wholesale organizations he might join. A careful study should be made of the advantages of each, the special services each provides, and the cost.

Before deciding whether or not to affiliate with an organization, he should determine detailed financing requirements, particularly for franchise fees, equipment, and inventory. If a lease guarantee is required this should be noted, too. This material, along with a detailed analysis of the proposed site, should be assembled and discussed with local banks or development organizations specializing in providing financial and technical assistance for the purpose of promoting minority enterprises. Many of these organizations can help direct qualified applicants to sources of financing. Potential applicants can demonstrate their qualifications by the care and thoroughness with which they prepare their preliminary studies and estimates and by the amount of their own funds they are willing to invest in the proposed venture.

It should be recognized by the new entrepreneur that successful convenience stores usually require 6 to 12 months to break even and about 2 years for profitable operations. Enough financing is needed for the new store so that initial operating losses can be adequately covered without impairing service.

PET SHOPS

I. Recommendation

The successful operation of a pet shop that satisfies the needs of pet owners and animals alike requires a strong liking for animals, a knowledge of their characteristics, and managerial competence. Individuals wishing to enter the pet shop industry in an entrepreneurial capacity should also bring considerable experience in the industry to their new business.

There are good prospects for success in the industry if it is located in the suburbs of a metropolitan area where pet ownership is the greatest. The new entrepreneur must be technically competent, willing to perform occasionally undesirable maintenance tasks, and able to keep abreast of the new trends in the industry, particularly as related to his trading area's demands. The risks in the industry can be minimized if the pet shop owner clearly defines and analyzes his market, keeps good inventory records to establish a pattern for stock turnover, and utilizes the many resources of advice available to him.

II. Description

A. Identification

Retail pet shops are classified under Standard Industrial Classification (SIC) 5999 which encompasses miscellaneous retail stores not elsewhere classified. Retail pet shops are involved in the sale of pets and pet products including food and accessories. They may also offer grooming services. Other segments of the pet industry which are not described in this profile include pet breeders, wholesalers and distributors, manufacturers of pet products, veterinarians, and trainers. Pets and pet products are sold at retail by independent pet shops including franchise operators, department stores, chainstores, discount stores, and variety stores. This profile will be specifically concerned with the operation of a retail pet business by an independent entrepreneur operating either under his own name or under a franchise.

B. Dimensions

There are now an estimated 12.5 million American households with one or more dogs and 5.3 million with at least one cat. The estimated dog population is 25 to 28 million, the cat population about 33 million, and the fish population about 300 million, with each type of pet having particular needs that may be met by the pet store. It is estimated that eight million households have birds—75 percent of which are parakeets. The industry has shown continued growth, especially in the area of pet supplies. In 1970, owners spent about $3 billion on their pets—almost three times as much as they spent in 1960.

A most important part of business is an analysis of future trends in the area of interest. Currently there is a strong demand for pets, pet foods, and accessories, with a high probability of bringing good profits to the owners of pet shops.

The demand for particular pets, such as dogs, cats, birds, and fish, always has existed, but the rate of demand is increasing rapidly. Tropical fish are a good example of people's desire to own pets. One of the largest tropical fish farmers in the world shipped over 20 million tropical fish throughout the United States last year, and his records reflect that his output doubled in the span of 3 years. Industry experts report that tropical fish have become America's second largest hobby, behind photography. There are about 15 percent more hobbyists yearly, with the number now exceeding 20 million.

Other factors reflect the growth potential for the pet industry. Research and development departments of pet shop supply manufacturers and supermarkets are placing heavy emphasis on pets in their projections for the next 15 years. Supermarket studies have led to conclusions indicative of the anticipated pet population growth. Grocery industry statistics indicate that retail sales of cat and dog foods have climbed from $600 million in 1965 to $1 billion in 1969. Pet products as a category of goods stocked by grocery stores has been one of the standout performers in the past 5 years. Projections show that in the next 5 years pet products will be among the top four grocery categories in terms of annual tonnage sales gains.

What are the external influences affecting growth? One of the primary causes may be found outside the pet industry itself—in the continuous growth and expansion of the American economy. Population is expected to rise to 213 million in the United States by 1975 and 225.5 million by 1980. Demographic data indicate that urbanization (settlement in areas with populations of 50,000 and over) will be the trend. The A. C. Nielsen Company estimates that, of the 26 million additional consumers expected by 1980, 20 million new residents will settle in metropolitan areas including city suburbs. Since the pet ownership tendency is greatest in these areas (with 50 percent of pet owners living there), this growth means a sales market with great potential.

Disposable income, too, is expected to grow rapidly, reaching over $1 trillion in the United States by 1980, nearly double the 1968 figure of $588 billion. This trend has led Progressive Grocer to say that "more people plus more people moving to cities and suburbs plus more money to spend equals more pets."

Market data such as the above indicate that the pet industry is well established, yet has plenty of growth potential. The business establishments that service this market demand reflect these characteristics. In 1967 the Census of Manufactures indicated that there were between 4,500 and 6,000 pet shops in the country, with about 300 new shops being added to the industry annually. More recently, a trade publication entitled Pets/Supplies/Marketing Magazine indicated that there were over 8,500 retail pet supply outlets in operation with an even higher outlet growth rate. The exact value of annual industry receipts is not known to the Census of Manufactures. The approximate value of industry receipts can be gauged, however, by the fact that the annual sales volume of the retail pet store usually ranges from $40,000 to $175,000, with some stores reaching $1.5 million.

The retail pet shop has become a more specialized operation in the past decade. There are still a great many stores that carry a wide variety of pets and accessories, but large numbers of pet shops specializing in dogs and fish have sprung up to fill the demand for these types of pets. Some shops also emphasize grooming services as well. The growth of specialty shops is closely related to increasing customer interest in knowledgeable advice and a wide range of products and services for their favorite pets.

C. Characteristics

1. Nature of the Product

What do pet stores offer? The product as described consists of pets, nonprescription medications, accessory items, recommendations as to the purchasing and care of pets, and possibly grooming. The stock of the store will obviously depend upon whether the store is of the all-inclusive type or is a specialty store. The average all-inclusive store will have the following breakdown of pets on the basis of average volume of sales:

Dogs	30%	Fish	25%
Cats	15%	Miscellaneous	10%
Birds	20%		

Pets tend to satisfy human needs for companionship, love, education (especially on the part of children), and protection. Pet shop owners address themselves, consequently, to a combination of the needs of the pets and the needs of the owners or prospective buyers. Through the understanding of the needs of both a pet and its owner, a pet shop owner develops the essential expertise to allow him to recommend suitable animals for his customers and suitable products for the pets' needs.

The animal's need for the food and nonprescription medicines dispensed by a pet shop are obvious. The fact that the so-called pet toys are a necessary part of an animal's life is perhaps less evident. Toys fulfill the absolute necessity of providing the animals with a form of recreation and exercise, particularly essential to those city animals kept indoors for so many hours every day. Most owners of pets buy their products on impulse, through seeing a particularly appealing item in the display window or on the shelves in the sales area. (Hence the need for good advertising, a well-organized store, and knowledgeable personnel.)

Although many items are necessary to the health of a pet, they are actually not regularly purchased items, primarily because of the durability of the equipment (cages, aquariums, animal houses, and beds) and because of the irregular and often seasonal occurrence of many of the diseases. Food is perhaps the most regular sales article, although it constitutes only about 12 percent of the receipts of the average pet store. Most larger stores carry a complete variety of pet foods for dogs, cats, birds, fish, and other small pets. Dry foods and pet "treats" are usually the particular specialty of the pet shop, however, and the vast bulk of retail pet foods is sold in volume through grocery stores and other food outlets.

The pet business, despite recent progress in stabilizing sales levels through the addition of products and the emphasis on pet care, is still a seasonal one. The two slowest months are July and August, and sales usually peak around the Christmas season.

The services rendered by pet shops obviously depend upon whether the shop is of the all-inclusive type or is a specialty store. In all of them, however, most of the business is conducted when customers come into browse, although those businesses that have branched into grooming do business by appointment. The technique most often used in promotion is the placing of stock in the display windows. Cleverly arranged windows will attract the attention of passersby. Customers will continue to patronize a store only if they see that the animals are well cared for and healthy and if they receive sound advice from the personnel on first aid products, foods, accessories, and pet care in general. Only through this personalized service can pet shops compete with the grocery stores and chainstores, which offer similar products at a lower price but on an impersonal basis.

2. Nature of the Customer

The wide distribution of pets among our population and the strong growth rate in the industry suggest a fairly broad base of market demand to support the business of new pet shops. The key influences on consumer purchases of pets and pet supplies, however, include place of residence, household size, income, and emotional factors.

a. Place of Residence

Over 50 percent of all pet owners live in suburban areas, and these owners spend the largest amount of money per family on their pets, according to a 1965 Stanford Research Institute study of the pet industry. Within Standard Metropolitan Statistical Areas, a steadily increasing percentage of families spend money on pets as the distance from the center of the SMSA increases.

The types of dwellings that characterize an area are another important influence on the area's market demand for pets and pet products. Families living in single-family detached dwellings are almost twice as likely to own dogs as persons living in apartments, for instance. The following figures illustrate dog ownership by type of dwelling and by population size of city in which the owner lives:

	500,000 or more	50,000-500,000	under 50,000
Multiple-type	16%	24%	26%
Single-family	34%	40%	49%

The spread between the types of dwellings is not so noticeable for cats and most other animals, since apartment living lends itself better to the smaller and quieter pets.

There are also variations in pet ownership among the several regions of the country. The South has the highest number of dogs per capita and has correspondingly high numbers of other animals. The north-central and northeast regions follow closely behind the South in the extent of pet ownership.

b. Income and Households

According to a 1965 Stanford Research Institute study on pet products, the proportion of households owning pets tends to rise fairly rapidly as incomes rise to the lower middle income level, when it appears to flatten out. Average expenditures of pet owners, however, continue to climb with income, thus indicating a greater expenditure per animal in the middle and upper income levels.

Consumer units with after-tax incomes under $6,000 account for only approximately 25 percent of total expenditures on pets, though accounting for over 50 percent of total consumer spending units.

Consumer units with after-tax incomes of $10,000 and over account for over 35 percent of total pet spending, but less than 20 percent of all consumer spending units.

Studies regarding the unmarried consumer reveal that aggregate spending is lowest for this group, being only about 6 percent of the total.

Per capita ownership of pets is highest in families of over two persons, while average expenditures on pets are highest in families of only two persons. Aggregate spending by families of two persons accounts for about 29 percent of the total and by families of more than two persons, 65 percent. The over-65 families account for less than 10 percent of total expenditures.

The rising affluence of the consumer, the need for apartment-adaptable pets, and a certain quest for status among many pet owners have created a trend toward exotic pets. Monkeys, ocelots, snakes, margays, and other such animals are gaining popularity, and other small animals are being added to the stock of the larger pet stores and specialty shops every year. These animals are particularly useful as an attraction for the street-side display windows of the shop.

The minimum population required to sustain an average pet shop or a full-line pet shop is 20,000. All other factors being equal, profit will rise with increase in population. (Exceptions to the rule have been found, of course. Those pet shops supplying exotic pets have been known to attract customers from many miles away.)

Several factors must usually be considered in establishing a retail pet outlet. Since over 50 percent of all pet owners live in suburban areas, it is usually best to establish in areas with this high population concentration or in areas with a potential for population expansion. The urban-oriented pet shop may best be located in a business area bordering on the residential sector. Residential areas of apartment buildings are not good site selections in general, however, because most apartment buildings do not allow pets. In small communities, the main street is desirable; in large cities shopping center pet shops are most popular. In fact, a clean, odor-free pet shop is an asset to a shopping center, largely because it attracts additional pedestrian traffic and generates impulse buying. Also, because of new techniques for creating odor-free, soundproof shops, it is sometimes possible to lease space from a department store and create a pet shop as a department within the store. (Pet shops selling both pets and accessories are usually placed in the back of the department store because they will generate interest on their own behalf and will attract customers through other parts of the store. Those offering only accessory items are placed in the front because their drawing power is not nearly as great.) In any event, it is a prerequisite to check with State and local licensing and zoning regulations to make certain pet shops and the related services are allowed.

Loyalty is usually based on services rendered, congeniality and knowledgeability of staff, location convenience, and atmosphere of store. Customers patronize pet shops where they get good professional service and advice. Therefore, pet shops with a strong, reliable reputation can survive in an out-of-the-way location. A new shop, however, in an out-of-the-way place will take longer to develop.

Understanding the market, the types of customers, their needs and reactions, and the factors surrounding location are all important. Also important is the need for comprehension of the necessary "technological" skills.

3. TECHNOLOGY

The manpower requirements of a pet shop will to some extent be dictated by the size and orientation of the establishment and its services. The owner of a pet shop must be extremely knowledgeable about all the animals he sells, for not only will he be responsible for the business management, but he will also be providing advice and consultation to his customers. The owner will be considered the expert on all matters of health care. Thus, it is necessary that the owner have some background or experience. A 1969 survey showed that the average pet shop dealer had 9 years of experience in the trade and 8 years as an owner of a shop. The pet shop owner should have a working arrangement with a local veterinarian, and obedience school, and a boarding kennel, the former to care for the health of the pets, and the latter two to recommend to customers.

The pet store manager may be able to obtain needed information about pets or operating practices by contacting pet journals for reprints on specialized topics. These reprint services often can provide useful knowledge to the manager on a wide variety of pet subjects.

Most pet shops are open Monday through Saturday including evenings (approximately 51-55 hours per week). Some shops are open on Sundays, but surveys in the trade show that Sundays are not as desirable as evening hours. Part-time employees are needed in staggered shifts to feed animals and clean cages and maintain the sales area. Knowledgeable employees are important to the store, since there must always be one employee available to answer questions and to give advice and service. The part-time employees must like animals and should have over-the-counter sales experience.

If grooming services are offered, a trained groomer must be affiliated with the shop. Grooming services consist of brushing to remove snarls and matting, clipping to obtain a pattern, shampooing and drying, reclipping to smooth off the animal, and a general scissor cut. In addition, many groomers will clean ears and clip toenails. The art of grooming has long been in existence. It was practiced in kennels and by local veterinarians, and in rural areas it is still these industries that are almost exclusively responsible for grooming. The vast majority of grooming establishments or pet shops with grooming facilities are located in the city or nearby suburbs. Many established groomers received their background as dog show exhibitors or by grooming neighborhood dogs.

The rise of the poodle in popularity precipitated the trend towards grooming salons or facilities within pet shops. As the demand rose for groomers, a demand for training facilities was created. Today, there are at least 10 groomers' schools in the country. Licensing for groomers is at this time an almost meaningless term. In many areas licensing is not required, and in those areas where it is, there are few standards. An emphasis on professionalism within the industry is increasing, however, and licensing of only proficient groomers appears to be the standard being sought by trade associations and pet owners.

The locational determinants for grooming shops are the same as for pet shops in general—population and, to a lesser extent, income. Grooming can be a factor to induce buying of other merchandise in a pet store. Its attraction is not as strong a factor as window displays and other forms of promotion, however.

Competition in grooming takes place on the basis of quality and proficiency in work. It is the opinion of one grooming establishment that there are never enough groomers for the demand and that the internal competition only reinforces quality.

Charges for services vary from area to area. They are based on the breed of dog, size of dog, type of cut needed, labor (time required to do the job), and markup to cover overhead.

There are ample opportunities for ownership of pet shops among men and women of all educational levels. A husband and wife combination is very popular and common in the ownership of pet shops.

4. COMPETITION

The rapid growth in market demand for pets and pet products has created a large number of retail outlets and a wide variety among them. In addition to the approximately 8,500 retail stores (either independent or franchised) in the industry, there are at least 4,000 "pet departments" in variety, discount, and department stores. About 90 percent of discount-type stores have pet departments. Variety and discount stores are expected to handle an increasing share of nonfood pet products. Grocery stores also play an important role in the pet industry. Between 75 percent and 85 percent of all dog and cat foods are now marketed through grocery stores. Over 10 different varieties of foods are currently offered to the consumer, and research and development departments are constantly finding new ways to improve what is offered and enlarge upon the scope of prepared pet foods.

The retail pet industry is dominated by the independent proprietorship. Franchises are available from any of the 12 pet store franchises listed in appendix B, but franchises have not made the inroads in the pet industry that they have in certain other lines of business. The pet industry includes several strong wholesalers, and the Pet Industry Distributors Association includes wholesaler members from around the country. Both wholesalers and franchisers are likely to be a valuable source of information to the prospective pet store owner.

The franchise is a fairly popular new vehicle for entry into the pet industry. The better franchises offer assistance to the new entrepreneur in planning, display, and inventory purchase and control. Some franchisers provide brief training courses to new franchisees and place franchiser staff members in the new store to assist the franchisee in hiring and training staff, ordering inventory, and coordinating the events leading up to and immediately following the store's opening. Another common form of franchise assistance is the assumption by the franchiser of the advertising responsibilities of the local franchisee.

The possible disadvantage of a franchise, however, may reduce its appeal to some entrepreneurs. Franchise fees may range as high as $60,000 (for those franchises which provide plant, equipment, and retail inventory), and the relatively limited line product of most franchisers that their franchisees are obligated to market occasionally prevents the store manager from appealing to the particular needs of his local market.

Competition among these outlets is based on price, service, quality, and types of products offered and developed. The independent pet store, which handles over 60 percent of the total volume in non-food pet products, has encountered competition from other retail outlets, particularly the variety stores. The smaller stores are the ones hardest hit, and penetration of their share of the market is likely to continue. The well-run, well-stocked, and innovative pet stores will continue to benefit from the interest in the pet industry. Tropical fish shops and dog specialty stores, above all, will continue to reflect buoyant growth.

5. EASE OF ENTRY

The retail pet industry has few barriers to entry for the prospective entrepreneur. There are, however, several special factors, in addition to a thorough review of the pet market in the several areas of potential location, that the new pet entrepreneur must consider before opening for business. One of the most important hurdles for the new entrepreneur to clear is the establishment of a satisfactory working relationship with the regional pet supply wholesaler. These wholesalers can often be helpful to the person interested in owning a pet shop by suggesting good locations for a store, and they usually offer valuable advice to the new manager on inventory matters. The wholesaler can thus be a valuable resource of information to the retailer as well as the source of appealing and attractive pets and supplies.

Licensing and locational requirements vary from area to area, but the State requirements are similar. One must obtain the usual vendor's license, consult the local health department about its requirements, and inquire as to the zoning ordinances of the area.

Currently, however, some States are considering the enactment of laws in the sphere of the pet industry for the protection of public health. California is perhaps a forerunner in this cause, having imposed quarantines on the South American monkey (raising their cost to the consumer by 200 percent), outlawed the sale and display of piranhas, and required all cats sold in pet stores to be altered. At the present time, the State legislature is considering placing temporary quarantine restrictions on any animal brought from outside the United States. The longrun ramifications of such restrictions will definitely be seen in the cost of ordering, maintaining, and selling these animals.

Another potential drawback to entry might stem from qualified personnel. Part-time staff is essential to the small pet shops, and the costs of training people can be great if turnover is high.

6. FINANCING

There are three types of capital requirements for establishing a pet shop of any description:

    a. equipment and fixtures,
    b. basic inventory,
    c. working capital.

Total shop investment typically runs $15,000, $22,000, and $30,000 for small (22 by 60 feet), medium (50 by 60 feet), and large (60 by 90 feet) shops, respectively.

The average dealer in 1969 spent $20,000 for livestock. The average markup for livestock is 50 to 55 percent. This covers care and feeding of the animals and the high risk of animals becoming ill. The average small pet dealer spends about $250 per month in rent. A breakdown of earnings conducted by the trade in 1968 indicates that, for every dollar of sales, 65 percent goes into new inventory and 35 percent into operating expenses and profit.

To finance such a business one may utilize such sources of funds as personal acquaintances, banks, lending establishments, and the Small Business Administration. There are no special sources of financing for those interested in pet shops. When dealing with a franchise, the franchise company may arrange for financing part of the business.

7. PROFITABILITY

There are many factors that affect pet industry profitability—location, population, size of shop, whether it is all-inclusive or a specialty shop, managerial expertise, types of stock will all affect the profit potential. Estimates have been projected by the Small Business Administration (SBA), however, that may provide a general picture of the annual sales over a 15-year period (assuming continuance of the growth rate prevalent in the late 1960's):

	Small	Medium	Large
First year	$30,000	$45,000	$ 55,000
Second year	36,000	55,000	65,000
Third year	48,000	65,000	80,000
Fourth year	55,000	75,000	95,000
Fifth year	60,000	85,000	110,000

Factors other than annual sales projections suggest the high profit potential associated with the pet shop industry. The average gross margin for the industry is 66.66 percent, a relatively high figure for retail businesses. The fact that the average inventory turnover in the industry is five to seven times yearly is indicative of the fact that there is a frequent return of cash to the business.

III. Feasibility Analysis

A. Review of Key Factors

The following factors are essential to the successful operation of a pet shop:

1. Management

The owner/manager of a pet shop should possess both technical competence and experience. Experience is recommended in both an apprenticeship role and a managerial role, with a 9-year background experience being the average in the industry. Extensive knowledge of the products with which he is dealing, precise identification of his market, a good rapport with the wholesaler and breeders with whom he deals are all prerequisites to success. Some of the most successful new pet shops are managed by younger pet fanciers with a business background.

2. Market

A very specific market should be identified to assure feasibility. A sound pet shop market is the following:

a. An area with a population of at least 50,000 is considered to be the best location for a pet shop. Interviews with wholesalers can help identify the existence and magnitude of the market. Predictions should be made regarding the future of the area.

b. Competition in the area must be carefully judged, remembering that a minimum population of 20,000 is essential to support a pet shop and an aquarium store. Competition for this market will come from department stores and discount shops as well as pet shops.

3. Location
Single-family dwelling units as the norm, as opposed to apartments or multiple-family units, are preferred since the highest pet ownership concentration and tendency are found in this category. Some of the most successful pet shops are located in shopping centers or malls with considerable customer traffic, since the pet shop depends heavily on "impulse" sales.

4. Service
The pet shop must offer sound advice to the customer on the care of pets. It must offer a high level of personal service by both the owner and the employees. The atmosphere must be one of cleanliness and orderliness, the latter so that the customer, who often buys on impulse, may see the full range of products offered.

B. Projections of Attainable Returns in the Pet Industry
Two common forms of participation in the pet industry have been portrayed below to represent the financial returns available to a pet shop owner.

Franchise Store

The hypothetical franchisee is required to have a minimum capital investment of $60,000, which includes leasehold improvements, fixtures, equipment, and $25,000 of retail inventory. Of this $60,000, the owner's cash requirement is $30,000, the balance to be financed through a Small Business Administration loan or an SBA guaranteed bank loan. The franchiser requires a training program and provides technical advice continually through each step in setting up the operation. The location selected is a suburban shopping center where the target market is a middle to upper income level area with the population residing primarily in single-family dwellings. An "exclusivity clause" is included in the lease to prevent another pet shop from leasing store space in the shopping center. The shop has 2,000 square feet of selling space and a frontage display window running the length of the shop, which faces the main walking concourse for maximum exposure. The store stocks a variety of livestock including puppies, kittens, birds, tropical fish, and exotic animals. The inventory includes a variety of pet supplies. Livestock and supplies are purchased from the franchise company, which offers higher discounts off list price than can be obtained through local wholesalers.

Projections for the 1st year are made on the basis of facts known about the industry.

First-year operating projections are as follows:

Net sales		$250,000	100.0%
Cost of goods sold		112,500	45.0
Gross margin		137,500	55.0
Operating expenses		125,000	50.0
Rent	$10,000		4.0%
Payroll	65,000		26.0
Advertising	15,000		6.0
Maintenance	10,000		4.0
Supplies	3,750		1.5
Telephone and utilities	3,750		1.5
Other	11,250		4.5
Loan interest and amortization	6,250		2.5
Net profit before taxes		$ 12,500	5.0%

Small, Independent Store

An investment of $20,000 is made in a small pet store operation. Financing is accomplished through $10,000 in owner's equity and $10,000 from an SBA guaranteed commercial bank loan. The store selected has 1,000 square feet of selling space and is located among a group of five other small businesses on the fringe of a downtown business district and the edge of a middle to upper income residential area. The store's front display windows are located on either side of the entrance and have been fixtured for displaying exotic animals rather than the more conventional livestock. The store's inventory includes puppies, kittens, birds, and tropical fish. It emphasizes its collection of exotic animals, however, as well as a variety of pet supplies.

Good trade relations have been established with two local wholesalers for pet supplies and livestock. The livestock wholesaler was selected and contacted particularly because of the rare types of animals he is able to obtain. Both have extended trade credit. Other livestock and supply wholesalers are used as needed to fill occasional inventory needs.

Some additional problems in fixtures have to be dealt with because of the unusual types of animals stocked. Four additional employees are required, three to help with sales and the handling of the animals and a fourth to care for the animals. Finding trainable staff experienced in handling a variety of animals poses a problem and is expected to entail a slightly higher wage expense. A fairly large amount of advertising in local newspapers, radio, and the regional shopping advertiser is planned, especially in the 1st year, to inform the public about the store and its interesting collection of unusual animals.

First-year operating projections are as follows:

Net sales	$100,000	100.0%
Cost of goods sold	47,000	47.0
Gross margin	53,000	53.0
Operating expenses	48,000	48.0

Rent	$ 6,000	6.0%
Payroll	23,000	23.0
Advertising	8,000	8.0
Maintenance	2,000	2.0
Supplies	1,500	1.5
Telephone and utilities	2,000	2.0
Other	4,000	4.0
Loan interest and amortization	2,000	2.0

Net profit before taxes	$ 4,500	4.5%

IV. Establishing the Business

A. Approaching the Market

Whether the potential entrepreneur is contemplating a franchise or a small, independent pet shop, he should have a precise definition of his market, substantiated by interviews with wholesalers and a "drive-through" tour of the potential site in order to pinpoint potential competition.

The approaches to the prospective market must be based on local customer needs, both real and potential. Inventory based on demands of the chosen trading area must be readily available and logically displayed. Most wholesalers will be glad to assist the new store in the selection of initial inventory. The selection of a local prime wholesaler, therefore, may provide valuable marketing information to the new dealer.

Advertising, as well as personal service, will contribute to the success of the stores. It has been estimated that pet shops have spent 3 to 8 percent of their annual sales volume for advertising Costs obviously will vary, depending upon the dealer's selection of media.

Newspaper ads are the most widely used form of advertising. Some pet shops take advantage of dealer ad mats and co-op advertising from the manufacturers. Other devices suggested are the tailoring of ads to seasons and holidays and the reutilization of particularly successful ads. Many pet shops advertise in the classified section in the "Pet" column. They may also run large ads for promotional events, i.e., pets for special holiday gifts or announcements of new animals.

Advertising in the Yellow Pages has proven to be an effective means of making all pet services known to the customer when he is ready to buy. The Yellow Pages have the advantage of reaching outlying communities to achieve full coverage of the trading area.

Radio and limited television spots are becoming more and more popular with businesses of all forms and have proved particularly beneficial to pet shops located in a tourist area during the vacation season (since more and more people are traveling with their pets). Time contracts provide a dealer with an easy, effective way to save money on spot radio advertising and guarantee special times for the broadcasts (which helps build up the recall value of the business with listeners).

A unique form of promotion is available to pet shop owners because they have access to unusual animals. An exotic animal or a group of puppies in the window is the best method of attracting customers into the store.

Some pet shops have built promotional strategies around the offering of community services—having school children, scout troops, and similar groups visit the pet shop to learn about various kinds of animals and their care.

B. Requirements

1. Space—Interior

The minimum square footage requirement for a small pet shop is 1,320; 5,000 to 6,000 for a large one. The store must provide for window display space facing onto a street or concourse. Most pet shops are arranged with one main display and sales area visible from the street through the window. Some of the new and larger stores have separate rooms for various groups of animals.

If grooming services are offered, a small room to the side or in the back must be available. There must also be a storage space for stock and cleaning equipment, as well as for food for the animals in the shop. A new pet shop, in order to compete successfully, must be well-lit, extremely clean, and odor free. Excellent ventilation is essential; in most locations, central air-conditioning is a must.

2. Space—Exterior

A carefully planned window display with frontage on a heavily traveled pedestrian way is the most important requirement for exterior space. Parking facilities are desirable but do not necessarily have to be adjacent to or in front of the store. Municipal parking provisions will be satisfactory. Access to pedestrian traffic is most important for pet shops, as it is for any business catering to impulse buying.

Outdoor space is not required for an urban retail store. Zoning ordinances in most cities and suburbs prohibit commercial kennels, thus automatically eliminating the need for outdoor space.

3. Equipment

Minimum capital equipment needs for the sales and display area would include the following:

> Animals: Dogs, cats, birds, tropical fish and aquatic animals, small pets such as hamsters, gerbils, and any of the more exotic animals desired.

> Food, clothing, and grooming accessories for these pets.
> Cleaning equipment.
> Refrigerator for perishables.
> Tropical fish tanks with aeration pumps.
> Goldfish tanks with running water.
> Heating and lighting equipment for fish tanks.
> Cages for animals and birds.
> Display gondolas.
> Tables, stands, and display shelves.

Supplies for a grooming area would include:

> Bathtub with adjustable water flow and spray hose.
> Grooming table.
> Galvanized iron or stainless steel cages.
> Electric clippers, scissors, combs, brushes, etc.
> Shampoo, towels, electric dryers, etc.

Advice on equipment and display may often be obtained from the wholesaler or distributor. He should be able to arrange for the prospective entrepreneur to visit some other retail shops he supplies to see how they stock merchandise or arrange displays. The trade journals give advice about equipment and provide directories of wholesalers of both animals and stock items. Information on associations, franchisers, and trade shows is contained in the appendices.

C. Obtaining Requisite Financing

The best sources for start-up capital for the new pet shop are personal savings, funds supplied by acquaintances, loans through banks, the Small Business Administration, or the franchises. There is also credit available to the entrepreneur through his wholesaler. Trade credit is a good way to finance open inventory. There are no known special sources of capital for new minority pet shop owners.

D. Employing a Labor Force

Employing a labor force specifically equipped to deal with the animals is sometimes difficult. Since most of the pet shops need part-time help, it is perhaps advisable to locate in an area where there will be students (who constitute the majority of part-time employees in pet shops). This will insure a fairly reliable source of labor, although the turnover is relatively high.

PHOTOGRAPHIC STUDIOS

I. RECOMMENDATION

A variety of opportunities exist for individuals to participate in the sizeable growth of the photographic industry. One of the most accessible opportunities for industry participation is as the owner-manager of a photographic studio that does portrait work for individuals or general photographic work for organizations and commercial enterprises. The photographer who opens such a studio has the opportunity to realize both a high degree of professional satisfaction and an attractive return on a modest investment if he serves his chosen market with insight, current techniques, and competitive prices. The photographic industry itself is, however, as turbulent as it is fast-growing. In 1969, equipment and photographic supplies stores experienced the highest failure rate of all retail businesses. The studio photographer must be able to keep abreast of the latest developments in photographic technology if he is to succeed in this easily-entered, highly competitive business. But his success is dependent primarily upon his skill in using photographic equipment to satisfy people rather than his possession of modern equipment. The photographic studio business will continue to be based on reputation and customer service, with the rewards going to those who are more than just eager amateur photographers.

II. DESCRIPTION OF THE INDUSTRY

A. Identification of Industry Activities

The photographic studio covered by Standard Industrial Classification (SIC) code 7221 is engaged in portrait photography for the general public and somewhat broader photographic services for commercial clients. It may develop film and process prints, but firms primarily engaged in processing and developing are not covered in this profile.

B. Dimensions of the Industry

The number of photographic studios has risen rapidly in recent years. From 1963 to 1967, for example, the number of studios rose from 19,544 to 26,558 while the value of their receipts climbed 50 percent to three-quarters of a billion dollars. The number of employees in studios has kept pace with the rise in the number of establishments: the 1969 figure of 42,500 photographic studio employees indicates that the industry continues to be characterized primarily by one- or two-employee operations. Individual proprietorships, in fact, make up about 80 percent of the industry by number of establishments, although they share equally with corporations in volume of industry receipts.

The growth in photographic studio operations is, of course, directly related to the rapidly increasing importance of photography in our daily lives. The 620-percent increase in the value of photographic equipment and supplies shipped to the American consumer from domestic and foreign producers between 1950 and 1969 represented nearly three times the rate of growth in Gross National Product in the corresponding period. And this growth only suggests the extent to which the American public has come to rely on accurate photographic representations of people, places, and events to communicate with each other.

The results of this increased reliance on photographic representation has had a mixed effect on the business and the professional photographer. He is more and more bypassed as the source of routine pictures, but he has been able to profit by the general public appreciation of skilled craftsmen and quality photographs created by this technology boom. The significant turnover among photographic studios indicates no lack of entrepreneurs willing to take a chance at proving their photographic skill in the marketplace.

The importance of the customer in this industry suggests a relatively attractive business opportunity for the skilled minority photographer, and minorities have already begun to penetrate the market. A recent survey by Flourney Coles indicates that photographic studios comprise about 20 percent of the black professional service businesses in seven cities with large black populations. Spanish-speaking communities also contain a number of studios serving their ethnic market. The extent to which these photographers have tapped the larger market usually is limited, however.

C. Characteristics of the Industry

The photographic studio's product is more than a picture of a particular subject. The customer—whether he be an individual portrait-sitter or a business advertiser—seeks a photographic representation of his ideas about the subject being photographed. The photographer who is technically proficient in the use of camera, lighting, and development material may fail to satisfy if he cannot relate to these ideas. Particularly successful photographers not only convey the image that the customer seeks, but have the creative talent to discover new ways of expressing the concept that the customer has of himself or his product.

This understanding of the professional photographer's role suggests the range of activities in which he may engage. Commercial studios generally perform a range of photographic work in advertising, recordkeeping, and public relations for commercial clients. These studios may also take photographs of events in their locale on contract to other commercial clients. Portrait photographers specialize in portrait photography in their studios, at institutions such as schools, and on location elsewhere. Portrait photographers also cover the growing field of wedding photography. Only about 20 percent of all studios engage in both portrait and commercial photography.

The market for each of these two types of studios continues to grow strongly. Audiovisual expenditures rose to a new high of $1.37 billion in 1969, with schools and business accounting for over half a billion dollars apiece. Over 26,000 photographic studios currently compete for this commercial market with about 6,000 corporate photo departments and even more photographers employed full- or part-time by schools and companies. Business management's growing awareness of the value of photography for obtaining information, selling products, and keeping records has afforded expanding opportunities for all these industry participants.

The portrait studio, considered the more traditional part of the industry, is also riding some significant growth trends. The Professional Photographers of America estimate that one-third of all households buy at least one professional portrait in a 3-year period, and this figure is expected to rise with the growing affluence of the population and increasing acceptance of the photograph as an essential part of new life styles. The increase in the number of memorable events at which professional photographers are usually preferred— weddings, graduations, and births—is another source of strength for the portrait photographer who does onsite photo work. School photography in particular has been an excellent source of business for the studios. An industry survey taken in 1970 showed that the high school senior market alone was worth over $100 million, and at least 70 percent of all school children are photographed for class pictures every year. This business is not only profitable—the average price of a portrait package for each photographed elementary school-child was $4—but serves as an excellent device for introducing the studio product to a large number of homes in the area. Follow-on contracts for school yearbooks are often quite lucrative.

The volume of business available and the relative ease with which a photographer can acquire the necessary equipment and developing facilities combine to keep the competition among studios high. Customer needs for photography are usually continuing ones, however, and a photographer who breaks into a market with price discounts or artistic flair can often hold his customers with attentive service and timely reminders. Industry sources indicate that customers place the greatest volume of repeat business with studios in which they feel comfortable. This characteristic of the photography business undoubtedly accounts for the considerable number of minority-operated studios operating in larger cities and suggests that these studios have a natural advantage in serving customers from their communities. While minority portrait studios are expected to capture at least some of the extra business from increasingly prosperous minority households, there are fewer minority commercial studios that have been able to compete successfully within the commercial market. Minorities moving towards the commercial market have usually done so after establishing themselves as portrait specialists, often using "affinity group" photography (church, social, recreational, civic) to obtain work in the wider business community.

The market orientation of the industry encourages the location of the studio in an area that is easily accessible to its customers. Studios have usually been located either on the fringes of commercial areas serving the target community (portrait studios) or in downtown business districts (commercial studios). Photography is not usually purchased on impulse, so space in an office building or a walkup in the chosen commercial district is usually satisfactory, and a store front is not a requirement. Some studios find it more profitable to send out their undeveloped work for processing, reducing their space needs and rental expense at the studio. For those studios that do their own development and processing work, however, the darkroom and other necessary facilities are invariably on the premises. The commercial specialist does much of his work on location and often satisfies his minimal office needs in a location close to his clients. Both types of studio are heavily dependent on a personal vehicle for transportation to worksites.

The photographic studio is seldom a lucrative venture for a new entrepreneur. Profits for the new studio photographer are usually heavily dependent on the extent to which he includes the value of his own contribution of time and talent to the business. The small proprietorship, which typifies the industry, can usually begin operations with a minimum of investment and at a low overhead rate, and a photographer who does his own portrait and development work, marketing, and accounting and clerical work can draw over 20 percent (from which his own draw or salary will be provided) of his total sales volume. Many individual proprietors hire part-time office staff for clerical and administrative functions as their time becomes more valuable and the increased volume of work justifies such a step. A survey taken in 1967 by the Professional Photographers of America indicated an average net profit before taxes (and owner's salary) of 15 percent of gross receipts. The survey can be expected to be biased towards the more successful studios and is based on only a small portion of the industry. Of greater significance, however, is the fact that surveyed studios were not asked to estimate, and include in their profit computations, the value of services rendered by the proprietor himself. The net profit projections of 21 percent to 25½ percent of studios grossing less than $100,000 annually are, therefore, overstated by the amount of the owner's (usually the photographer's) draw. Studios grossing over $100,000 annually include most corporations in the industry; they indicate salary costs of about 25 percent and a net profit before tax of about 9 percent.

D. Requirements for Entering the Industry

The photographic studio business is easily entered by the ambitious photographer. The studio owner must, of course, be more heavily capitalized than the freelance photographer, but industry sources indicate that a one-man studio can be started for about $6,500. For a sales volume of up to $50,000, minimal space requirements call for an office or reception area, a shooting room of at least 15 by 20 feet, a work and storage area, a small dressing room for clients, and darkroom space if the studio does its own processing.

An important decision for the new studio operator is whether or not he will operate his own developing facilities; the inclusion of a darkroom will about double space requirements and increase initial capital requirements by an amount between $1,000 and $1,500. Most one-man studios patronize commercial processing laboratories.

Trade sources indicate an allocation of initial investment for a one-man shop as follows:

a.	Photographic equipment and fixtures	$4,200
b.	Supplies	500
c.	Rent deposit	200
d.	Initial promotion	500
e.	Working capital	100
		$5,500

The photographic equipment investment can be further broken down as follows:

a. Camera, including lenses and tripod (twin lens reflex or
   2¼" by 2¼" single lens reflex) .... $1,000 to $1,500
b. Office equipment .... 600 to 700
c. Lights, meters, filters, etc. .... 500 to 800
d. Inventory (frames, flashbulbs, etc.) 1,500
e. Miscellaneous 200

The actual outlays for equipment depend on local prices and on how much equipment is already owned or easily secured secondhand by the entrepreneur. The quality of the equipment chosen is not as important to the new studio operator as the skill with which it is used.

The typical new entrepreneur finances a major portion of his studio setup costs out of his own pocket. A limited amount of debt financing may be available from commercial banks, especially if the applicant has contracts in hand (commercial, school, civic portraits) to support his sales projections.

Franchising has extended into the photographic studio business as it has into many others in recent years. Though not a significant force in the industry, the dozen or so franchisers provide assistance to the franchisee not only in financing startup costs but in equipment selection, advertising and promotion, and training. Several franchisers also do all the developing work, supplying the franchisee with film in the process.

III. FEASIBILITY ANALYSIS

A. Business Opportunities in the Industry

The photographic studios of both commercial and portrait types are currently handling about $1 billion worth of business per year. The average studio, however, has gross billings of only about $40,000 per year, and many marginal studios are business ventures in name only. Success for the new enterpreneur, no matter what his background, is difficult in this competitive industry and depends on two critical factors.

The primary ingredient of a successful studio photographer is his ability to combine technical proficiency and artistic ability with his "reading" of the client so as to produce a picture that assists the customer in expressing himself or his idea. Whether the subject is an individual or an ad campaign, the cameraman who can capture his insight into the customer with a perceptive portrait or picture is likely to establish grounds for continued business. The ability to empathize with the customer is demonstrated by many photographers and is generally considered to be an important factor in their success. This skill is obviously useful in insuring the comfort of the customer during what can be a trying experience. The ability of a person with similar ethnic and cultural background to more easily convey this empathic quality probably provides some advantage to a new minority entrepreneur who intends to service his community's photographic needs. Industry surveys tend to support this segmentation of the market for photographic work. As the studio develops, the work of the photographer—displayed at the studio and distributed throughout his market—conveys his style and image more effectively than most forms of advertising, permitting a certain self-selection to take place among his new customers over time. The new photographer, who correctly matches his personal and professional style to his chosen customer group, has strong possibility of success.

The second critical determinant of financial success in the studio business is the extent of the entrepreneur's profit drive. The lack of this business profit motivation is identified by industry sources as the single most important cause of studio failure or "reversion to amateur status." The photographer tends to be an artist, and the temptations to sacrifice cost control to artistic excellence and to sacrifice administrative and management performance to photographic enjoyment undoubtedly prove enticing to the new studio photographer. The new studio photographer will seldom have enough business and working capital to go first class at the beginning, unless he leaves an established firm with a block of his own customers. The new studio invariably requires the 40-plus-hour weeks required of any new small business and the avoidance of costs that can be achieved by a one-man organization. Every buying and hiring decision can be justified only if it leads to more than enough revenue to cover the additional cost. Since the new studio owner will spend a good part of his day marketing, the developing (if done in-house) and administrative work must often be done at night. Judicious use of part-time help, sales commissions, and subcontracting can help the busy photographer in his growth to a two- or three-employee shop.

The studio photographer—especially if he is alone—must, of course, possess a good knowledge of camera optics, film and paper emulsions and speeds, darkroom and lighting techniques, photographic chemistry, and projection equipment.

B. Projections of Attainable Returns in the Industry

Two of the most likely scales of operation in the new photography studio venture are the one-man portrait studio and the three-man commercial and portrait studio operation. These levels of operation are representative of the industry in general and are particularly illustrative of the minority-operated studios in urban centers. The projections are based on a 1967 industry survey.

One-Man Studio

The one-man portrait studio is assumed to be located in a shopping center or commercial district patronized by the chosen customer group. The developing and processing work is sent out daily to a processing facility located downtown. The studio itself contains 750 square feet of work, supply, and reception space, with 20 feet of sidewalk frontage. The owner works 6 days a week; a part-time book-keeper types records and correspondence. The studio was financed by $3,500 of owner's equity and a $3,000 loan from a local Minority Enterprise Small Business Investment Company (MESBIC).

Gross receipts		$25,000	100.0%
Portrait work	$24,000		
Film developing (commissions)	1,000		
Direct expenses		$10,000	40.0%
Processing services	$ 6,250		25.0
Photographic supplies	3,750		15.0
Overhead expenses		$9,250	37.0%
Rent	$1,250		5.0
Repairs	250		1.0
Taxes, license, and insurance	1,000		4.0
Utilities	500		2.0
Office supplies and postage	500		2.0
Telephone	375		1.5
Advertising and promotion	1,125		10.0
Auto expense	375		1.5
Clerical salary	2,500		10.0
Depreciation	750		3.0
Interest on equipment debt	250		1.0
Other	375		1.5
Net profit/owner's draw		$5,750	23.0%

Three-Employee Studio

The three-employee studio is the most common single size in the industry. The owner of the proprietorship employs a darkroom man and a portrait photographer in his downtown commercial center location. The studio performs both portrait and commercial work, with the owner servicing the local business market and schools during the spring season. He also performs at numerous social events and weddings in his community. The studio does its own developing, processing, and mounting. The business was financed for the present scale of operations at $12,000, with the owner putting up $6,000 and a local bank the remainder under the stimulus of a Small Business Administration (SBA) guarantee.

		$50,000	100.0%
Gross receipts		$50,000	100.0%
Portrait work	$20,000		
Commercial work	26,000		
Film developing	4,000		
Direct expenses		$27,500	55.0%
Salaries	$17,500		35.0
Photographic supplies	10,000		20.0
Overhead expenses		$11,000	22.0%
Rent	$1,500		3.0
Repairs	500		1.0
Taxes, license, and insurance	2,000		4.0
Utilities	750		1.5
Office supplies and postage	750		1.5
Telephone	500		1.0
Advertising and promotion	1,750		3.5
Auto expense	500		1.0
Depreciation	1,000		2.0
Interest on equipment debt	500		1.0
Other	1,250		2.5
Net profit/owner's draw		$11,500	23.0%

The return on owner's investment in each case is negligible if he takes the net proceeds out in the form of owner's draws, but retained earnings can be built up in such a business by living modestly during the startup phase. The reserves set aside to cover depreciating photographic equipment are tempting for a new business to "consume," but if the studio is even to finance its own growth it must cover future equipment needs out of operating proceeds.

IV. GUIDANCE IN ESTABLISHING A STUDIO

The first step in establishing a photo studio is to ask what unfilled or inadequately served photographic need exists in an area. If there is no such need and plenty of local competition, it is probably best to remain employed and/or an amateur photographer. It is estimated that 5,000 to 10,000 persons are required to support a photographic studio. A quick check of the volume and profitability of potential competitors may also be useful in defining opportunities.

Location of a new studio must be accessible to the chosen customer group. Of perhaps greater importance than the general area of the store is the type of neighbors surrounding the studio. The new photographer may find that a particular setting does much to enhance or detract from his chosen image. Other locational determinants are relatively unimportant.

The new photographic studio should give great care to the planning of its marketing effort. Emphasis should be on showing work samples and demonstrating technical competence. Several suggestions from trade sources may be helpful.

1. *Commercial Studios*

   a. Portfolios of varied commercial and industrial photographs that convey strong messages can be a useful device to obtain business for the new commercial studio.
   b. Advertisements in business magazines and trade journals are useful for introducing the firm's name and special talents. The Yellow Pages are also good.
   c. A cheaply printed flyer announcing the new firm's talents and hand-carried to potential clients by the photographer along with quality work samples may be another way of introducing the new firm.

2. *Portrait Studios*

   a. Portrait studios must rely more on representing their particular style of work on studio display windows and using the better pieces of early work in sample portfolios for viewing by "affinity groups" and chosen customer organizations. Contacts made in the studio, if pleasant, can lead to a large volume of outside work.
   b. Schools and other large groups are often susceptible to price discounts in their purchases of photography, and a new photographer may be able to break into a large new market with low-margin pricing on several key jobs. School contracts in particular are worth a great deal in community advertising. The contract to provide high school senior photographic work can lead to work for yearbooks, university applications, job applications, and graduation announcements; these young people may return for business the rest of their lives.
   c. Careful use of newspaper announcement sections may alert the studio to opportunities for work—solicited with congratulatory cards—in weddings, births, and graduations. Mass mailings to past customers before large family holidays is also helpful.

The new studio owner need not start out with new equipment; a more important requirement is that his equipment be well known by the operators. For those new entrepreneurs who might require new equipment, suppliers and distributors of photographic equipment in a particular local area can perhaps best be located through the telephone directory. Other sources of information are journals such as The Professional Photographer; Photographic Trade News: *Master Buying Guide and Directory Annual;* or the *Popular Photography Directory and Buying Guide.* Also of interest in determining specific equipment needs is the Printing, Graphic Arts, Photography category of publications prepared by the U.S. Government.

SMALL RESTAURANT

I. Let's Take a Look

You may be a factory or an office worker who has been cooking as a hobby for years. Or you may be a serviceman about to be discharged from military service. Perhaps you are a cook, or a dining room host, or a salesman, or small businessman. For that matter, you may be just a senior in high school planning his career.

Regardless of your present position, you do have one burning ambition: some day you want to run a restaurant of your own. Can you do it? Should you do it? Can you afford it? Is it worth the risk? Is it worth the headaches? Is there a future in it? These are the questions which must be going through your mind—and these are the questions this book will attempt to answer.

One thing to keep in mind right from the start: The restaurant business is a highly competitive and complex business. It is true that "everybody likes to eat" and that a good restaurant operator makes many friends. It is also true that many people who open restaurants do not succeed. A little later, you will find some of the reasons for such failures in greater detail.

Remember that to be among the good operators, you must have certain characteristics: Personal integrity, business ability, patience, a liking for food and for people, a pleasing personality, imagination, experience, know-how, determination, and ambition are some of them. You must also have adequate financial resources. Without any one of these, you may fail. With all of them, you may still fail.

Add to these requirements foresight, planning, and a resolution to maintain a high standard of quality, and you may very well succeed. It is the purpose of this book to help you do it.

JUST WHAT IS A RESTAURANT?

Statisticians tell us that the average American family is currently spending approximately 25 percent of its food dollar on food eaten outside the home, and that this amounts to $18.4 billion each year. The restaurant industry (or "food service industry," as it is called in the trade) is, in fact, the fourth-ranked industry (in terms of retail sales) in the United States.

Technically, any business enterprise which sells prepared food for consumption outside the home is part of the restaurant industry. This includes many types of businesses which have very little in common: fancy night clubs as well as hot dog stands; doughnut shops and hospital kitchens; industrial cafeterias and railroad dining cars. And as restaurant technology progresses, the eating places of the future may have even less in common with those of today. Nevertheless, despite the great variety in restaurants, and the rapid changes in the field, there are some features that are common to practically all types of restaurants.

● **What restaurants have in common.** Some of the common features are:

They prepare and serve food to the public, or to segments of the public (as with club restaurants).

They must be licensed by the community or State in which they operate.

They must comply with sanitation and health regulations.

They are business enterprises and, with few exceptions, operate for profit.

They must please their customers, since they depend on their returning or recommending them to other people.

A restaurant operator (also known as "restaurateur") thus has a challenging and responsible job. In preparing and serving food, for example, he has to exercise the greatest care to handle it in a sanitary manner and to make it appetizing.

Dirt, improper refrigeration, improper cooking, unwashed hands, and various sanitary violations can bring about the loss of the restaurant man's license. This kind of carelessness also can cause food poisoning to customers.

The restaurateur must know how to please his customers, and to serve food in a manner and in an atmosphere that will enhance their enjoyment of his dishes. He also must become acquainted with customers, for their pleasure depends, to a great extent, on his personal hospitality. A customer who will happily munch on a lukewarm hot dog at a ball game, may send the roast beef back to the restaurant kitchen, if it doesn't strike him as being cooked "just right."

People's moods and tastes are very personal feelings. In England, for instance, beer is served at room temperature. In the United States, it is served ice cold.

● **Some of the Differences.** A friendly, middle-aged widow in a small country town opens a small restaurant and stresses "home cooking." A large nationwide drive-in chain proclaims in neon signs that they have sold 500 million hamburgers. A modern, glass-enclosed doughnut shop on a highway, serves 28 different kinds of doughnuts. Meanwhile, downtown an inconspicuous luxury-type restaurant serves its steaks, chops, and roast beef in a Victorian atmosphere under gaslight lamps.

A factory worker may eat his lunch in an automatic vending cafeteria where he must completely serve himself, and may take his wife to dinner in a fashionable restaurant where four or five people wait on him at one time, and where even the napkin is spread out for him.

A modest wedding may call for the service of punch and sandwiches on the church lawn, while another wedding may be catered at the same time in the grand ballroom of the local hotel.

You will notice, from the above, that some of the differences among restaurants are primarily ones of size, others of emphasis, others of types of food, and still others of service. Some restaurants may not interest you at all, but others may be just like the kind that you have been thinking about.

PROBLEMS OF SMALL OPERATORS

Most successful restaurant owners started their business in a very small way. After being successful with a small restaurant, and after having established a reputation for good food and friendly service, they then expanded step by step over the years until they eventually achieved the status of large-scale successful restaurateurs.

Your future may some day be the same. But it is much more difficult now to "start in a small way" than it used to be 10 or 20 years ago. There are several reasons for this:

● **Today's diners expect first-rate eating facilities.** Except for eating places in small towns or rural communities (where folksiness is the most important ingredient), a new restaurant in the United States should have stylish and well coordinated furniture and fixtures.

● **Commercial food service equipment is expensive.** A household range is not designed to stand up under the hard treatment to which a piece of cooking equipment in a commercial restaurant is exposed. Commercial equipment is, therefore, built for harder and more continuous usage. It is also three or four times as expensive. Nevertheless, in order to run an efficient operation and reduce labor costs, certain pieces of equipment are absolutely essential. Twenty years ago, perhaps, an operator could have done without dishwashing machines, slicers, and mixers, but not now.

● **Labor costs are high.** At one time, the most important cost to the restaurant operator was the cost of food. At present, however, the cost of labor (with its related payroll costs and fringe benefits) amounts to almost as much as the raw cost of food and, in some operations, to even more. If you and your wife were to open a restaurant, and employed just one person as dishwasher and porter, you would require sales of at least $700 per week to justify the salaries which you would be paying to yourselves and your hired man. For each $100 of additional payroll, you would need a minimum of $300 to $400 of additional sales.

● **Profits are modest.** Profits from food alone are often small. In recent years, the average net profit of restaurateurs, before income taxes has been less than 5 percent of their total sales. It happens that in successful small operations, this percentage often has been higher. But even then a net profit of 10 percent of sales is considered high. Thus a person planning to open a new small restaurant and hoping for a profit of $100 per week (in addition to the salary he may pay himself) would require sales of at least $1,000 per week or $50,000 per year.

● **Turnover is limited.** "Seat turnover" is the phrase used in restaurants to describe the number of times that each seat is used by customers throughout a given meal or period.

Suppose you planned to open a restaurant with just 20 seats. If you then decided to make it a luxury restaurant for leisurely dining, you might expect an average turnover of 1½ or perhaps 2, during the dinner hours of 6:30–9:30 p.m., since each party would spend about 1 to 1½ hours in your establishment.

On the other hand, if you opened a drive-in on a busy highway, you might have a turnover of 10 or more during the evening, with the average customer staying perhaps only 20–30 minutes.

Unless you are operating a take-out business, therefore, your business is very much limited by the number of seats that you may have, and this, in itself, can make a very small restaurant uneconomical to run.

Since it can be risky, as noted above, to start a very small restaurant under present conditions, you should consider waiting to make your start until you can afford to do it on a scale that will provide the basis for success. Meanwhile, you might seek additional experience by working in a restaurant. Or you might try your hand at operating a related business, such as a small concession stand at a beach or amusement center, or some other kind of small operation in which food is prepared and sold.

II. Restaurants You Might Start

If you are ready to open your own small restaurant, you should first consider the types of operation that require the least capital and also, perhaps, the least practical experience.

SPECIALTY RESTAURANTS

An interesting development of recent years is the success of the many restaurants which sell only one or two specialty items—but of these, they sell a lot! Examples of such places can be found in doughnut shops, pancake and waffle shops, fried chicken houses, or clam bars—also, in the hamburger-and-french-fries stands all over the country.

More and more of these places are operated successfully as franchise operations in which the new owner may get all the specifications and advice from the parent company. There are also many specialty restaurants, which were started and are now being run successfully by individual owners—some with little or no previous food service experience.

Certain features can contribute to the success of this type of operation:

● **A Superior Food Product.** The main reason for the fame of specialty restaurants is that they usually concentrate on one or two items. These are unusually appetizing and appealing. The doughnuts are fresh and light and come in 27 varieties. The waffles are crisp. The pancakes are topped with fresh, creamy, whipped butter. Hamburgers are juicy and tasty and are offered in extra large sizes or at a very low price. Other hot sandwiches come in interesting combinations (such as chopped smoked pork sandwiches on bun with barbecue sauce and home-made baked beans).

● **Favorable Location.** A good location, with adequate parking space, is practically a must for a specialty restaurant. Most are on highways, preferably on the outskirts of towns or where they can enjoy both transient traffic and local trade.

● **Imaginative Merchandising.** Many specialty houses have unique methods of advertising and putting together their products. Pancakes are shaped like silver dollars. Chickens are served in the basket with honey. Hamburgers are given special names, special envelopes, fancy cartons, served in unusual buns, or with an unusual garnish. The buildings are attention-getting. They usually have distinctive neon signs. The staff may wear special uniforms in line with the general theme of the restaurant.

● **Popular Prices.** Specialty houses aim to appeal to everyone—but many of them attain success through pleasing the economy-minded. The success of the 15-cent hamburgers and the 19-cent milkshakes is evidence of this fact. A successful specialty house will make it possible for a customer to satisfy his hunger for a small price—and at the same time will try to offer additional enticements to increase the amount of the average check.

● **Takeout Business.** The advantages of taking ready-prepared snacks home for supper, or of eating them in the car, have made the sale of takeout food increasingly popular in the United States. And specialty houses depend on this business for a part of their volume.

● **A Checklist.** The following is a list of important points taken from the operational manual of one of America's largest pancake house chains, and published in *Restaurant Management*:

1. Pleasant, warm, neat exterior.
2. Availability of parking.
3. Friendly greeting.
4. Pleasing exterior.
5. Good table impression.
   a. Comfortable table and chairs.
   b. Attractive table settings, clean and sparkling.
   c. Friendly, helpful waitresses.
   d. Interesting menus—fair prices.
   e. Immediate offer of coffee.
6. Fast service.
7. Good food.
   a. Top quality cakes, waffles, and other foods.
   b. Use of hot plates for foods.
   c. Use of unchipped, good quality china.
   d. Attractive arrangement of cakes on plate.
   e. Tasteful decoration of cakes.
   f. Use of warm syrups and whipped butter.
   g. No delay between production and serving.
8. Courteous cashier.
9. Clean washrooms.

The list ends with this remark:

"Many factors contribute to forming the total impression, and while they are all important, the most important is still the production of top quality pancakes and waffles, attractively served. Everything else is supplemental to, or complementary to, this objective."

SHORT-ORDER RESTAURANTS

If you are interested in offering a little more variety than a specialty restaurant, you might consider a "short-order restaurant." Actually, there is no such category in the prevailing terminology of the restaurant industry. But for simplicity you can include in this category all the various kinds of food service which offer primarily quickly-prepared and easy-to-make snacks, such as hamburgers, steak sandwiches, milkshakes, and french fried potatoes. Drive-ins, fountain-luncheonettes, and various types of snack bars are examples of short-order restaurants. They usually have the following features:

● **A Variety of Menu Items.** In a drive-in or luncheonette you usually have a good choice of hot and cold sandwiches, also some heavier meals that can be prepared on the griddle or in the deep fat fryer. Often there will be one or two hot dishes, that require advance preparation on the range.

● **Quick-service.** Patrons usually wish to eat their meals quickly. Therefore, the entire menu in a short-order place should be geared for almost instantaneous service—usually at a counter or in booths. In this connection, it is important to have a menu which the customers can read quickly.

● **Heavy Lunch Business.** Short-order restaurants usually do most of their business at lunch. People eat their evening meal either at home, or if they go out to dine, they prefer restaurants with more complete table service.

● **Low Check Average.** Because of limited menus, and since customers are consuming primarily snacks or light meals, the average check is considerably less than in a table-service restaurant.

● **High Seat Turnover.** The average customer in a short-order place eats a meal in 20 minutes or less. This means that every seat can be occupied many times during each lunch period. Enough help should be available to clean up after a customer has left, and prepare a setting for the next one.

For you, there might be several advantages in starting with a short-order operation.

First, limited experience in quantity cooking would not be too great a handicap, if you learned to prepare and serve the few items that you featured in a tasty, clean, and appetizing way.

Second, you would require a minimum of help, since the persons who serve the counter often also do some of the short-order work.

Third, and very important, you could gain a fairly high volume of business with a relatively small investment, because of a high rate of seat turnover.

On the other hand, there are also some important disadvantages. The most serious is your low check average. You will find that, in spite of serving hundreds of customers each day, your total sales volume will be disappointingly small. It will take imaginative merchandising and extraordinary salesmanship to get your customers to spend more. Another disadvantage is the lack of dinner business.

COMBINATION OF COUNTER AND TABLE SERVICE

By far the largest single group of restaurants in the United States is the "all-purpose" group. These are the luncheonette, and the neighborhood or highway restaurants which have a counter or two, a number of booths, usually a juke box, and a combination cashier-and-candy stand. Usually, some of the short-order cooking equipment and food-dispensing equipment is located on the counter and on the "back-bar" behind the server. Kitchen and dishroom are in the back.

These restaurants offer a fairly extensive menu, including both short-order items and prepared meals. Baking, especially of pies, is often done on the premises.

A disadvantage of this type of restaurant lies in the larger initial investment in equipment, a larger staff, and the necessity for you to have a greater knowledge of food preparation than for a specialty or short-order restaurant.

THE TABLE SERVICE RESTAURANT

A table service restaurant is one in which all food and beverages are served by waiters and waitresses, usually in an atmosphere conducive to leisurely dining. The phrase "adventurous dining" applies perhaps more to table service restaurants than to any others, since ideally, everything in the restaurant—the food, the service and the atmosphere—have been carefully combined to create an exciting and memorable experience.

The food is largely prepared or cooked to order according to the customers' tastes. The service is very personal. The decor and general atmosphere often express an overall theme designed to stir the imagination of the clientele.

You may hope, some day, to own such a restaurant. This is a logical goal, and it can bring you much personal satisfaction in addition to a good income.

It can also give you many headaches. Equipping a table service restaurant is very expensive. Its cost has been estimated at between $500 and $1,500 per seat. Actually, some fine table service restaurants have been built for less, and some for considerably more. Nevertheless, you can see that in order to open a relatively small restaurant having, for instance, 100 seats, you might need a minimum of $50,000—if you leased your space.

In addition to your high initial cost, you would also have a very high overhead in such a fine restaurant. You would probably have to pay a high salary to your chef. You would use linen tablecloths and napkins at dinner. Your food inventory would have to be large to take care of a gourmet menu. Your taxes, entertainment, rent, and promotion expenses would all be higher.

Seat turnover would be very low, especially at dinnertime. Since you would stress leisurely dining, you could not expect your patrons to rush through their meals. The average dinner period extends from 6:00 p.m. to 9:30 p.m., which means that even at full capacity you could only get a turnover of three guests per seat. Your average would probably be closer to 1 or 1½. This might not give you enough volume to cover costs.

To illustrate the above, look at the actual figures of a restaurant with 150 seats in its public dining room and with seats for 250 banquet guests in its private dining rooms on the basement floor.

The restaurant is located in a suburban area, across the street from a shopping center, and is very busy at lunchtime. At dinnertime, it caters to families. Because of a shortage of banquet facilities in the area, the restaurant's banquet business has been very good—an average of 250 banquet guests per week, with an average banquet check of $2.49 per person. Other "vital" statistics of the Plaza* Restaurant are as follows:

---

*The name of the restaurant is disguised as are the names of all establishments and all people mentioned in this booklet. Data on the "Plaza Restaurant" on this and following page is reproduced with permission of the copyright holder, the Ahrens Publishing Co.

THE PLAZA RESTAURANT

Statement of Profit and Loss for a Calendar Year

Sales:	Amount	Ratio (percent)
Food...	$306,500	82.93
Beverage.....................................	63,100	17.07
Total sales................................	369,600	100.00
Cost of Sales:		
Food...	116,600	*38.04
Beverage.....................................	22,300	*35.34
Total cost of sales.........................	138,900	37.58
Total gross profit..........................	230,700	62.42
Operating Expenses:		
Salaries and wages:		
Preparation............................	58,800	15.91
Service................................	24,100	6.52
Cashiers (engaged occasionally part-time)....	400	.11
Bartenders............................	11,100	3.00
Total salaries and wages..................	94,400	25.54
Employees meals.............................	5,800	1.57
Laundry and dry cleaning.....................	7,900	2.14
Uniforms expenses less collection for uniforms......	(300)	(.08)
Licenses....................................	2,000	.54
Menus......................................	1,600	.43
Cleaning and paper supplies..................	4,500	1.22
Kitchen utensils and supplies................	700	.19
Bar supplies................................	300	.08
China, glass, and silverware.................	2,600	.70
Flowers and decorations.....................	200	.06
Kitchen fuel...............................	1,800	.49
Mechanical music...........................	1,200	.33
Miscellaneous expenses......................	1,900	.51
Administrative and general..................	27,800	7.52
Payroll taxes and employee relations.........	5,500	1.49
Advertising and business promotion...........	11,500	3.11
Heat, light, and power......................	5,800	1.57
Repairs and maintenance.....................	11,400	3.08
Total operating expenses...................	186,600	50.49
Operating profit............................	44,100	11.93
Cigar stand and other income.................	800	.22
Profit before rent..........................	44,900	12.15
Rent.......................................	23,100	6.25
Profit before depreciation...................	21,800	5.90
Depreciation...............................	14,700	3.98
Net Profit (before income taxes).................	**7,100**	**1.92**

*These ratios are computed in relation to their respective sales. All other ratios shown in relation to total sales.

Source: *Pinpointing Your Profits*, Ahrens Publishing Co., 1958, p. 25.

Hours of service: 11:00 a.m. to 1:00 a.m.
Number of days: Six days per week (closed Tuesdays)
Seating capacity:

Public dining room.. 150
Private party room.. 250

Total.. 400

Customers per year: 144,000
Number of employees: 45
Daily food averages (approximate):

	Sales	Number served	Average check	Turnover ratio
Luncheon........................	$210	151	$1.40	1.0
Dinner..........................	640	257	2.49	1.7
Supper..........................	27	12	2.30	.1
Banquets........................	105	42	2.49	.2
Total or average..............	982	462	2.13	1.2

Note that the return (less than 2 percent of sales) is relatively low. On the other hand, since your salary as owner-manager would probably be included in Administrative and General Expenses, the profit of $7,100 would be additional income.

While the profit potential of a fine table service restaurant is great, so is the risk. Much of the success or lack of it will depend on you, but there are some things beyond your control. General economic conditions, construction of new competing restaurants, relocation of existing highways, for instance, can be serious threats to your success.

When you enter the restaurant business, you must be dedicated, be willing to work hard and long hours, and have high standards of food quality.

You must be imaginative, and willing to grasp new opportunities that may offer themselves.

You must be patient. It took Bill several years to build his reputation as a restaurant operator, and again several years to do so in the catering field.

Your restaurant can serve as a food production center for other income-producing activities. In Bill's case, he used his first restaurant to prepare food both for occasional banquets, and for his highway restaurant.

Once you have proven yourself a successful operator, it is much easier to find the funds for expanding your operations.

III. Franchise Operations

One of the easiest ways to get started in the restaurant business is to purchase a franchise from a reputable and successful franchise organization. A franchise, technically, is the right to sell certain goods or services within a specified area. Actually, it enables a person to lease, build, or purchase a standardized operation which, right from the start, is part of a statewide or nationwide chain, although it is often owned or partly-owned by the operator himself. The holder of the franchise, that is, the operator, in return for the right to represent the parent firm, may pay a "franchise fee" or a commission on gross sales, or agree to buy his equipment and supplies from the parent company.

In the restaurant business, franchises fall basically into two categories:

1. Those which feature a product or a patented process which can be incorporated into existing operations.

2. Those which offer the operator a complete business, preplanned in every detail.

The growth of franchise organizations in the restaurant field has been phenomenal since World War II. Many of the people involved—both those who formed the parent firms (the franchisors) and those who bought the franchises (the franchisees) have done exceptionally well. Others have not.

For a variety of reasons, some franchisees have lost all of their savings in ill-conceived ventures, sometimes promoted by individuals out to make a "fast buck."

The three most essential ingredients to success in this field are:

● **A Good Franchise.** The most valuable asset of an existing franchise is a time-tested record of success. Have other operators made money on the same kind of franchise obtained from the same franchisor?

● **A Good Location.** The success of a restaurant in one place is no automatic guarantee that a similar restaurant will succeed in another. Each type of franchise requires a certain kind of location. Some need to be near highways, some in downtown areas. Some need ample parking. Without a suitable location, a new unit may well be doomed before it starts.

● **A Good Operator.** Since franchise operations are individually owned, the personality and business ability of the owner are just as vital as in any other small business. The most successful franchise operator is the man who has a fine reputation in the community, good business sense, ambition, and willingness to work hard, and who operates his own unit.

PRODUCT FRANCHISES

The purchase of a franchise for a popular, nationally-known food item can produce a great change in a small restaurant. Suddenly it will attract the attention of people who normally would have passed it by. The reason is that the American public is alert to advertising, and is more likely to have confidence in an eating place if it features a popular product.

This does not mean, of course, that every restaurant should purchase a franchised product. Many have developed a fine reputation for their own dishes, and their own methods of doing things. Such places may not need the extra stimulation that a franchise can bring.

A franchised product can bring other advantages besides good publicity and more customers. When a small drive-in restaurant, for example, takes on one of the many popular fried chicken franchises, it can suddenly become an "around-the-clock" operation, whereas before it may have sold mainly "in-between-meal" items such as hamburgers, hot dogs, milk shakes, and so on.

The typical product franchise is not expensive. Often there is no franchise fee at all, with the parent firm being content to make its profit from the sale of the product ingredients, or the promotional material, the necessary cooking equipment, or a combination thereof. Sometimes there is a small royalty or a down payment or similar charge.

Among the most popular product franchises are those for fried chicken. Coming in a variety of catchy names, each chicken franchise offers something a little different: a secret batter, a special type of fryer or griddle, or a special formula. Actually, the value of such a franchise to the operator is that a great deal is done for him which he couldn't do as well by himself. For instance:

An imaginative chicken platter is conceived. The food ingredients are clearly specified or are centrally purchased.

The platter becomes well known through national advertising and through standard promotion and handling among the franchise holders.

Special serving materials, such as platters, napkins, takeout containers, and paper bags are printed and sold to the franchisee at wholesale prices.

A great many promotional materials, such as backbar stickers, cardboard signs, radio and TV tapes, and menu stickers, are sold to the franchise holder practically at the parent company's cost.

An outdoor lighted sign is, perhaps, sold to him at a low price.

The parent firm's representative stops at his place regularly to make suggestions on how he can improve his operation.

BUSINESS FRANCHISES

The development of franchise organizations which sell a whole "business package" to a franchisee, has brought about a major change in the complexion of the restaurant industry and, to some extent, also in the eating-out habits of the American public.   It has enabled many people to become restaurant owners who, at the start, knew absolutely nothing about the business.

It has given the parent concerns the advantages both of individual ownership and of a large chain operation.   It has enabled many families to eat out very inexpensively, or to purchase complete meals, already cooked, at only a little more than these meals would have cost if they had been cooked at home.   It has raised the standard of quality and cleanliness in many restaurants.   This last is because under the terms of their franchise, the individual operators must live up to certain standards of quality and sanitation   Meanwhile, competitors, noting that the public appreciates good food served in a clean place, have followed suit.

STEP-BY-STEP PROCEDURE

If you become interested in obtaining a franchise from a national franchising organization, here is what you will probably need to do:

● **Make preliminary inquiries.** The mere fact that you have seen a nice-looking and busy franchise restaurant is never enough.   If you are seriously interested in a similar operation, you should contact (and preferably visit) the parent company's home office.   You should obtain satisfactory credit references and personal references concerning the principals in the parent organization.   You should also obtain reports from a national credit reporting organization and the local Better Business Bureau.   You could secure additional information on how to proceed from your restaurant association, or from a franchising trade association for instance, the International Franchise Association, Inc., 333 North Michigan Avenue, Chicago, Ill.

● **Apply for a franchise.** Your willingness to purchase a franchise is no guarantee that one will be granted you. For one thing, you must apply in a territory not already assigned to another restaurant man. For another, your own professional and personal background must satisfy the franchisor.

One franchisor expressed it this way: "Once we sign a franchise agreement with a franchisee, this becomes as binding as a marriage contract. We feel a peculiar sense of responsibility to the franchisee. Therefore, before we sign, we examine quality.

"What we want to know is this:

"Do they pay bills on time?

"Are they accepted in the community?

"Are they solid financially?

"Can they talk to people?

"Can they operate at a good profit?

"Have they had previous restaurant experience? (It happened that this particular franchisor considered previous restaurant experience a liability rather than an advantage. This attitude would not necessarily be that of other franchisors.)

"Are they going to operate the unit themselves? Or will they turn it over to others, who would be strangers to us?"

● **Meet with franchisors.** Even if you have conducted a thorough inquiry, there is no substitute for meeting the principals of the parent firm in their offices. In preliminary conferences, every detail of the franchise agreement should be explained, a copy of the agreement given to you for inspection by your lawyer, and preliminary plans made for completion of the agreement, if everything seems satisfactory.

● **Tour existing operations.** You should insist on visiting several present franchise holders and on talking with the operators privately. If most are happy, especially after operating under the franchise several years, chances are good that you may feel the same way several years hence.

● **Select a location.** The parent firm's experience in real estate negotiations can be a big help to the new applicant in site selection. To get good locations, many parent firms recommend a long-term land leasing arrangement, by which the landloard is assured of a land rental of from $600 to $1,500 per month, depending on the size and location of the property. One parent company, whose franchise covers pancake houses with a seating capacity of from 70 to 150 seats, makes two types of operations available to its applicants: the "off-the-street walk-in" type, or the standard drive-in type. The latter requires a lot of 150 x 150 feet which allows him parking space for 50 cars, and a building of 50 x 70 feet. These lot and location requirements vary, naturally, with each franchise and depend on such factors as size of building, type of operations, and size of the town.

● **Sign lease, franchise license, and arrange financing.** Once all the preliminaries are concluded, the applicant signs the papers which will make him a franchisee. While there are some franchises which may cost less, most applicants for a business franchise will need to have from $15,000–$25,000 of their own money. The parent firm can then usually help them get the rest financed at relatively low rates of interest.

● **Get advance training.** While the new building is being constructed (in accordance with exact specifications and supervision by the parent firm), the new franchisee will probably participate in a preliminary training program. This may be in another operation, in the parent firm's offices, or both. During this period, he becomes familiar with business techniques, food preparation techniques, service, and various other things. The products in this type of franchise operation are relatively few, the procedure rigidly standardized, and every operating step prescribed. An intelligent person therefore usually can learn the fundamentals in a few months or perhaps even weeks.

● **Opening the restaurant.** Opening your restaurant will not be easy. But the experience of the parent firm can help you greatly. They can help with advance promotion, and in getting the full publicity value out of the opening. Of course, as in any opening, your employees must be prepared to handle the onrush of curious patrons without stumbling. The impression created on that first day may make you or break you during your first few months. The opening period is so important that many parent firms send their supervisors to work with the new franchise holder for several weeks, until both feel that the supervisor's presence is no longer needed.

ADVANTAGES OF FRANCHISE OPERATIONS

The preceding pages have indicated, that if you are inexperienced but you want to run your own restaurant and you are willing to work hard and to follow someone else's ideas and suggestions, a good franchise business may be the best plan for you. The advantages can be summarized as follows:

- **You purchase a "package deal."** Many of the worries involved in opening a new business have been solved for you by the parent company. Presumably, they have made certain mistakes in their earlier units, and you get the benefit of their trial-and-error experience.

- **You handle a proven product.** The product or products which you will be serving already have been accepted by the public. The method of preparation and the techniques of service have been worked out and you, the new franchise holder, are the beneficiary of this past experience.

- **You benefit from national reputation.** Because there are many places which look and operate exactly as you do, the goodwill which they earn will benefit you.

- **You benefit from national promotion.** If the parent company does effective national advertising, you are the beneficiary. (One parent firm collects an extra 2 percent of sales as an "advertising assessment.")

- **You get professional assistance.** The parent company has a vital stake in your success and sends out people to help you solve problems. (If you had to pay for it yourself, such consulting advice would be costly.)

DISADVANTAGES OF FRANCHISE OPERATIONS

In addition to the advantages discussed under the last heading, there are certain distinct disadvantages of franchise operations. These include:

- **Limited menu.** Most franchise restaurants are geared to the low-cost, fast service trade, usually to the automobile customer. Menus are limited. This not only holds down the check average, but also restricts the ability of the franchise holder to expand. While some parent firms are more liberal, few of the large ones will permit a fundamental change in the menu and price structure.

- **Lack of freedom of action.** Although the franchisee is the owner (and usually operator) of his business, his franchise agreement stipulates that he run his business a certain way. He, therefore, does not possess the freedom to make changes that the independent operator has. Few of the large firms will permit an addition or change in the building.

● **Purchasing obligations.** Most franchise agreements stipulate that the franchisee must buy certain materials from the parent company. These may be food, promotional items, equipment, or all three. Unless it is specifically spelled out in the agreement, the franchise holder does not even have control over the price he is charged for such items. In fairness, however, you should know that usually the cost of these items is lower than you would pay elsewhere.

AUTOMATIC VENDING BUSINESS

I. Is the Vending Business for You?

WHEREVER YOU LOOK THESE DAYS, there's a coin-operated device. Your small change will buy everything from a candy bar to a full lunch, from a paper towel to a load of clean laundry, from a massage for your feet to a comb and tonic for your hair. You can get a quick photo or a photostated birth certificate, a newspaper or a parking space, a postage stamp or a phone call—all from coin-operated machines. The list is endless. You know it's a big and growing business even if you don't know that the 4-million-plus machines vending merchandise and services in the United States sell more than $4 billion worth of goods every year.

In some ways, the vending business is very young. The first American venders got their start in the 1890s, but vending didn't develop as a business until the early 1930s, when cigarette, candy, and gum machines were introduced. The real expansion came after World War II. The need for round-the-clock snack service in defense plants and the invention of the coffee machine in 1946 paved the way for the rapid spread of in-plant vending, and further expansion has brought vending service to hospitals, colleges, and similar institutions. Today, the average American drops more than six times as many coins into merchandise vending machines as he did in 1946.

Starting your own merchandise-vending business looks like a promising way to become your own boss in a growing industry—but what does it take? What, actually, are your chances? How do you get started? What does a vending operator do?

There are many kinds of coin-operated machines, but the expression "merchandise and service vending" usually refers to machines dispensing a product to be consumed or used on the spot and to a limited number of services, such as scales, toilet locks, photo machines, shoeshine machines, and so on. This booklet is concerned with merchandise vending; it does not include coin-operated services.

What a Vending Operator Does

Whether you vend in Pittsburgh, Pa., or in Ruraltown, Calif., your business will operate on the same basis. As a vending operator, you will carry on these activities:

Purchase machines.
Place them on location.
Stock them with merchandise and change as required.
Refill and service them at regular intervals.
Repair them when they need it.
Collect, count, and deposit the coins.
Maintain a suitable headquarters where you keep merchandise, supplies, and parts and have facilities for repairs, coin counting, sanitation, and bookkeeping.

Since you can't make the rounds on foot, you must have a station wagon or truck, no matter how small your operation. Your vending business will be organized much like a milk or dry-cleaning route. Locations for your machines will fan out from your headquarters in such a way that they can be reached in an organized fashion.

If you're in a small town, the whole area is your "route." In larger cities, you should limit yourself to one section at first. Later, you can build the business up into several routes laid out so that the machines can be serviced and maintained in a convenient travel pattern. These routes are the basis of every vending business.

It isn't practical to extend your routes beyond a radius of 30 to 50 miles. There are large vending operators with routes in several cities or States, but additional headquarters have to be set up when the operation expands beyond a certain point. Even the largest companies are locally operated.

Vending machines sell a product or service in two general types of situations:

1. At a time and place when other retailing methods can't do the the job as well.
2. When round-the-clock sales over a counter aren't profitable.

When you vend through a machine, you rely primarily on impulse buying. Perhaps there's no candy counter nearby or open. Or, because your machine is there, the customer is reminded that he'd like a quick refresher or a pack of cigarettes. He buys "on impulse." That's why many vended sales are extra sales—the customer buys only because the machine is handy. And it's why the location of the machine is so important. The successful vending operator knows the right spots from experience and by intuition.

Each vending machine is a little like one shelf in a store. Therefore, the average volume of sales per machine is low. When you consider the investment needed to buy the machines and the expense of traveling to each outlet for servicing and stocking, you see that the profit per machine is very thin. You must rely on getting enough volume per machine and in your *total operation* to earn a profit on your investment

How "Automatic" Is It?

Because the description has been oversimplified here, running a vending business may sound as easy as moving pawns on a checkerboard. Don't be misled. It isn't.

First, you have to find profitable locations and persuade each owner to let you install your machine. Usually, the location owner shares in your profits through monthly commissions based on sales at his location.

Second, like the owner of a hardware store or drugstore, you have to be a merchandiser. Just placing the machine won't sell enough products. Which brand you stock, how you rotate products, how you place the machine—these are among the merchandising skills needed in what is often spoken of as "automatic merchandising." Only the actual dispensing is automatic.

You must also know what model and size of machine does the best job in each location; where to buy it; what licenses and regulations apply in your city and State. And there's the basic requirement of bookkeeping and adequate records of several kinds. More of that later.

Types of Vending Operations

If you had been a vending operator back in the 1930's, you would have been in the peanut, gum, candy, cigarette, or penny scale business or a combination of these. It wasn't too complicated. But now—in the mid-1960s—vending, like everything else, is more varied. Some vending firms operate in only one line of business and make a success of it— for instance, candy, or cigarettes, or milk, or ice cream, or coffee, or postage stamps. In fact, 18 percent of the vending operators still specialize in one kind of machine, and another 14 percent offer only two different product lines. But the majority—58 percent—handle four or more types of products.

In some product or service lines, the vending operators tend to avoid adding other items—for example, operators vending postage stamps, cosmetics and grooming aids, school-supply items (such as pens, pencils, notebooks), and gum balls (commonly known as bulk vending). Such operators are less likely to diversify because often their machine loca-

---

Some Vended Products and Services [1]

Bags	Hair dryers	Photographs
Bait	Handkerchiefs	Pies
Batteries	Hosiery	Pizza
Candy	Hot chocolate	Popcorn
Casseroles	Identification tags	Post cards
Charcoal	Ice	Postage stamps
Chewing gum	Ice cream	Potato chips
Cigars	Insurance policies	Pretzels
Cigarettes	Laminations	Puzzles
Coffee	Laundry supplies	Razor blades
Combs	Magazines	Salads
Cookies	Massages	Sandwiches
Cosmetics	Milk	Sanitary napkins
Crackers	Milkshakes	Shaves
Eggs	Newspapers	Shoeshines
Facial tissues	Notebooks	Soft drinks
Film	Paperback books	Soup
Film slides	Pastry	Tea
Flashbulbs	Peanuts	Tickets
Flowers	Pencils	Toothpicks
Fruit	Pens	Towels
Fruit juice	Perfume	Voice recordings
Greeting cards	Phonograph records	Water
Groceries	Photocopies	

[1] Laundry, cleaning, and amusement devices are not included.

tions are not suitable for multiple-line operations. Cosmetics and grooming aids, for instance, are usually vended in or near washrooms. Also, machines in these lines cost less than most other types, and many of their operators don't care to risk the larger amount of capital.

For most operators, however, growth has come through the addition of new lines. From candy, cigarette, milk, or coffee routes, they have expanded into a full offering of machines and products. Many vending companies today offer the customer a number of different machines that vend coffee, soft drinks, juices, milk, ice cream, candy, gum, cigarettes, hot canned soup, cold and hot sandwiches, salads, pastry, desserts, cookies and crackers, and even complete hot entrees or casseroles.

Such "full line" installations are especially widespread in industrial plants, office buildings, colleges, hospitals, military installations, and other places where a complete snack or meal is offered to employees, students, or visitors. Because machines that vend different products can easily be ranged in uniform rows, the services available are very flexible. "Area decor" is often used to blend the machines into the lunchroom, and machine "fronts" give equipment from different manufacturers a uniform appearance.

Full-Line Vending vs. a Smaller Operation

The shorter lunch hour, the trend to employee fringe benefits that include on-the-job refreshment and food facilities, the high cost of conventional serving methods—all these have combined to offer vending companies a vast new market and an incentive to expand into full-line vending. A small vending operator who takes on this type of account must be ready to grow, to add personnel, to raise additional capital, to learn new skills.

Many have. But this type of business is handled not only by vending companies but by conventional food-service contractors who have added vending departments. The potential market is large, but the competition is intense. Full-line vending is not a field for amateurs.

The majority of vending machines, however, are still installed in small offices or plants, theaters, restaurants, cocktail lounges, transportation terminals, service stations, motels, and similar places where one or two machines are the rule. Here, the small vending company can compete on more or less equal terms with larger operators. Here, several factors offer a challenge to the qualified small vending operator—close personal contact with the location owner and his customers, the ability to turn a profit on smaller volume, the large number of such locations still not served, our expanding economy. Many new operators come into the vending business every year through just such locations as these.

What Are the Pitfalls?

You probably suspected even before you started to read this booklet that there's more to vending than stocking machines and collecting coins every few days. In any case, you know it now. Here are a few of the special pitfalls you'll have to look out for if you decide to go into the business.

Poor equipment. Many a beginning vending operator has bitten the dust because he started out with poor equipment. A machine out of order means loss of sales—and every nickel counts. More important, customers won't return if the machine doesn't work properly. And the owner of the location will soon ask you to move your machine out of his place of business.

Fraud. Sometimes beginners fall victim to dishonest vending-machine promotions. After paying exorbitant prices for equipment, they find themselves saddled with shoddy machines that won't work—and by that time the promoter has usually skipped town. It's always best to deal with reputable machine manufacturers and to compare machines offered by different companies before you decide which to use.

Obsolescence. Obsolescence is just as troublesome with vending machines as with your car. Sometimes more so. Refinements in machines—or even entirely new approaches—can be problems for the small operator. For instance, when the fresh-brew coffee venders began to make inroads on those using instant coffee, many small operators had to upgrade their operations or face the loss of their established locations. Operators with the new machines threatened to capture the business of operators still using the old equipment. The same thing happened when the soft-drink machines that automatically dispense ice into the cup made their appearance.

Commissions. Probably the most dangerous pitfall for an inexperienced operator is the mistaken belief that any new location is good business. You will find sooner or later that if you want to stay in the vending business very long, it is essential to keep proper records of each machine, to evaluate sales against your costs, and to allow a sound profit margin.

This need for care in providing for a sound profit margin applies particularly to the size of the commission you pay the location owner, which is usually a percentage of gross sales. "Buying" new business through too-large commissions will force you to cut corners on service and product quality. It won't be long before such practices will eat into your profits and undermine your ability to build a reserve for expansion.

Vandalism and burglary. Vandalism and burglary can plague your outdoor locations. Where supervision is impossible, thieves consider vending machines a likely target, and vandals can cause costly damage to your equipment. Strong locks and burglar alarms can help, but it's often a question of where you place equipment.

Slugs. A problem that will really bother you is the passing of slugs or foreign coins. If the slug artist's worthless token delivers him your merchandise, you have the same expenses as if he had paid in full, but you get no income or only a less valuable foreign coin. Slug artists often come in waves and even sell their fake coins.

Fortunately, there are laws against the use of slugs, and often police authorities can trap the offender. The problem continues to plague vending operators from time to time, however.

II. What Are Your Chances for Success?

IF YOU LOOK at different types of vending businesses, you'll see that the operators started with varying kinds of experience. Not all of them had the same background when they went into vending.

Take Virgil Lund.[1] He had an average job with an accounting firm in a town of 126,000. Then his father-in-law suggested that he try his hand in the family vending business. Lund had no vending experience, but his business background and training in accounting came in handy. He didn't exactly start at the bottom; and now that his father-in-law has retired, he is the manager. But he still goes out on service calls.

Jack Peebler, on the other hand, was a service-station mechanic in a suburb of Boston. Several times, he had used his mechanical skills when the soft-drink machine where he worked was out of order.

He thought he saw an opportunity in the many small offices and factories in his neighborhood and inquired about how the managers were taking care of the coffee breaks. With some financing and other help from a vending-machine manufacturer, he placed 12 instant-coffee machines, servicing them in his spare time. Because he was good with machinery, he could handle service and repair problems in the evenings and on weekends. Accounting and other recordkeeping were harder to manage; but his wife had taken a business-college course, and she took charge of the bookkeeping.

Within a few months, Peebler saw possibilities for expansion. He quit his job and now works at his vending business full time.

What Skills and Experience Do You Need?

Mechanical dexterity and sales ability are among the skills you need to be a successful vending operator. It will help if you have been a salesman or a service representative. Or the manager of a small restaurant. A successful milk or drycleaning routeman would also have some of the basic requirements, because handling vending routes resembles in some ways the work such routemen do.

---

[1] Names in all examples have been changed.

How About Your Market?

Because few communities today are without vending operators, it is wise to take a good look at the companies already active in the vending business in your town.

How many are there?
How big are they?
What kinds of accounts do they seem to serve?

Don't just take a quick look at some service stations. You can assume that all have some vending. Look in companies with large offices, in factories, restaurants, airports, and other places where many people gather. Check with the location owners. Are they satisfied? Have sales in their machines been holding up?

Check also with local bankers. Many of them have vending companies as customers. They will know whether the vending business is successful in your town.

It Could Be You

Finally, unless you're in a town or area that is declining, keep in mind that vending is a young business. Its best growth and diversification are still ahead. If you meet the qualifications discussed in this chapter; if you like competition, hard work around the clock, weekend hours, the satisfaction of providing a service, attention to detail, tinkering with machinery, keeping careful records, the problems and joys of dealing with people; if you are dependable, courteous, and thorough—then you might want to take a closer look at becoming shepherd for a flock of vending machines.

You'll be in good company. Nearly every successful vending-machine operator started small, most of them with little prior knowledge of the business. Many entered the business after World War II, and it is still possible to start from scratch today. Even though mergers of independent local operators have created multimillion-dollar vending corporations, small local operators still thrive. Of 6,000 vending operator companies, nearly 2,000 have no full-time employees except the owner. Another 2,000 or so have 3 or fewer employees.

In other words, much of the vending business consists of small, independent local firms. Not all of them manage to stay ahead of competition. Many fail to survive. But the average sales increase for the industry in the last decade has been about 8 percent a year. Somebody is achieving those averages. It could be you.

III. Getting Off on the Right Foot

ALTHOUGH MANY VENDING OPERATORS started their businesses without any prior experience in vending, there is probably no better way to learn the business than to work for a good vending operator. Many routemen or supervisors have, after working in the business for some years, gone to another city and set up routes of their own, either alone or with a fellow employee. They have the advantage of knowing vending equipment; which machine models are best in each product category; how to set up a route system, stock controls, and servicing schedules; and so on.

Other vending operators have worked at one time as field servicemen for vending-machine manufacturers or as salesmen for suppliers of vendible products. In the course of calling on vending operators and helping them with day-to-day problems, they acquired a basic knowledge of the business. This helped them avoid mistakes when they started their own vending business.

But more than likely, you've been no closer to vending machines than putting coins into them. If you have a good head on your shoulders and have had some business experience, you can still get started in the vending business. Two basic approaches are possible.

1. Start by developing a small route, either part time or full time. You may not be number one in your area right away, but you'll be learning fast with a minimum of financial risk. When you make mistakes—and you will—they will be relatively small ones. If you buy equipment and products from reliable suppliers, they will be helpful from the beginning. They can give you general information; and in larger cities, they may have special service departments to help you over the first few weeks.

2. Buy a small route or a small operation with several routes. This way, you acquire experienced help who can carry on with a minimum of supervision while you learn how to manage the business. The danger is, of course, that you might not select a sound operation. It's important that you have previous business experience that will enable you to check the books and other indicators of whether the business you are buying

is in good shape. If you start this way, the former owner may be able to give you advice while you are getting your bearings.

Remember this, though. When a good vending operation goes up for sale, other local operators are usually interested in bidding for it. If you seem to be the only eager buyer—be careful!

Start Small?

The answer to that question is easy. Yes.

No matter where you live, local vending companies are already operating. It would be almost impossible to get enough profitable locations to start on a big scale—even if you had the money to buy hundreds of machines.

There are other reasons, too. Assuming that you still have a lot to learn about the business, you'd be better off to invest in just a few machines at first. That will keep your overhead low while you're learning the business. Anyhow, you'd find it impossible to hire enough qualified routemen and mechanics for a large operation.

Also, the larger your operation, the greater your risks. For instance, suppose you started out with several large industrial accounts (though this is seldom possible under existing competitive conditions). You'd find yourself in trouble if there should be a strike or a slowdown in the economy. As a new operator, you'd be hard pressed to last out the famine, with no revenue coming from your machines while your overhead and payments on the machines went on and on. There's no ready market for used vending machines to help you in such a case—most manufacturers accept used equipment only as trade-ins when you purchase new machines.

How Small Is Small?

Remember the story of Jack Peebler, the garage mechanic who started a vending route in his spare time? If you start the way he did, almost any number of machines can work out for you. Say 25 gum venders. Or a dozen coffee machines. Or 20 cigarette and candy machines. You can add more as your judgment and success suggest.

But if you expect to start in the business on a full-time basis, you'll need to be more specific. First, of course, you'll have to decide which part of the business you want to enter. Let's say candy machines. Here's one way to figure it:

·According to national statistics of the vending industry,[1] the average candy machine grosses about $600 a year. Small operators whose

---

[1] From *Operating Ratio Study of the Vending Industry*, 1964, sponsored by the National Automatic Merchandising Association and compiled by Price Waterhouse & Co.

business is primarily in candy make an average net profit, before income taxes, of 4 to 6 percent on gross sales. Thus, if you had 50 candy machines (you could service that many alone), your gross sales might come to $30,000 a year and your net profit, at 5 percent of sales, to $1,500 before taxes. This is in addition to your salary, which would be included in the expenses of operating the business. The national average for owner's salaries is 15 percent of sales—in this case, $4,500. (Remember that these figures are national averages. Results for individual vending operations vary considerably, depending on local conditions and the skill of the operator.)

For illustration's sake, let's compare the candy-machine business with a small coffee-vending operation.

One man couldn't service 50 coffee machines—30 would be more like it. On the basis of average annual sales of $2,650 per coffee machine, with 30 coffee venders you'd gross $79,500. The average annual net profit for small operators who specialize in coffee vending ranges from 6 to 10 percent of sales. Thus, you might net $6,360 before income taxes (based on 8 percent). Figuring your salary again at 15 percent of gross sales would give you a salary of $11,925.

Does this make you want to rush into vending coffee rather than candy? Wait—you haven't heard the whole story yet.

At an average cost of $300 per machine, the candy equipment would require an investment of $15,000 (if you pay cash). Thirty coffee machines (average cost $1,200) would require an initial outlay of $36,000. Also, it might be harder to place 30 coffee venders than 50 candy machines, and the investment in headquarters facilities, servicing equipment, and so on is higher for a coffee operation.

These two examples are only illustrations, not typical case histories. But they do point up the importance of starting small, learning as you go, and expanding only as you get on solid ground.

Where To Get Advice

Fortunately, a number of people are ready to help you think your way through these questions—and the many others that will come up before you put the first candy bar in your first vending machine.

Manufacturers. A reputable vending-machine manufacturer is always glad to help the beginning operator. If you get past the first hurdles, you'll be a grateful customer in the future. Also, having his equipment in the hands of well-qualified operators strengthens his reputation. So he has all the reason in the world to help you get started right.

All good manufacturers know this and act accordingly. Some will have a service representative work with you for a few days and then check back from time to time. Some have special schools for operators and their personnel to make sure that you will be able to set the equipment up properly and make necessary repairs.

Some vending-machine manufacturers use distributors located in different territories. These distributors are in business for themselves, and they try to keep in close touch with customers at the local level. They, too, maintain training schools for vending operators and have service personnel to work with their operator customers.

Most of the manufacturers who sell direct from the factory base their contact with you on personnel located in the field. These fieldmen travel constantly to give help and, of course, to sell equipment. Some manufacturers operate field offices combined with parts depots and equipment showrooms. Through these regional offices, they offer immediate delivery of equipment and parts and conduct training schools similar to those of distributors.

Suppliers. You can expect help from the many companies that sell products and supplies to vending operators. Firms that distribute coffee, soft-drink sirups, cups, coin mechanisms, creaming agents, candy, cigarettes, gum, and a host of other products rely on field representatives to make their sales and to help their vending-operator customers.

A coffee salesman, for instance, can help you get the best quality out of your machines by showing you how to adjust the product "throw" on all coffee venders. He knows how to get the right water temperature and whether your local water needs softening or purifying.

One gum-company representative prides himself on showing operators how to arrange the gum column in candy machines for maximum sales. Similar advice is readily given by supplier representatives who furnish cookies and crackers. Unless you turn them away, manufacturer and supplier representatives are always ready to help you.

Local distributors. A special source of help in many parts of the country is the distributor who handles products and parts from many manufacturers. Large vending operators buy direct from the manufacturer, but small operators often buy from these local distributors.

Since such a distributor depends on small firms like yours for his livelihood, he is especially knowledgeable in your method of operation. He knows your problems. Not only will he deliver in smaller quantities, but he may be able to put you in touch with other small operators who do business nearby but do not compete with you. Some of these operators may be willing to share information, since their territory does not overlap with yours. Of course, their opinions may not be as valuable as some other sources of help.

Trade groups. Don't overlook this important source of help. Nearly every State and many cities have organizations of vending operators.

There are groups of bulk-vending operators, cigarette-vending operators, independent State organizations of full-line operators, and State councils affiliated with the National Automatic Merchandising Association. The State councils can be especially helpful. Some have full-time offices, and all hold regular meetings to help members improve their vending operations.

You may wonder why you should consult all these people before you're even in business. It's a good question, because your first interest would seem to be to get well enough established so that you will have time to join organizations and talk with suppliers. But consider this:

Let's say you start off with just candy-vending machines. There are more than half a dozen first-rate machine manufacturers and more than 100 companies making candy bars for vending operators. Who has the best machine for your type of operation? What bars should you offer your customers? What about gum and crackers in your machines? With coffee or soft-drink vending, the problems are even more complicated.

So talk with several machine manufacturers before you start in business. Compare their equipment, their sales stories, their prices, the help they can offer you. Listen to the advantages of several product suppliers and base your selection on your own comparison of their presentations. Finally, get independent advice from other operators, from vending associations, and, if possible, from your bank. The money and headaches you'll save will make it well worth your effort.

IV. Financing Your Enterprise

IN THE CANDY AND COFFEE route examples, it was assumed that you would pay cash for your vending equipment. In reality, you probably won't. But there will be other outlays besides what you put down on the machines that sell your merchandise. Even the smallest operation needs money for a center from which to operate, a truck, licenses, taxes, supplies, and other expenses. What financial resources do you need, then, to get started?

How Much Capital Does It Take?

The amount of your initial investment depends on which part of the vending business you want to enter. On your city. On the types of accounts you seek. On the products you want to vend at the start.

Take the case of Ed Boyer,[1] who lives in a typical Los Angeles suburb. Until he got his fingers burned in a fraudulent popcorn-machine promotion, Boyer had never seen a vending machine from the inside. Having learned his lesson by dropping $6,000 in the popcorn deal, he was wiser when he started again a little later. For an $800 downpayment, he bought 30 compact candy venders. Within a few weeks, he added a small coffee vender, making a $200 downpayment on the purchase price of $500. A month later, he ordered 30 more candy machines, and within 5 months he needed 10 more coffee machines.

Six months after he started, Boyer was operating 60 candy machines and 11 coffee venders. His cash investment then totaled $1,600 for the candy venders and $2,200 for the coffee machines, or $3,800 all together. For another $1,000 he laid in some supplies and basic parts.

Since his equipment was financed by the machine distributor, Boyer had to take a job from 4 p.m. to 12:30 a.m. in order to keep up his payments. He serviced the machines during his off-the-job hours. Of the $20 in monthly sales from a typical candy machine, $4 went for payments on the machines, $11 for candy supplies, and $2 for rental

---

[1] Names in all examples have been changed.

to the location. The remaining $3 was available for other expenses that might come up and for profit.

Boyer hoped to own 20 instant-coffee machines and 130 candy venders within another few months. He expected to be able to quit his job by then and devote his full time to the vending business. His total cash outlay for machines would then come to $7,800 (some of the later candy venders would be larger). Probably another $2,000 or so would be needed for additional supplies and other cash outlays.

The minimum. Ed Boyer's case is probably typical for a small operation. In other words, a vending business of this type will require close to $10,000 cash as a minimum. Only a bulk-vending operation (such as gumball vending) can be started for less—bulk-vending machines are smaller and simpler. On the other hand, it would take longer to build a bulk-vending business into a full-time occupation.

Obviously, Boyer had bought the smallest available machines, and he placed them in service stations, bank buildings, a small dairy, carwashes, and the like. His example represents *the minimum*. It would not work out in a highly competitive market.

What about the larger machines? To place machines in high-volume industrial locations, you would have to buy more expensive equipment. As the examples in chapter 3 indicate, launching a small coffee route with standard-sized coffee venders would cost far more than Boyer spent, using the small venders. List prices for the larger-capacity, fresh-brew coffee machines run from $800 to $1,600.

About 20 of the large machines would be the most that one man could service. One model that vends fresh-brew coffee is priced at about $1,400. With the best credit rating, you could buy it at 10 percent down, with from 24 to 36 months to pay the balance. Thus, your down-payment for 20 machines would come to $2,800. Your monthly install-ments, including finance charges, would be perhaps about $40 for each machine, or a total of $800 a month for 36 months.

As a beginner in the business, however, with only average resources, you might have to pay 15 to 20 percent down ($5,600). Your contract might call for 24 monthly payments of about $50 per machine.

Furthermore, leaving 20 coffee venders with a 1,000-cup capacity to themselves while you hold down another job is usually not practicable. You'd have to spend most of your time keeping the venders filled and sanitized, answering service calls, finding better locations, and so on. This means you'd need money for business and living expenses until you could build up your business. Because locations for this type of machine are seldom within a short distance of each other, you'd probably have no choice but to get a small truck right away; and your investment in tools for servicing, supplies, and parts would be greater.

Placing 20 machines in profitable locations the first week may seem easy on paper. In reality, you might have to "carry" some of the equipment until you could place it where it would sell enough coffee to earn a satisfactory return.

So—how much capital will you need? Under most circumstances, you will need at least $10,000 to start a vending business. You may need more. It depends on the type of vending business you decide on and the location—a large city, a small town, an industrial center, a resort, or what.

This figure doesn't include working capital and living expenses while you're getting started. The requirements here are flexible. Normally, receipts from the machines carry the average small operator well enough after the first few months. But allowance has to be made for expansion and for problems that can't be foreseen, such as strikes and reductions in the work force at your factory locations, loss of locations to a competitor, fire, theft, and so on.

Where To Get Financing

The American vending industry has made such constant progress since the late 1950s that capital to supplement your savings will probably be available from various sources. Among the major financing agents interested in vending companies are machine manufacturers, vendible-products suppliers, banks, factoring companies, special vending investment companies, and equipment-leasing companies.

Machine manufacturers. Most of the machine manufacturers and many distributors offer their own financing plans. Terms may depend on your credit rating and, as you become established, on the lender's knowledge of your locations and your proved ability as a good vending operator.

Product suppliers. A number of leading suppliers of coffee, dairy products, and soft-drink sirups have worked out special financing plans for their vending customers. Interest rates are usually about the same as those charged by banks, and the financing is often done through a bank chosen by the supplier. In effect, the supplier company, through its bank, guarantees a conditional sales contract for machines. The charges under this arrangement can be less than financing terms from the machine seller, but the plan is usually available only to established customers of the supplier company.

Banks. Many banks handle daily deposits for vending operators, and this has alerted them to the soundness of vending companies as borrowers. In fact, some well-known banking institutions have special vending departments.

One banker [2] has recommended that loans to vending operators be based on the five "C's" of credit: character, capacity, capital, conditions, and collateral. For the bank officer, he outlined this 4-point checklist:

1. The number of machines operated.
2. The type of operation. (Is it confined to one operation, or is it diversified, with two or more operations?)
3. The type of equipment. (Is the vending machine of standard type, so as to ensure an efficient operation?)
4. The value of the equipment. (The purchase price, if new; the current market value if it is used equipment.)

A typical bank loan agreement, reprinted from the article, is shown in exhibit 1.

Commercial finance companies. These companies usually provide financing for the machine distributor, based on paper generated from their customers' vending operations. In some cases, their dealings may be directly with the operator.

Special vending investment companies. A few investment companies have been organized to lend capital to established vending operators. As security for the capital furnished, they are usually given options to acquire stock or a part interest in the vending operation. Your banker or trade association will be able to tell you how to get in touch with one of these companies.

Equipment-leasing companies. Equipment-leasing companies offer service vehicles or vending machines to the vending operator on a lease basis, sometimes with options by which the operator may purchase the equipment under certain conditions. Most leasing plans are better suited to established vending operators than to the beginning operator.

Which one to use? It is usually best to examine several possible sources of capital. Compare the cost, the conditions of obtaining the loan or lease, and so on before you make formal application for a loan.

If borrowing is necessary and you can't find a commercial lender, the Small Business Administration may be able to help—by participating with a bank in a loan, by guaranteeing part of a loan made by a bank, or by a direct Government loan. If you need SBA help, get in touch with the nearest SBA field office.

---

[2] R. J. Erfle, former vice president of the Broad Street Trust Co. of Philadelphia, in an article in the March 1962 Bulletin of Robert Morris Associates.

V. Where to Get Machines and Supplies

Y OU'VE WEIGHED the pros and cons. You know the pitfalls are real. But you've decided to take the risk. You are going into the vending business.

So you want to buy machines—and fill them. Where do you go?

Vending Machine Manufacturers

According to the current *Blue Book of Automatic Merchandising,* a directory published by the National Automatic Merchandising Association, more than 150 American companies manufacture vending machines. All but a few of these manufacturers produce only one or two kinds of machines. Fewer than 10 make a full line of vending equipment.

Which manufacturer do you contact? Well, what type of vending business do you want to enter? If you're interested in a stamp-vending route, you'll deal with one of the single-line producers in that field, because none of the major full-line manufacturers make that kind of equipment. The same is true of several other specialized lines. For the more common candy, cigarette, coffee, pastry, milk, soft-drink, and food machines, you have a wide choice among both the full-line companies and the smaller, specialized producers.

All these companies are used to dealing with newcomers to the vending business. Most of them are able and willing to give you guidance.

The marks of quality. What can you expect of a good vending-machine manufacturer?

• A good manufacturer sells equipment at an established uniform price. Discounts, if any, are only for the large-volume purchaser. Therefore, beware of special deals.

• A good manufacturer is ready to supply spare parts, service manuals, troubleshooting hints, and conversion kits (for adapatation to special needs).

• A good manufacturer will have obtained approval under various State, local or national health codes for machines that vend perishable merchandise. Such approval is required in many local and State jurisdictions before you can place the machines. It is furnished through the evaluation programs of the National Automatic Merchandising Association or the National Sanitation Foundation. Be sure the equipment meets these certifications as required by your State or local health authorities.

• A good manufacturer is always willing to demonstrate the working of the machines to you. He will not play down the importance of know-how in servicing and repairing the equipment.

• Several leading machine manufacturers work through local or regional distributors. The majority deal with their customers through direct-from-the-factory salesmen in addition to maintaining regional offices and depots.

• The manufacturer depends almost exclusively on you, the operator, for his business. The better you know your business, the greater his chance for repeat sales in the future. Therefore, most reputable machine manufacturers will help you get started as an operator only if they believe you are well qualified for the job.

• Continually upgrading machines, developing new types of machines, adding refinements for easier and less costly servicing, improving the merchandising and eye appeal—all these functions are carried on by quality vending-machine manufacturers whether they are large or small, diversified or single-machine producers.

Used equipment. A few vending-machine companies specialize in reconditioning and selling used venders. If such a dealer is reputable, his equipment will be reliable, and it will cost less than new machines. But most owners of prime locations won't knowingly let you place used equipment in their establishments.

As a result of the rapid expansion of vended service, many location owners have become very knowledgeable. They know the machines well. They get offers from several operators, and secondhand equipment will not help your chances of getting new locations.

Vendible-Product Suppliers

As a vending operator, you are a retailer who gets vendible merchandise from many sources. You are like the corner grocer, in a way. He produces none of the products on his shelves. The candy bars he has for sale come from a number of factories and often from more than one distributor. So it is with all his products.

This is true of the vending operator, too. You will rely on various producers or distributors for the products you sell. Take coffee vending. You must buy cups, coffee, creaming agents. For most coffee venders, you will also need tea, hot chocolate, and even soup concentrates. So, with just a simple coffee-vending route, you may have from two to four suppliers.

If, like most vending operators, you handle several product lines, you will soon find yourself dealing with from 4 to 20 supplier companies. Even with the simplest vending route, you should contact competing suppliers to compare their quality, prices, and services.

Suppliers' services. You will find all supplier companies interested in you, even if yours is a small operation. Getting in on the ground floor with a new operator is important to them. You are an outlet of extra sales. Moreover, in some products—such as candy, cigarettes, and soft drinks—vending machines offer suppliers a valuable opportunity to win new business. A casual sampling of root beer from your machine may produce a new customer who will buy a six-pack in the supermarket.

Knowing this, many suppliers have training schools where the operator can learn about their products. They will teach you everything from better merchandising of gum to how to brew better vended coffee. Don't hesitate to seek the advice of suppliers who are willing to give it. Their salesmen contact many successful operators in other localities and can pass on to you valuable hints and experience.

Another important service of many product suppliers is that they will deliver small quantities. Some will even let you return products that have been stored too long. Most of them want to make sure that only fresh and appetizing merchandise is sold from your machine.

Preselling. Equally important is the "preselling" done by many suppliers. The constant advertising of cigarettes, certain brands of candy, brand-name soft drinks—all this is a direct selling aid to your vending operation. The supplier of a given candy bar, for instance, helps make the sale from your machine by creating recognition for the brand through advertising, even though the advertising may never picture the product in a vender.

Training for You and Your Employees

As a small businessman with your mind on many day-to-day details, you will find it hard to keep up with innovations in the vending industry. Improvements in vending machines, a new kind of hot-beverage vending cup, a cheaper way to service your equipment, and many other developments can come along without your being aware of them.

That's why the solid machine manufacturer, supplier, or distributor will send out field-service men or organize special training schools for operators, routemen, or mechanics. Usually, there is no charge for these courses. They may last a few evening hours, all day, or several days.

Beware of Deceptive Promotions

It's not hard to find reputable vending-machine manufacturers. But it's just as easy to fall victim to the deceptive promoter who sells cheaply made equipment at inflated prices and promises exaggerated profits.

Such deals are usually offered in the "Help Wanted" or "Business Opportunity" classified-ad sections of local newspapers. They often cite well-known name brands, require a minimum investment, and promise a profitable return from part-time work. Some of the most respected local and national newspapers have carried these ads. The copy cleverly conceals the real nature of the offer.

Beware especially of ads that offer machines already on location, or tell you, "Our salesmen will help you get locations." Reputable manufacturers seldom do this. They wouldn't use their own salesmen to help you compete for locations with their present operator customers.

What lures many intelligent persons is that the deceptive promoter "looked so honest. And he really knew the business." Of *course* he looked good! That's the only way he can deceive you. But after fleecing dozens of unwary investors of their savings, he will skip town and set up shop elsewhere. How do you guard against this fringe element?

• Never buy machines on the basis of newspaper ads without comparing the offer with equipment and prices offered by established manufacturers. Do this on your own without letting the advertiser know about it.

• Check the ad with the Better Business Bureau. They may already have received complaints from other victims.

• Show the literature and the proposed contract to an established vending operator in your community and ask his opinion.

• Never sign *any* paper without having your attorney check it carefully.

• If at all possible, contact a vending trade association for other information.

VI. Putting Your Machines Where They'll Pay

L OOK FOR BUSINESS where the need is greatest. In other words, seek out high-volume locations suited to your type of equipment. But keep an open mind. Experienced operators constantly report unlikely locations that turn out to be high-volume producers.

Exhibit 2 shows how sales volume affects operating profits. The profit resulting from sales of 25 cups a day from 1 coffee machine is compared with the profit resulting from sales of 75 cups a day from the same machine. (Since prices change and conditions vary from one locality to another, the figures should not be taken literally but only as an example.)

Each product has its own characteristics and markets, but a typical case will illustrate how to get and keep good locations.

A Case Study

George Bruening started out with compact candy venders and a few coffee machines. Some were already on location when he bought them. For the rest, he concentrated on service stations, a few small motels, truck terminals, a motor-parts outlet, and a swimming pool.

By purchasing only small machines, Bruening avoided competition with larger, established firms that rely primarily on high-volume locations. Most of the places he contacted had never had coffee machines.

Although he didn't know it at the time, he had selected two products that usually return a higher net profit than other products. (The national profit average for coffee is about 10 percent of gross sales; for confections, nearly 6 percent.) He avoided the pitfalls of starting out with pastry or sandwiches—their perishability can cause loss instead of profit for the beginner. And Bruening's town was small enough so that he could go after all potential locations without worrying about his route pattern. In a larger city, he would have been forced to concentrate on a limited area to keep his travel for servicing the machines from consuming too much time.

He soon found that sales at one of the truck terminals slowed down for 2 weeks a month. This cut into his sales, and he decided to leave only the candy machine at the terminal. His wife had heard about a new carwash, and he moved the coffee machine there after convincing the carwash owner that the extra income from commissions would be worth the space the machine would take.

Low volume eventually forced Bruening to relocate other equipment; but as he worked, he learned. Prospecting for new locations seemed to follow certain directions:

1. Bruening watched the newspapers for information about new businesses and new construction.

2. He cased all prospective locations for the number of employees, traffic, age and earnings pattern of potential customers, and nearness of competing outlets such as drugstores, restaurants, and so on.

3. He cooperated with another vending operator who specialized in milk-vending machines. Since the two men were not competing with each other, they referred business from one to the other.

4. He avoided offering overly high commissions to location owners. Instead he stressed his service and the convenience of vending machines.

5. Experience taught him to turn down business where the location owner insisted on fancy, large-volume coffee machines even though the sales potential didn't justify the investment.

6. He never stopped looking for potential new locations. He enlisted his family, his friends, and his relatives to give him tips and ideas.

Before long, Bruening had learned enough about the business to zero in on locations of his competitors. As he upgraded his own equipment, he found potential customers who were dissatisfied with the vending service they were getting. In several of these cases, he was able to gain a foothold through referrals from satisfied customers.

How To Sell Your Services

Selling techniques in the vending business vary as much as the 6,000 vending-service companies do. The largest firms have full-time sales departments; but in the average vending company, selling is one of the many jobs performed by the owner.

The first steps. One of the basic steps in getting new locations is to build a "logical prospect" list. Put down all the possible types of loca tions you are interested in serving.   One such list in a typical city included more than 70 different kinds of locations ranging from Airports to Zoos.   An even longer list is shown as exhibit 3.

In the beginning, your selling methods may be very simple.   As you cover your route, simply keep your eyes and ears open to possible new

Exhibit 3

Have You Tried These Vending Locations?

(From *National Bottlers' Gazette,* June 1959)

Automobile laundries	Employment agencies	Parking lots
Automobile showrooms	Exhibitions	Post offices
Academics	Excursion boats	Picnic grounds
Arenas	Firehouses	Pawnshops
Amusement parks	Fishing piers	Points of interest
Arcades	Fishing camps	Plant locker rooms
Airports	Factories (all types)	Photo studios
Athletic fields	Ferry stations	Police stations
Armories	Fairs	Public buildings
Art galleries	Farmers' markets	Playgrounds
Athletic stadiums	Funeral homes	Parks
Aquariums	Federal buildings	Rifle ranges
Archery ranges	Five-and-ten stores	Riding academies
Apartment houses	Fruit stands	Resorts
Auction houses	Fraternity houses	Racetracks
Beaches	Golf courses	Railroad stations
Bait stations	Golf driving ranges	Recreation centers
Boatyards	"Miniature" golf	Restaurants
Bowling alleys	courses	Stores (all types)
Billiard parlors	Gymnasiums	Shipyards
Banks	General stores	Skating rinks
Bars	Gas stations	Supermarkets
Barbershops	Garages	Sanitariums
Beauty salons	Grocery stores	Schools
Broadcasting studios	Hostels	Stadiums
Boards of trade	Hobby shops	Swimming pools
Bus terminals	Hospitals	Shoeshine parlors
Community centers	Hunting lodges	Ticket agencies
Construction projects	Hotels	Train terminals
Courthouses	Historical sites	Telephone companies
Community buildings	Lumberyards	Travel bureaus
Convention halls	Laundries	Tourist camps
Concert halls	Lodge halls	Taxi stations
Cafes	Libraries	Tobacco stores
Candy stores	Lunchrooms	Theaters
Clubs	Military posts	Trucking terminals
Carnivals	Model homes	Trailer camps
College dormitories	Massage parlors	Union headquarters
Doctors' offices	Marine-gas barges	Western Union
Drawbridge booths	Meeting halls	Warehouses
Drive-ins (banks, etc.)	Museums	Youth centers
Dance halls	Motels	YMCA
Drugstores	Night clubs	YWCA
Department stores	Office buildings	Zoos

locations. Drop in on the owner of the prospective new location and ask him whether he's ever considered installing a candy machine. Explain the convenience for his customers and employees and the extra traffic your machines will produce (if he runs a service station or store). Describe your policy of providing machines free of charge and doing all stocking, servicing, and repair work. Explain how you will share your profit with him (if you do) in the form of a commission for letting you place the machine.

Another source of new business is your own workforce. Vending operators often reward employees with special bonuses for furnishing leads that result in new accounts. In some companies, it is part of the routeman's job to go after new business.

Selling for growth. As your business grows, you'll need to organize your selling effort more thoroughly. Establish a card file of potential locations, and set aside a definite amount of time each week for calling on prospects. Have your business listed in the yellow pages of your telephone directory. Consider advertising in your local newspaper or in special-events publications.

A good method of advertising is a direct-mail program based on your prospect list. (Several machine manufacturers help with tailormade campaigns.) A direct-mail campaign should start with a letter and a reply card set up so that you follow up on a prospect within a week after he returns the card. Follow up even if no card is returned.

It's important to know who is "the person to see." In a service station, it's usually the owner or manager. In a factory, the place to start is usually the personnel manager or the purchasing agent.

Since you can't bring the machine on your first call, carry illustrated literature of your machines. (Most machine manufacturers are glad to furnish colorful tearsheets of advertisements for this purpose.) Offer to demonstrate the equipment at your other locations, and invite the prospect to check on your performance with present customers. Often, the recommendations of people or organizations he respects carry more weight than all the sales talk or benefits you can offer.

If the machine manufacturer's representative is in your area, ask his advice. Many of these representatives are trained to give you suggestions based on the experience of other customers.

As you expand, you will probably want to make use of a special sales-presentation folder. Put the following items in it:

A list of quality brand products you carry in your machines.

A list of present customers, preferably with photos of some installations.

A statement of your company policy. (This can be useful for employees as well as for sales purposes.)

A list of the business and civic organizations to which you belong.

For larger customers, it's good salesmanship to be able to say that you are a member of your State or national vending association. Don't hesitate to seek ideas on selling from trade associations, trade journals, and other sources. The basis of the vending business is selling and merchandising. Very little of it is "automatic."

Should You Have a Firm Contract?

A contract with the location owner ensures, in addition to continuity, a better understanding of what the vending operator offers and what responsibilities the location owner assumes. A properly drawn contract should spell out clearly the agreement between the vender and the location owner as to what each is to do or not do, when and for how long he is to do it, and the amount and method of payment.

A contract is simply good business, especially since you are offering to place an expensive piece of equipment at the disposal of the location owner—and at no charge. If he should suddenly decide without cause to have you remove it, you will still have to complete payments on the equipment, even though your income from it has been cut off.

The contract should always be drawn by a competent attorney. It should include these basic items, at the least:

Duration of the contract.
Who has title to the equipment.
Payments to be made by the operator (commissions) or by the location (subsidies).
Termination provisions.
Security provisions (reasons for termination, protection against competing selling methods, responsibility in case of vandalism, and so on).
Freedom to operate (recordkeeping, changes in selling prices).
Assumption of risks.
Safety provisions.

You will avoid problems if you make yourself thoroughly familiar with the details of location contracts. A guide, *How To Use Location Contracts,* is available from the National Automatic Merchandising Association and from the Magazine *VEND,* where it was first published. A sample contract from this guide is shown as exhibit 4.

Keeping Your Locations

A successful vending operator doesn't think only of *getting* locations; he is equally concerned about *keeping* the ones he has. The same principles apply to both goals.

Exhibit 4.—Location contract

Single Machine Agreement

In consideration of the mutual promises and convenants set out herein it is agreed by and between _____ of _____ (street & number) of _____ (city and state), its successors and assigns, hereinafter called "Company" and _____ Automatic Vending Company of _____ (street and number) _____ (city and state), its successors and assigns hereinafter called "Operator" that:

1. Company grants operator the exclusive right to install and operate cigarette vending machines at mutually agreed on location(s) on the premises owned (operated) by the Company at _____ (street and number), Chicago, Illinois.

2. Operator agrees to install and properly service, maintain, clean and keep stocked with standard brands of cigarettes to the proper operating level the following machine(s):

Kinds(s)   Serial Number(s)

1. ....

2. ....

3. ....

It is agreed that operator may change the machine(s) listed for machine(s) of similar quality and capacity without in any way affecting the other terms and provisions of this agreement and without changing this agreement to list the machine(s) so exchanged. The machine(s) so installed may also be exchanged at any time upon written consent by both parties to this agreement without in any way affecting the other terms and provisions of this agreement.

3. Company will furnish all necessary electrical and service connections for operation of the machine(s) and will keep the area around the machine(s) in a clean and orderly condition.

4. Operator agrees to pay Company for the exclusive right to sell cigarettes on the described premises _____ per cent of the gross receipts of sales through the machine(s). Operator will submit to the company, by the 10th day of each month, a statement covering the sales through the machine(s) for the preceding month together with a check for the sums due the company under the agreement. State, city, county or other required licenses and all sales taxes shall be deducted from the gross receipts from the machine(s) before computing the sums due and payable to the company.

5. Company agrees to notify the Operator promptly of any failure of the machine(s) to function properly and of any other matters affecting the proper operation of the machine(s), and further agrees to permit only authorized agents of the operator to remove, open or tamper with the machine(s) at any time. Operator shall have access to the described premises at all reasonable times in order to service and maintain the machine(s) properly.

6. It is understood that the provisions of this agreement are based on state, federal, local and other taxes and cigarette costs on the date of this agreement. It is agreed that in the event of an increase in such taxes or costs which are not reflected in an increased retail price of cigarettes sold through the machine(s) that the payment to company set out above may be reduced by an amount equal to the increased costs of operation resulting from such increase.

7. It is understood that the machine(s) are and remain the property of the operator who will cause the machine(s) to be removed within thirty (30) days upon having given to Company or received from Company written notice by registered or certified mail.

8. Operator agrees to comply with all federal, state, local or other laws or regulations applying to the machine(s) or products.

9. Operator agrees to carry and continue in force the following insurance: General Liability and Property Damage (if applicable Workmen's Compensation and Product Liability). A certificate is available on request.

10. This agreement shall remain in full force and effect for a period of one year from the date hereof, and, unless canceled by proper written notice, is deemed to be automatically renewed for periods of one year thereafter without notice.

11. This contract is entered into by the Operator on the express warranty and representation that Company owns and operates the business conducted at the above described premises.

12. This agreement may not be assigned by either party without the written consent of the other.

Dated _____

Proprietor _____

Secretary _____

Company Name _____

Vending Company _____

Address _____

Address _____

City and State _____

City and State _____

Since a vending operation depends on machines and on the products they sell, excellence of equipment and of products vended is the key to successful operation and to getting new locations. But your competitors have equal access to top-quality machines and top-quality products. So it is also important to offer top-quality service. This is the only point at which one company can—with the right effort—do better than its competitor.

"Good service" covers many points:

• It requires round-the-clock servicing and therefore full-time phone service in case of malfunctioning or other problems.

• It requires constant attention to the training of employees—to brushing up skills previously taught as well as to presenting new skills, new aspects of the operation, new equipment.

• It requires strict attention to sanitation. Laxity here will cause problems with health inspectors, unfavorable reactions from customers, and loss of sales.

• It requires machines that are well designed, well made, and well taken care of.

• It requires prompt attention to refunds when a machine malfunctions or a customer has trouble with it. All your equipment should be posted with your name, your phone number, and information about how refunds can be obtained. (Too many operators still neglect this step, but many location owners are beginning to require it.) Refund policies are one of the criteria that distinguish excellent service from haphazard operation.

No skill in selling or in building good relations with a location is more important than the attention you give to providing topnotch products, good equipment, and first-rate service. They are the keys to keeping the accounts you have and to getting new ones.

RETAIL MUSIC STORE

M USIC STORES are of many kinds and varieties. Formerly, the high-grade music business in the community featured pianos or was solely a piano store. Other stores handled only the smaller musical instruments.

Today, too, many stores handle musical instruments and accessories but do not sell pianos.[1] Some of these were begun by music teachers who opened teaching studios for accordion and guitar or by band directors for teaching band instruments of all kinds. At first, they handled only the sheet music used in the studio, but gradually their activities covered a wider and wider range. Some developed small bands or orchestras. Some taught baton twirling.

With the growing popularity of the phonograph and the aggressive promotion of record manufacturers, many of the better music stores undertook the sale of records. By now, there are

---

[1] Throughout this booklet, references to "musical instruments" will exclude pianos and console organs, which are known in the trade as "keyboard instruments."

many shops that specialize in records and in high-fidelity record and tape reproducers as well as the many accessories now on the market. This is a multimillion dollar industry. Quality phonograph and reproduction systems with many loud speakers, installed to specifications, are elaborate and costly projects. And never has there been such a large and varied selection of recorded music.

The early 1930's brought rapid expansion of the radio industry. When people had only to turn a knob to receive their music free, the sale of pianos especially went into a slump. Radios, on the other hand, could hardly be built fast enough to supply the demand.

Many music stores became radio stores during that period. Later, combination radio-phonographs were featured and then, of course, television receiving sets.

Many music stores not only handled all these items but took on also the many new electrical appliances that were brought out in the 1930's and 1940's. Some people still tend to think of a music store as an all-purpose shop that handles electrical appliances, radios, television sets, musical instruments, sheet music, records, and accessories. The beginning dealer, however, should avoid this approach.

Opportunities in the Retail Music Business

There has never been a time with so many opportunities in the retail music business as today. True, there is some tendency on the part of large dealers and manufacturers to set up chains of retail music stores; and many other types of retailers—including mail-order houses, department stores, drugstores, food markets, and others—handle goods formerly pretty well restricted to music and record stores. But as yet these are not discouraging factors. There is no question but that opportunities in the music business are increasing as people have more leisure time.

As a music merchant, you will be in a position to serve your community well. You will deal mostly with the cultural element in the community. Your sales will be largely semiluxury items, and quality is relatively easy to sell. If you run a music studio, you will meet many parents who are vitally interested in their children's welfare. If you sell records, there will be buyers in your store all day long.

For the careful operator, profits in the music business are as good as the average in other businesses. Furthermore, the small retailer can handle his operation with a minimum of help, and the work is pleasant.

Are You Qualified?

Most music dealers are independent small businessmen. They started with limited capital, but they had a general knowledge of some aspect of the music business—as a former teacher, school music director, or salesman in a music store.

But not everyone is qualified to own and manage a music store even with capital and experience. John Hayes[2], an excellent piano and organ salesman, went into business for himself. He sold pianos on time. Some of his sales the bank financed; some were turned down.

But Hayes was a better salesman than financier. He thought his banker was too tight on credit, so he began to carry some of the paper himself. He'd sell, for a $50 down payment, a $700 piano that had cost him $350. This meant that he needed $300 to replace that one piano.

It was only a matter of time before his reserves were gone. He went out of business because he was too good a salesman, too poor a manager.

The owner-manager of a music store needs training and experience in management as well as in some phase of the music business. A small dealer must understand financial management or he will fail.

Nor need everyone interested in music own his own business. The compensation to salesmen, both retail and wholesale, is above average. Many branch-store managers are earning good incomes without the financial responsibility that ownership car-

---

[2] Names in all examples have been changed.

ries with it. So consider carefully whether you really want to take on the responsibilities and risks that go with owning and managing a music store of your own.

What Kind of Music Store for You?

Suppose you've decided that you really do want to own and manage your own music store. Very early in your planning you should make up your mind just what kind of music store you are going to have. This decision will depend partly on you—your background and what you'd like to do, partly on where you decide to open your store, and partly on how much capital you have to start with. Sometimes two of these factors are involved, sometimes all three. The first two are involved in the following case.

Robert Thomas, a band director in a community of 10,000, got the idea that since he wasn't very busy in the summer, he'd open a small music store in his town. He planned to feature recreational instruments, which are inexpensive and don't require too much capital, and popular records for young people.

He began selling guitars, other stringed instruments, and records. Soon he found that he could repair band instruments, and then he gradually added new band instruments to his inventory.

For a time the business prospered. The town, however, was too close to a larger city. The competition of the city stores, plus the fact that Thomas didn't want to give up directing his band, caused him to close shop. Basically, he was not retail store-owner material.

Kinds of music stores. Music stores can be classified according to the types of merchandise they handle as follows:
1. Pianos and organs (keyboard instruments) only, new and used
2. Pianos, organs, and musical instruments only
3. Musical instruments and accessories only
4. Musical instruments and band and orchestral music

5. Pianos, musical instruments, and sheet music
6. Studios and sales (piano, organ, or other)
7. Records and sound equipment only
8. All musical merchandise—a music department store

To these eight basic groups can be added radios, television sets, and appliances, plus service in any or all areas.

Limit your field. It's easy to make the mistake of expanding with lines for which the demand in your area is too light to be practical. If your music store is in a small community, remember that you can get from the wholesaler or manufacturer on short notice almost any article in the lines you carry. You don't have to stock items for which you rarely have a call.

As a small music dealer, you must study carefully the lines you will carry, and not just from the investment and turnover angle. You must also remember not to spread yourself too thin. Ask yourself these questions:

"Why am I in this business"

"What do I want to do and how best can I do it?"

If you are a teacher with limited capital, don't try to carry too broad an inventory. If you are a salesman and want to go into business for yourself, beware of having too many irons in the fire.

Location Problems

Where to establish your store?
Other questions have to be answered
before you're ready to decide.

O NE OF THE FIRST decisions to be made in preparing to open
a retail music business is where to open your store. A
small dealer with little capital can't afford a mistake in selecting
his location. You must study very carefully the factors that make
a location good or bad for the type of store you want to open.
Even a musical-instrument dealer who will be calling on band
directors and can draw prospects to his store by personal contacts
must pay careful attention to location problems.

Types of Merchandise

In thinking of a location for your music store, keep in mind
the buying habits of the people you hope to win as customers.
Buying habits are the basis on which marketing experts classify
goods as convenience goods, shopping goods, or specialty goods.

Convenience goods are usually purchased often and at the
most convenient place. The price per unit is relatively small,
and the customer doesn't want to put too much time or effort

into making the purchase. A supplier of these goods therefore tries to offer them where as many customers as possible will be sure to see them.

Convenience goods are sometimes bought on impulse and therefore should be sold where they are exposed to heavy buying traffic. This type of buying has increased greatly in the last few years, and a great variety of products are now offered for impulse buying. Popular phonograph records are often bought on impulse. The same is true of recreational musical instruments, musical toys, and even popular sheet music.

Shopping goods are items for which the buyer wants to compare styles, price, and quality. He usually visits several stores before he finally makes a purchase.

A music dealer may choose to combat this desire to shop around by playing up his studio facilities and superiority in teaching. Otherwise, good locations for a shopping-goods store are in downtown districts, regional shopping centers, or near competitors.

Specialty goods are usually high priced, and exclusive in style and quality. They are purchased for long-time possession.

Stores handling items of this kind rely on reputation and prestige. The purchaser will go out of his way to find the items or stores. For this reason, a location near such stores may be a good one for a new music dealer.

Location and Types of Music Merchandise

Pianos, organs, and musical instruments are generally considered shopping goods, except for the highest priced instruments. Most music dealers, however, handle other items along with these, so a music store can be said to carry shopping goods and some convenience goods.

If you are interested only in the sale of pianos and organs, you should consider locations near similar stores. Retail "grouping" is of two kinds. One is the grouping of stores of the same general class. That is, piano and organ stores can group with furniture stores, antique shops, jewelry stores, and so on. The other grouping is competitive grouping, where each store can profit from being near stores handling similar items. This is often the situation in downtown areas.

Many music stores begin as music studios. For a teaching studio and sales center, a neighborhood or suburban shopping center, near schools and easily reached by prospective students, is a good location.

A small music store that caters to band directors and supplies band instruments to schools should be near the downtown area. It should be easily reached by car and have considerable space for storage and/or repair. Such stores are usually located in low-rent areas, however, because much of the owner's time is spent out in the field calling on band directors.

If you are planning to open a band-instrument store, be sure you are in an area where there are plenty of bands to service. Also, you must be in a position to handle repairs either in your shop or through a nearby repair center, or perhaps through a large general repair center such as can be found in many large cities.

If yours will be the only store selling records in a small community, choose a downtown location. Complete music stores, too, are usually in the downtown area, though many of those in big cities are branching out into the suburbs.

Selecting a Site

Every community has different problems for the prospective owner of a music store seeking a location. If your store is to be in a small city or town where you are likely to be the only business of your kind, the best location is in the center of the retail area or near it. Parking isn't too great a problem. If you plan to be in a large city, it may be wise to be near your competition if a cluster has already been established. If there are shopping centers in your area, you may choose one of these for your operation.

Leased Departments

*If you choose this sort of operation,
study the contract before you sign—the
advantages—the disadvantages.*

SOME MUSIC RETAILERS, some wholesalers, and even some
manufacturers operate leased music departments in department stores. The basic reasons for a retail store's leasing one or
more of its departments are these:

To get expert merchandisers in areas not familiar to
the department-store owner.

To expand without more inventory investment and
with the least possible capital outlay.

To get superior purchasing facilities.

A number of leased music operations have been very successful in large department stores in cities of 100,000 or more
throughout the country. Even some music retailers have used
leasing arrangements in order to offer merchandise for which
they lack know-how or capital.

Sheet-music wholesalers, for example, have leased departments in music stores and in radio and phonograph stores, as
well as in department stores. Piano and organ departments
have also been operated as leased departments. So have record
departments, music-instrument departments, and music studios.

Advantages and Disadvantages

If you plan to start your retail music business as a leased department, you should know the advantages and disadvantages of such an operation. One of the biggest advantages to you—the lessee—is that the store—the lessor—pays the cost of preparing the premises. Other advantages include these:

1. You start with a location in a developed market where traffic is assured.
2. You gain the prestige of the store's name.
3. Credit and delivery services are usually already established.

There may also be some disadvantages, however. The less favorable points include the following:

1. You aren't sure of a permanent location—the store may not renew the lease when it runs out.
2. You don't have as much chance to build personal good will.
3. You have to accept the store's credit terms, collection procedure, employee rules, and hours. (In some cases, leased teaching studios have been located in such a way that they could be open at hours when the rest of the store is closed.)

The charge paid by the lessee varies from 12 to 25 percent of the net sales.

A Typical Leased-Department Arrangement

If you are considering a leased department, study all provisions of the lease very carefully and have your lawyer go over it with you. Be sure you understand exactly what your rights and responsibilities are. Following is an outline of a typical leased-department contract:

CLAUSE 1 describes the location of the premises to be leased and lists the merchandise covered.

CLAUSE 2 states the basis of the charge to the lessee—what percentage he will have to pay of sales less returns and repossessions, less occupational taxes, less trade-in allowances, less carrying charges and interest.

CLAUSE 3 provides that the lessor shall take charge of all funds, keep accurate records, and provide the lessee with monthly financial statements on or before the 15th of the month following the period covered by the statements.

CLAUSE 4 provides that charge and deferred-payment sales are to be treated as cash sales.

CLAUSE 5 provides that the lessor may change the location of the department in his store and that he is to pay the cost of any such change.

CLAUSE 6 states that the lessee is to supply the necessary fixtures; that the fixtures are to be approved by the lessor as to style, color, design, and so on, so that they will harmonize with the rest of the store; and that the lessee is to contribute a specific amount on any new construction said to be the property of the lessee.

CLAUSE 7 provides that the lessor is not liable for damage to lessee's property by fire, water, or other casualty, or theft.

CLAUSE 8 states that the lease is not assignable and the leased department cannot be subleased or transferred.

CLAUSE 9 states that if the lessee moves, he may not advertise that his stock was formerly on the premises of the lessor.

CLAUSE 10 states that the lessee shall employ his own employees and may pay them their salaries, including uniforms if any, but that these employees shall agree to abide by the rules of the lessor. If any employee is objectionable to the lessor, he shall be removed.

CLAUSE 11 specifies that the lessor shall supply light, heat, electricity, elevator service, cashier service, wrapping service, wrapping materials, porter service, salesbooks, local telephone service, and delivery service (except pianos) in metropolitan areas. This clause also provides that lessee is to deliver all merchandise to alley loading platform of lessor, and lessor is to deliver it to location.

CLAUSE 12 provides that insofar as the public is concerned, the department is to be conducted as an integral part of the business of the lessor. The lessee has no right to incur any debt or other liability in the name of the lessor, however.

CLAUSE 13 states that the lessee is to advertise in the name of the lessor but is to pay for the advertising himself. The lessor is to approve all advertising, which must conform to the type and style used by the lessor.

CLAUSE 14 states that in case of fire the lease will terminate if it is impossible to carry on the business.

CLAUSE 15 provides that if either party goes bankrupt or makes assignment for the benefit of a creditor, the lease is to terminate.

CLAUSE 16 provides that the lessor is to fix the hours the leased department will be open.

CLAUSE 17 reserves to the lessor the right to make adjustments or settle claims of customers.

CLAUSE 18 provides that the department shall be conducted in a first-class manner and kept adequately stocked with representative merchandise at all times.

CLAUSE 19 provides that window space shall be available to the lessee for advertising.

CLAUSE 20 states that lessee will indemnify and hold lessor harmless of any act of commission or omission on the lessee's part.

CLAUSE 21 requires that lessee carry adequate workmen's compensation insurance and public-liability insurance indemnifying lessor.

CLAUSE 22 provides employee discounts for lessee's and lessor's employees and provides that lessor shall be paid the lease percentage on these accounts.

CLAUSE 23 states that the lessee shall pay all taxes arising from operations of his departments.

CLAUSE 24 states the lessor's agreement not to sell merchandise similar to that of the lessee.

CLAUSE 25 provides that the lessor will deduct and retain carrying charges on time-payment or other credit accounts.

CLAUSE 26 states that the lessee shall repurchase goods sold by him and repossessed, and provides for determining the balance due lessee and lessor when repossessed goods include goods purchased from both.

Your Building and Equipment

The home for your business—
keep it simple—
but pleasant and comfortable.

T HE SIZE OF YOUR STORE will depend partly on the volume of business you expect to do. Size is related to rent, and your rent should be based on what you estimate your sales volume will be after a year's operation.

Occupancy expenses—that is, rent plus such expenses as maintenance salaries and supplies, repairs, insurance, heat, light, power, and so on—shouldn't total more than 5 percent of gross sales. So if you expect sales to level off at $100,000 at the end of the year, you can figure on $5,000 a year, or $400 a month, for occupancy expenses.

The size of the store is also directly related to the kind of merchandise you carry. If you sell only pianos and organs, 1500 to 2000 square feet will be enough to start with. A frontage of 20 feet with a depth of 100 feet will give you room for handling a representative line of pianos and organs as well as for office and repair facilities. If you plan to carry other instruments as well, you'll need more room. If possible, the store should open onto an alley in the rear for receiving and shipping.

The Rooms You Need

Your business office and, of course, the repair room should be separated from the sales floor. Especially if you sell organs, it is well to have soundproofed studios for teaching individual beginners. Group or classroom teaching can be carried on in the evening when the store is closed for regular business. The studio operation is discussed further in chapter 5.

A couple of small closing rooms will give the salesman a place to take his customer for the final steps in a major sale—drawing up the contract for time payments, recording credit information, and so on. Two chairs and a simple desk are all the equipment you need in each closing room. Keep the desk clear, with contracts and other information filed away conveniently in the drawers.

Interior Finishing

The floor of your show window should be about 8 inches above the selling floor. It's a good idea, too, to elevate some of the spinets on the floor itself. If possible, have your floor carpeted to give a warm, homelike atmosphere.

The interior color of the store and the lighting are important. Warm pastel colors are best. You'll need adequate lighting fixtures of a type that brings out the best in the wood of the instruments. Consult a good electrical-goods supplier or the electric power company in your community for advice as to the best kinds of light for your products.

The store should be air conditioned and should have good acoustic properties. Ventilation is important in all rooms.

Your Display Window

Everyone passing your store will judge it from your show windows. They are the face you present to the passersby. They must be clean and attractive and protected against moisture, condensation, frosting, fading, and heat damage. You'll need awnings or marquees, or perhaps tinted glass. The floors should be carpeted. Have the windows cleaned daily, and change the displays every week.

The background of the windows can be open, partly closed, or completely closed. Most music stores favor an open back, but this means that the entire store can be seen from the street. The layout behind the windows as well as the windows themselves has to be carefully planned.

The lighting of your display window is important. You'll need plenty of light, but the lights themselves should be concealed. There should be no shadows on the merchandise.

Furniture, Equipment, Supplies

You don't need—nor want—many pieces of furniture on the sales floor or in your display window. If you want to have a brief display showing a room layout, you can borrow the furniture and accessories you need from nearby dealers. Just be sure to display a card crediting the merchants.

Office equipment you'll need consists primarily of desks and chairs, a typewriter, an adding machine, and—if you carry small cash items such as sheet music, records, or accessories—a cash register. Get a good, fire-resistant file cabinet with a lock. After the first year, you'll need transfer files.

You must have recordkeeping materials, but don't invest in them until after you've talked with an accountant. Here the National Association of Music Merchants can give you some help. Their standard accounting manual, for instance, can be used as a basis for discussing with the accountant the exact records and forms you need.

Delivery Equipment

You may find it cheaper to farm out your deliveries than to own a truck and man it. Every community has commercial delivery firms who will pick up and deliver pianos and organs. They will also unload pianos shipped by freight.

If you plan to sell in rural areas, however, you'll have to lease or buy a van. If your community has no automobile agency that handles lease arrangements, go to the nearest large city and check the rental facilities there before you buy a truck.

The Studio Operation

*A store studio is part of the
sales effort. It is important to make
the best possible use of it.*

FOR THE PROSPECTIVE music merchant with limited capital—
and especially if he has teaching skill—a studio-sales
operation may be the quickest and simplest way to get started.
Some studio operations produce income from the rent collected
from independent teachers who contract to use the studio
facilities. The income from studio instruction, however, usually
goes to the teacher, although in some cases the music merchant
may withhold a small amount for his recordkeeping expenses.

Despite its small income-producing potential, the studio
operation is an important adjunct to the music store. It
produces the traffic necessary to sell both keyboard and other
musical instruments.

The music studio may be a part of a musical-instrument
store or of a store selling pianos and organs only. It may be in
the downtown area, in an outlying neighborhood, or in a shopping center. In the piano, guitar, or band and orchestra instrument field, it should be located where children of elementary-
school age have easy access to it. Organ studios, on the other

hand, can be located in business areas, since their appeal is to adults as well as children.

Types of Teacher Arrangements

Music-studio operations are carried on with two types of teacher arrangements. One is the independent contractor teacher, sometimes called the free agent. The other is the studio-employed teacher.

The independent teacher pays rent for the studio at an agreed-upon rate per lesson or per hour. A written contract covers all essential points of the arrangement. (Members of the National Association of Music Merchants can get a typed form of such an agreement by writing the association and requesting the comprehensive *Store Studio Manual*.)

The other type of teacher is an employee of the studio. Under this plan, teachers are paid by the lesson, by the hour, or by the week.

It is generally agreed that teachers should confine themselves to teaching. However, the store studio is basically a part of the sales effort of the retail music merchant. When a beginning instrument is sold or a rental plan started, the pupil should be assigned to a salesman, who should have free access to the teacher. The better teacher and salesman understand each other and their objectives, the better opportunity both have to profit.

The store manager must know at all times the status and progress of each student. Orchestras should be encouraged and pupils urged to take part in them after the first few lessons. Beginning bands also stimulate interest.

Commissions to Teachers

The matter of paying commissions to studio-employed teachers for selling instruments has been debated for many years. A small commission of from 1 to 3 percent for the teacher when a student buys a better instrument than he started with can usually be justified. More sales are likely to be made if everyone is constantly aware of the fact that the studio is in reality a sales office. Some teachers have a special ability to create new and higher sales.

Sometimes studios limit the number of lessons offered to the number necessary to get the best instrument sold and the customer satisfied. They then turn the pupil over to an independent teacher or even to a school of music for more advanced teaching.

Some music dealers do business through school-band directors who may or may not be paid for sales made. In a few instances, outside piano teachers have received commissions in sales made with their help. Many retailers publicly condemn the practice of paying commissions to band directors and teachers, but the fact remains that it is still carried on in many areas. Generally, it is an expensive policy, and it does raise ethical questions. Some States have laws prohibiting salaried officials of a government agency (which school-band directors are) from accepting payments of this kind.

Studio Lesson Plans

There are two basic plans for teaching and selling any instrument, from piano to organ to drums or guitar—a rental lesson plan and a sales lesson plan. From the standpoint of costs, it is important to get the fullest possible use from the studios, regardless of the type of plan used. Most studios will be very busy after school hours on weekdays (from 3 or 3:30 p.m. till 6 or 7p.m.) and all day on Saturdays. As much as possible, adult instruction should be scheduled in the morning or early afternoon.

Rental lesson plans. In the rental lesson plan, the studio grants the student the use of an instrument for the duration of the course. These loan plans may run as long as 20 weeks. Lessons may be group or private, or a combination of the two. A downpayment is usually required to apply on the last lessons.

Fees vary, depending on whether all group or all private lessons are offered. Usually, in these beginning rental plans, the full fee goes to the teacher, although, as previously mentioned, a small amount is withheld in some cases to cover recordkeeping expenses. Prices for private lessons on the piano range from $1.00 to $5.00 per half hour. Group lessons are usually less.

Sales lesson plans. Sales plans are often used to sell beginning musical instruments. Here is a typical beginning deal for a low-priced instrument:

Selling price of merchandise	$ 89.00
M.L.R.[1]—25 lessons at $1.00	25.00
Carrying charge	4.00
Tax on $89.00 at 3 percent	2.67
	$120.67

[1] Music lesson reserve, the account set up for payment to the teacher.

Typical payment terms would be a downpayment of $14.00 and $4.00 a week for 26 weeks.

At the end of the 25 lessons, another 25-week lesson course may be sold for $25.00, or the pupil can be placed in a band or orchestra. A charge may or may not be made for participation in the band or orchestra. If there is a charge, it is usually very low. When the student's progress suggests that he is ready for a better instrument or the teacher recommends it, a more expensive instrument can be offered.

Organ lesson plans. Lesson plans are widely used with organ sales, rentals, or trials. If a sale is made, it will be a substantial one, and so the dealer may offer a prospective buyer the chance to learn to play at little or no cost. Sometimes an organ is placed in the home for a trial period at a very low rent, and lessons are given in the organ studio at the store. Organ manufacturers have many practical suggestions for promoting sales.

Piano lesson plans. There is no reason why the piano, too, can't be promoted as the basic music instrument and leased or sold with lessons. Class lessons with groups of 4 to 10 can be handled easily by a competent teacher.

The past few years have seen the introduction of the electronic piano and the rapid development of class piano lessons not only in public schools but in dealer studios. A new day is dawning in the teaching of piano, and piano manufacturers are actively promoting it.

Physical Facilities

Studio sizes vary, depending on the type of instruction being offered. All, however, should be well ventilated and sound-proofed. This is not always easy, since air conditioning and heating vents are sound carriers.

For private lessons on band instruments, the accordion, and the guitar and other fretted instruments, the studio room should be just large enough to accommodate teacher and pupil comfortably. Larger rooms are necessary for private instruction on marimbas, drums, pianos, and organs, although size is not too important for beginning students.

If plans call for class instruction in groups of four or more, obviously larger studios are necessary. Group instruction on musical instruments should usually be limited to 6 students— 10 in the case of the guitar.

Rehearsal hall. There should also be a place for band or orchestra rehearsals. A recital hall isn't absolutely necessary. Recitals can usually be arranged in schools, lodge halls, church halls, or even homes. But it is an advantage to be able to hold the recitals in the store studio. The buyer traffic (parents) it creates is good, and the opportunity for you or your salesman to visit with the parents is valuable. It's also a good chance to display better instruments.

Electronic equipment. With the growth of class teaching and a decline in the number of qualified piano teachers, new group electronic teaching devices have been developed. Electronic techniques are now being used in both organ and piano teaching. As many as 24 pupils can be taught as a group. Confusion is avoided by the use of earphones.

Many leading piano and organ manufacturers have perfected instruments and courses of study. Schools of music and music departments of public schools, colleges, and universities are adopting the new methods.

Even the small music merchant should look into the opportunities in this area. For more information, write the National Association of Music Merchants, 222 West Adams Street, Chicago, Illinois 60606.

Starting Capital and Financial Management

It takes money to make money.
Know how much you need
before you start looking for it.

MANY A BEGINNING DEALER has failed because he wasn't farsighted enough to plan his money requirements accurately or because his expected financial support dwindled or disappeared. Others have sold themselves into bankruptcy by trying to expand sales faster than they could finance with the credit they had. Or changed economic conditions made loans harder to get, and their reserves weren't large enough to carry them through.

How much money will you need to get a retail music store safely started and to support it and yourself until it begins to make a profit? The answer to this question depends on many factors—the kind of merchandise you plan to sell, your location, current business conditions, the size of your operation, your fixture and equipment needs, even the time of year you plan to open for business.

Consider the following table showing a typical distribution by months of annual music-store sales of $100,000—obviously you'll need a larger starting inventory if you open your store in the fall than if you open in the spring:

January	$8,100	July	$ 6,500
February	6,900	August	7,800
March	7,800	September	8,500
April	7,200	October	9,100
May	6,200	November	10,100
June	6,600	December	15,200

Any figures mentioned in this section, therefore, are intended only as a guide to what must be considered. You'll have to work out yourself the estimates of what you will need in your particular situation.

Your Basic Needs

If you are opening a new music store, you'll have to provide for the following basic needs:

1. The building and its preparation for your use
2. Store fixtures and equipment
3. A starting inventory of merchandise
4. An accounting system and forms
5. Stationery and office supplies
6. Personnel
7. Delivery arrangements
8. Insurance
9. An advertising plan and program
10. A budget for 1 year—expense and income
11. A bank connection
12. Licenses, permits, utilities deposits, and so on
13. Legal and accounting services in connection with getting started
14. A reserve fund large enough to take care of your expenses—business and personal—until the business can bring in enough money to do the job

How Much Money Do You Need?

You can only estimate how much starting capital you'll need; but for that very reason, you should get all the information you can on which to base the estimate. Once you have a good idea of what size and type of store you want to have, you can get help in figuring how much you need for various items. Consult suppliers, real estate people, your banker, local authorities, and so on.

Inventory. Probably the largest single item in your estimate will be your investment in inventory. One way of figuring the cost of your beginning inventory is to break down the total sales you expect for the year by departments and work back from those figures. This method is illustrated in the following example:

Department	Esti- mated sales (1)	Gross mar- gin [1] (2)	Cost of mer- chan- dise [2] (3)	Turn- over (4)	Inven- tory require- ments [3] (5)
Pianos	$ 18,000	39	$10,980	2	$ 5,490
Organs	22,000	37	13,860	2	6,930
Music instruments	20,000	42	11,600	1.8	6,440
Accessories	6,000	32	4,080	1.8	2,270
Radio and phonograph	10,000	30	7,000	2.5	2,800
TV	12,000	25	9,000	2.5	3,600
Sheet music	5,000	30	3,500	2	1,750
Records	7,000	30	4,900	2.2	2,230
	$100,000		$64,920		$31,510

[1] Percent of sales [2] $\frac{\text{Col. 1} \times (100 - \text{Col. 2})}{100}$ [3] Col. 3 ÷ Col. 4

As explained in the discussion of inventory turnover beginning on page 44, if you can achieve a higher turnover, you can invest less in inventory. Because of uncertainties in shipping and the possibility of manufacturing shortages, however, you should start out with at least a 4 months' supply.

Operating expenses. You should have enough cash available to take care of your operating expenses for at least 2 months. First-year expenses, based on sales of $100,000, would probably run something like this:

Type of expense	Percent of sales	Amount
Salaries and commissions, including your own	16	$16,000
Occupancy	5	5,000
Advertising	5	5,000
Receiving and shipping	2	2,000
Office and administrative costs	6	6,000
Service	1	1,000
Total	35	$35,000

Startup costs. Lay out as little cash as possible on your physical setup—you'll need all you can save for expenses such as merchandise, advertising, and service. You can probably do much of the interior decorating yourself. Fixtures should be plain but attractive, chairs and desks primarily functional.

As for your opening day, you may be able to get a school-band group for a relatively small cash outlay. Or your future teachers will play. If you carry a single first line of pianos or musical instruments, the manufacturer may supply a name performer without charge.

Throwaways announcing the opening can be printed and distributed. If you own or lease a truck, have it carry an announcement sign. Window mobiles can be obtained from suppliers. A dignified newspaper advertisement will bring visitors if light refreshments are served.

You don't need to spend more than $500 on your opening. Painting, fixtures, and furniture should be held to $1,000.

Expected cash income. With these estimates of inventory requirements and expenses, you can figure your monthly outgo. Cash income for the year by months is much harder to estimate, but you should set up an income budget as well as an expense budget. You need to know how much cash the business is likely to generate in order to know how large a reserve you must have to carry you through.

Expect the unexpected. Be sure to allow a cushion for unexpected expenses. Most prospective businessmen underestimate the amount of capital they need, and the results can be disastrous. It's better to err on the conservative side.

FINANCIAL MANAGEMENT begins with good records. Unless you have had accounting training, one of your first steps should be to make a connection with a good, reliable accountant. He will help you plan and set up your accounting system and will explain its use.

If your records are well planned, reasonably accurate, and kept up to date, they will serve many purposes.

• They can show the financial status of the store at any time.

• They show trends in the store as a whole and in individual departments.

• They keep important facts about your business available at all times. This is especially important when you need a loan.

• They help you supply a distributor or manufacturer with information on which to establish your credit.

• They give you basic information with which to compare your business with similar businesses.

• They make it possible for you to plan intelligently.

• They will help to establish your claim for loss with your insurance company in case of fire, theft, or other loss.

• If you should decide to sell your business, they will help establish the price.

Many businesses have failed because their financial records were poorly organized or not kept up. Danger spots that good records would have brought to light were not discovered until it was too late. Too, some outside agencies have a right to be concerned about the company's facts and figures. Banks, bond companies, and other lending agencies must know what financial shape their clients are in. The city, State, and Federal governments are also concerned because of taxes and other matters.

Types of Expenses

A beginning music dealer often doesn't realize how many different items of expense have to be kept track of in the operation of a complete music store with teaching studios.

You'll need an accounting system that will provide for recording these expenses as well as all types of income. The system should enable you to keep your records up to date with the least possible expenditure of time, yet in a form that makes the information easy to use in managing your business. Without good records, you can be losing money and not even know it.

There are many advantages in using a standard accounting system. One of them is that you then have a basis for comparing your business with similar businesses. The National Association of Music Merchants has prepared such a system—the *Standard Accounting Manual for Music Stores*. The manual was developed from and tested in actual experience.

Inventory Turnover

Inventory turnover is the ratio of the cost of goods sold to average inventory—that is, the cost of goods sold divided by the average inventory. Usually, inventory is taken at the end of the fiscal year and the ending and beginning inventories averaged.

The turnover rate shows how fast your merchandise is moving—how many times your stock is sold and replenished in a given period of time—usually a year. A report published by the National Association of Music Merchants gives the following annual turnover ranges for complete music stores with sales of $100,000 to $250,000 a year:

Department	Turnover range	Typical
Pianos	1.5 to 2.3	1.8
Organs	1.2 to 2.0	1.6
Musical instruments	1.0 to 1.8	1.4
Accessories	0.9 to 1.9	1.6
Sheet music	1.1 to 2.1	1.3
Records'	1.8 to 4.2	2.4

Inventory turnover is an important clue. It is a measure of merchandising efficiency. If you can improve turnover, you can invest less in inventory. There is no greater waste of capital funds than in merchandise that doesn't sell.

Increasing the rate of stock turnover is probably more important in the music business than in many other businesses because the price per unit is high. Here are some of the advantages of a higher turnover.

• Your money is used more efficiently. The higher the turnover, the smaller your capital investment can be in proportion to sales. For example, suppose you are aiming for annual sales of $100,000, with the cost of goods sold at $65,000. If you can achieve a 5-time turnover, you'll need to invest only $13,000 in stock. With a 4-time turnover, you'd need $16,250 to reach the same sales level; with a 2-time turnover, $32,500. The small dealer with limited capital needs to watch his inventory and sales figures very carefully so as to make every dollar count.

• Interest, some taxes, insurance, and other expenses are lower in relation to sales. Less floor space is required, and handling costs per dollar of sales are reduced.

•Markdowns are fewer because with a faster turnover rate goods remain in stock for a shorter time. There is less physical deterioration.

• New styles can be offered more quickly.

It's possible, however, to overemphasize turnover rate. If you carry too little merchandise, so that you don't have a representative line to offer, you'll lose sales. It's wise to watch the experience of the trade as shown in national averages.

Recording Trade-ins and Repossessions in Inventory

Merchandise acquired through trade-ins or repossessions should be included in your inventory at its estimated purchase price in the local secondhand market, regardless of the amount allowed for the trade-in or the unpaid balance on repossessed merchandise. If you can't estimate the price of a similar secondhand unit accurately, use the following formula: estimated selling price minus profit margin and reconditioning cost = inventory price. For example:

Estimated selling price _____		$395.00
Profit margin (40 percent) ____	$158.00	
Reconditioning cost _____	175.00	333.00
Inventory price _____		$ 62.00

Rental Accounting

If most of your rentals, or a large percent of them, *do not* develop into sales, record the rental in the rental-income account. If many *do* result in sales and you apply the rent received as payment on the merchandise, you'll find it easier to record the deal as a sale in the first place.

Depreciation of rental pianos is handled as follows: Set up in your ledger a separate asset account, "Rental Pianos." Now suppose you buy a piano for a wholesale price of $500. From the date of purchase, the piano is carried in the "Rental Pianos" account as a fixed asset. It is then treated in the same way as office equipment or any other asset subject to depreciation.

First, establish the probable salvage value of the piano—say, 20 percent of the wholesale price, or $100. The basis for recording depreciation of the piano will then be $500 minus $100, or $400. Writing this amount off over 10 years at 10 percent a year gives a depreciation expense item of $40 a year. This $40 is a tax-deductible item each vear until the piano is depreciated to its salvage value.

If you can rent the piano for $25 a month, your income from it will be $300 a year. The piano will soon pay for itself and provide a good income.

Your Merchandise

*Pencil and paper can carry your planning
only so far. For some information,
you have to go where the action is.*

WITH SEVERAL HUNDRED manufacturers and distributors selling various lines of merchandise, you may feel over-
whelmed with high-pressure salesmen, each one wanting to sell
his company's products. Many dealers make the mistake of
overstocking and carrying too many lines. This slows down
turnover and restricts your credit.

Generally speaking, it is best to do business with a few reliable, well-established distributors or manufacturers who will be
sincerely interested in your long-time growth and success. Some
lines are exclusive, others are not. Usually, if you are granted
exclusive representation, you will have to sell a stated minimum quantity within a given length of time in order to keep
the franchise. This can be a dangerous commitment unless you
know your market potential, the quality and popularity of the
product, and how strong the competition is in your market.

All other things being equal, it is wise to deal with a source
that isn't too far away. You can't stock everything you might
have a call for. To be able to phone for what you need and get
overnight delivery often makes the difference between adding a

new customer and losing him. One test of a good supplier is his concern in filling emergency needs, whether the order is large or small. (This doesn't apply to pianos and organs, since they usually come directly from the manufacturer.)

Sources of Merchandise

The electrification of musical instruments of many types is evidence of the growing market for modern musical merchandise. As a prospective dealer, you should acquaint yourself with all these developments and with the principal sources for both the new and the more traditional types of merchandise.

Pianos and organs. Dealers in pianos and organs usually deal directly with the manufacturers. Because of the limited sale of these items, many manufacturers appoint only one dealer in a city or sales territory.

Changes in dealerships are constantly being made, however. If you are interested in a specific line of merchandise, write directly to the factory or seek out a traveling representative of the manufacturer. Or you can contact the manufacturer at the conventions of the National Association of Music Merchants.

Other musical instruments. Many kinds of nonkeyboard instruments, such as accordions, band instruments, and guitars and other fretted instruments, are sold through distributors, though some manufacturers deal directly with franchised dealers. Hundreds of salesmen travel over the country representing the many lines of music merchandise.

Sheet music. Sheet-music stock for small music stores consists of (1) popular vocal, piano, and organ music; (2) teaching materials; (3) the music on contest lists; and (4) band, orchestra, and choral music for schools and colleges. The best thing for you to do is to have a representative of a music publisher or distributor visit your store. Discuss the matter with him thoroughly before you venture into promoting and selling sheet music. In many market areas, the field has good possibilities. Study the opportunity in your community.

Sometimes a retail dealer supplies space for a rack jobber. The rack jobber sets up the racks, supplies the merchandise, and services the racks regularly to keep them up to date. The dealer sells the music, collects for it, and makes a regular accounting to the rack jobber, who then pays the dealer a commission.

Phonograph records and tape recordings. Phonograph records, tape recordings, and the instruments for playing them are highly specialized in their distribution. They are discussed separately in chapter 12.

Rental Instruments

The renting of pianos, organs, and other musical instruments is common in the music business. Some dealers rent only used merchandise; others rent both new and old. Many rent either new or old merchandise with option to buy.

A project of this kind requires a sizable investment of money, but you can begin on a small scale and plan a steady expansion. A rental stock is usually accumulated over a period of time by adding from 1 to 10 pianos to the rental "bank" each year

Information About Sources

A good source of information about suppliers or music merchandise is *The Purchasers Guide,* published every year by *The Music Trades Magazine,* 111 West 57th Street, New York, N. Y. 10019. This guide to the music industries—which every music dealer should have—lists the following:

Manufacturers of musical instruments, pianos, organs, and chimes
Harpsichord manufacturers and importers
Sources of piano, organ, and tuner-technician supplies
Piano-organ schools and literature
Used and rebuilt piano wholesalers
Publishers and wholesalers of sheet music
Music engravers and printers

Musical merchandise manufacturers and wholesalers
National music trade associations
Trademarks of the music industry
Trademark manufacturers' code

In addition to this guide, there are many monthly trade journals and magazines that will help to keep you abreast of the new and rapidly changing merchandise and marketing techniques in the music industry.

As soon as possible after you decide to open a retail music store, you should attend a convention of the National Association of Music Merchants and visit the manufacturers' exhibits. These conventions are held every year in June. They bring together not only the leading music dealers in the United States but also manufacturers, importers, and distributors of every type of music and music merchandise.

Pianos, organs, band instruments, stringed and fretted instruments, accordions, violins, sheet music, accessories of every description, both group and individual teaching methods and equipment, pianos and organ supplies, service equipment and parts—all are on display with salesmen to explain them. In addition, many sessions of the convention are given to discussions of the problems of music dealers, including financial matters, advertising, personnel, promotion, and general management.

Regional conferences are also held each year. These meetings, too, are challenging and informative.